America?

The End of America?

A Guide to the New World Disorder

Alan Friedman

Biteback Publishing

First published in Great Britain in 2025 by
Biteback Publishing Ltd, London
Copyright © Alan Friedman 2025

Alan Friedman has asserted his right under the Copyright, Designs and Patents Act 1988 to be identified as the author of this work.

All rights reserved. No part of this publication may be reproduced, stored in a retrieval system or transmitted, in any form or by any means, without the publisher's prior permission in writing.

This book is sold subject to the condition that it shall not, by way of trade or otherwise, be lent, resold, hired out or otherwise circulated without the publisher's prior consent in any form of binding or cover other than that in which it is published and without a similar condition, including this condition, being imposed on the subsequent purchaser.

Every reasonable effort has been made to trace copyright holders of material reproduced in this book, but if any have been inadvertently overlooked the publisher would be glad to hear from them.

ISBN 978-1-78590-957-3

10 9 8 7 6 5 4 3 2 1

A CIP catalogue record for this book is available from the British Library.

Set in Adobe Caslon Pro

Printed and bound in Great Britain by
CPI Group (UK) Ltd, Croydon CR0 4YY

For Gabriella

'An nescis, mi fili, quantilla prudentia mundus regatur?'
*('Do you not know, my son, with how very
little wisdom the world is governed?')*
AXEL OXENSTIERNA, 1648

CONTENTS

Prologue		xi
Chapter One	The Infant Empire	1
Chapter Two	The Emerging Superpower	21
Chapter Three	The Accidental Empire	39
Chapter Four	The Parabola of US Leadership	59
Chapter Five	The Empire Strikes Back	81
Chapter Six	Imperial Overreach: The Failed Wars of George W. Bush	101
Chapter Seven	Obama's Mismanagement of the Arab Spring	115
Chapter Eight	Trump and Other Miscreants	133
Chapter Nine	Putin's War on Western Democracy	157
Chapter Ten	The Chinese Century	175
Chapter Eleven	The Rise of the Global South	199
Chapter Twelve	The United States of Amnesia	217
Chapter Thirteen	The New World Disorder	233
Acknowledgements		251
Bibliography		255
Notes		259
Index		265

PROLOGUE

I remember listening to Gore Vidal talking passionately about the similarities between America today and the declining days of the Roman Empire. It was a humid summer evening in Rome, July 1998, and we were at a cocktail party and dinner reception for the former US presidential candidate George McGovern. Vidal was clearly delighted to see McGovern, the man who lost the election to Richard Nixon back in 1972 and a fellow former critic of the Vietnam War. McGovern was enjoying his role as the guest of honour, and he was being fawned over by the smart set in Rome. Then aged seventy-six, McGovern had just been appointed by President Bill Clinton as the new American ambassador to the Rome-based UN Food and Agriculture Organization. Vidal held aloft a glass of chilled Vermentino as he stood on the terrace of Rome's most aristocratic club, the Circolo della Caccia, and spoke scornfully of America. The main difference between Imperial Rome and twentieth-century America, he snarled, was the extraordinary brevity of the American empire, which had gone from global hegemony to decadence in less than half a century. Vidal's vision was that of a fairly rapid trajectory for an empire that had reached its pinnacle of strength and global power in the decades after the Second World War.

There was no greater champion of Washington's imperial destiny than Henry Luce, the media mogul who in 1941 published a famous editorial in *Life* magazine. Luce proclaimed the dawning of 'The American Century' and emphasised the idea that in the twentieth century, the United States was poised to play a pivotal role in shaping the political, economic and cultural landscape of the world. He believed that American values and influence would guide the course of history and would ultimately 'make the world safe for democracy'.* Vidal was famously pessimistic about America, as were other critics of so-called American imperialism, such as left-wing intellectuals like Noam Chomsky and Chalmers Johnson. Yet one need not employ an ideological framework of the left in order to understand the parabola of American power. It is the story of the rise and fall of a great power. Empires come and go; just look at world history. And some, like Rome, eventually collapse

---

* Henry R. Luce (1898–1967), journalist and founder of *Time* and *Life* magazines, in 'The American Century', published by *Life* magazine on 17 February 1941, urged Washington to enter the Second World War to defend democratic values and 'create the first great American century'. Luce's editorial echoed the words used by President Wilson in his message to Congress delivered on 2 April 1917, when he called for a declaration of war against Germany, saying that not only had America's rights as a neutral been violated but that 'the world must be made safe for democracy'. Americans must fight 'for the rights and liberties of small nations' and to 'bring peace and safety to make the world itself at last free'. See President Wilson's Declaration of War Message to Congress, 2 April 1917; Records of the United States Senate; Group 46; National Archives. Also quoted by Niall Ferguson, *Colossus: The Rise and Fall of the American Empire*, Penguin Press, 2009, pp. 65–6; and Stanley Karnow, *Vietnam: A History*, Penguin Publishing Group, 1997, p. 14.

or implode because of poor leadership, mismanagement or strained resources and imperial overreach. Other downfalls include assassinations, insurrections, civil wars and other internal divisions. These are, by the way, the kind of divisions and existential challenges that were prevalent during 2024. At the time of writing, America is in the wake of a turbulent presidential election season. With Donald Trump back in the White House, the future is more uncertain than ever. Washington is in upheaval, autocrats everywhere are encouraged and America's traditional allies wait anxiously to see the mercurial tycoon's next move. But the trajectory of America's decline will not change; it may even be accelerated.

Ultimately Gore Vidal got it right: there are few periods of imperial predominance that have been as short-lived as the parabola of US leadership between the 1940s and the 2020s. At the end of the Second World War, America was not prepared to step into the role of global policeman. Yet the United States would take up the mantle anyway, and it would do so with a mixture of altruistic-sounding rhetoric, naive and self-righteous promises of freedom and democracy on the one hand and cynical self-interest on the other. This contrast between utopian and moralistic US rhetoric, proclamations about the right of all peoples to self-determination and a post-war period filled with CIA machinations and regime change policies remains the greatest paradox in American foreign policy. In a rapidly changing world, American exceptionalism is no longer defensible.

It never was. Indeed, the very system of Western liberal democracy that America designed is currently under attack, with a motley crew of autocrats, terrorists, authoritarian and illiberal elected leaders on the one hand and the Global South plus the BRICS crowd on the other, all proposing an alternative vision of how to manage the world.*

We have kept the flag flying for nearly eighty years now, but the current phase is one of visible decline in American influence and the emergence of alliances that break with the old norms and practices of the post-war period. This is the price of the globalisation that created greater income inequalities, the effect of Putin's war in the Ukraine, of the pandemic, of the disruption of supply chains, of the rise of China, and it is also the result of deep fissures in US society. America, sadly, is broken. As the rockstar hedge fund manager Ray Dalio will tell you, every big cycle has a phase when you are on the way up and a phase when you are on the way down.† This book is the chronicle of the slippery slide down the big cycle and of how we are now living in a period of upheaval and realignment. America is weakened and distracted by an existential battle that is raging within its own borders. This is the story of the failure of American leadership at key moments in post-war history, both before and after the fall of the Berlin Wall in 1989, and a glimpse at

---

* BRICS is an intergovernmental organisation comprising Brazil, Russia, India, China, South Africa, Iran, Egypt, Ethiopia and the United Arab Emirates.

† Ray Dalio, also known as 'the Super Trader', is the founder of successful hedge fund Bridgewater and a very high-profile financial guru. His success in online trading was also a result of his approach to investment strategies based on a particular combination of finance and philosophy.

the increasingly dangerous and uncertain world that is now taking shape. There is no Big Bang moment in which America's influence comes to an abrupt end. It is more a question of the long arc of history, the inexorable and multiple forces that together are like kryptonite for the unruly giant. After a relatively brief period of Pax Americana, less than a full century, we now are entering a phase that future historians may one day call 'the New World Disorder'. In this period of history, early 21st-century America is on the defensive, riven by deep internal conflict and steadily ceding influence to China and other rivals. Trump is the ultimate manifestation of a full-blown societal crisis in America, and his xenophobia and isolationism appear to accurately mirror his nation's mood.

Gore Vidal would not be surprised. The truth is that we Americans have never been very good at managing empire. It is not really one of our skillsets. Most Americans would probably say the term should be applied only to the Roman Empire, or the British Empire, or to the empires of France or Spain and other European colonising nations. But not to America. We are not an empire! Perish the thought. After all, we were once a colony. We rebelled and secured our independence from the British Empire. We were told by Benjamin Franklin that we had created a republic, if we could keep it. We are not an imperial power. We have always seen ourselves as the Good Guys. We are idealists. We are America. We are that city upon a hill. We are the defenders of democracy. That is who we are. At least, that is what we were taught in school for the past century.

History, of course, is generally written by the winners, or by their acolytes; so many of America's history texts were written, until quite recently, by middle-aged white male historians. The telling of American history has been left largely in the hands of men who came of age in the past century, who learned the Pledge of Allegiance at school, whose *Weltanschauung* was formed by the Cold War. Fashions change, in history as in real life. These historians have tended to skip over some of the more awkward issues, like nearly 300 years of slave labour and a century of recurring genocide against indigenous peoples. Instead, we Americans have told ourselves a far more heroic story about 'manifest destiny' and the frontier crucible.* It is the Disney version of American history. We have pretty much convinced ourselves that we Americans have never had anything to do with imperialism or with imperialist behaviour.

'America has never been an empire,' George W. Bush proclaimed with vigour, and typically exaggerated swagger, during the 2000 presidential campaign. 'We may be the only great power in history that had the chance and

---

* The belief in the necessary expansion of the nation westward was called 'manifest destiny', a kind of faith in the American duty to settle the continent, conquer and prosper. The settlers were said to have overcome hazardous terrain and death to reach their 'promised land', the American West. American journalist John L. O'Sullivan is known for being the first to use the phrase 'manifest destiny' in his essay titled 'Annexation' in the *Democratic Review* to advocate in 1845 the annexation of Texas and Oregon, not only because Texas desired this – he wrote – but because it was 'our manifest destiny to overspread the continent allotted by Providence for the free development of our yearly multiplying millions'. Also, artists helped the American dream to strengthen. The fresco cycles for the Dome, for instance, served as propaganda to celebrate the greatness of the young nation and motivate many Americans seeking a brighter future. See Philip Kennicott, 'In 1898, the US was entranced by empire. The legacy lingers', *Washington Post*, 2 June 2023.

refused, preferring greatness to power and justice to glory."
The reality is that we have been in collective denial for a very long time. We have also been the victims of selective storytelling. We have deluded ourselves into thinking that nothing would ever change, that America and the American way of life would reign supreme until the end of time. Today, with the known American-led world order disintegrating, and with at least half of America retreating into a primordial isolationism, it is time to look at how we got here, and why America's de facto global empire is being displaced by the uncertainty of a New World Disorder. In order to understand why the Pax Americana is entering a twilight period and what may come next, we need first to examine the illusions and fairy tales we have lived with for such a very long time. What began as the colonisation of America's eastern seaboard by settlers and religious refugees from the Dutch and British Empires in the early 1600s, and then morphed into a republic by the late 1700s, would soon be transformed into a United States of America that for more than a century would press forth with a huge and unprecedented territorial expansion, a massive continental land grab, through petition, purchase, treaty, war, invasion and annexation. The phenomenon would continue throughout the 1800s and well into the 1900s. Today, in

---

* In a speech delivered on 19 November 1999 at Ronald Reagan Presidential Library, George W. Bush also stated that 'all the aims I've described today are important. But they are not imperial. America has never been an empire. We may be the only great power in history that had the chance and refused – preferring greatness to power and justice to glory.' See Niall Ferguson, *Colossus: The Rise and Fall of the American Empire*, Penguin Press, 2009, pp 6–7 and p. 170, and Ferguson, 'The "E" Word: Admit it – America is an Empire', *WSJ* Opinion, 7 June 2003.

the 2020s, American democracy is more fragile than at any time since the Civil War of the 1860s. And as the republic is torn asunder by deep social and political divisions, American power on the world stage is being weakened. America's de facto empire is in decline. This is the story of the failure of American foreign policy since 1945. It is time to admit the hypocrisy, the incompetence, the mismanagement of US power at times by so many American Presidents, from Franklin D. Roosevelt to John F. Kennedy, Bill Clinton, George W. Bush and Barack Obama. Not to mention Donald Trump. It is time to imagine a world without any order, a world in which the United Nations and the World Bank are no longer relevant, a world where NATO faces a terrifying threat in Vladimir Putin, a world of disorder in which multilateralism has been replaced by new crosscutting alliances, a New World Disorder where the laws of the jungle replace the International Court of Justice.

But first we need to understand the origins of American imperialism in the late eighteenth century. The idea of an American empire was first mentioned innocently by George Washington, but it would become a strategic reality under President Thomas Jefferson.

CHAPTER ONE

THE INFANT EMPIRE

The word 'empire' was not always taboo.

George Washington, with eloquent humility, would describe his country as 'an infant empire'.* Back in 1780, during the Revolutionary War, Thomas Jefferson would use the phrase 'Empire of Liberty' to describe his vision of a confederation of equal American states, based on a forceful westward expansion, as a kind of 'democratic' empire that could stand up to the powerful British Empire at the time. In Jefferson's vision, this 'Empire of Liberty' would be based on acquiring new lands and guaranteeing access to overseas markets. He specifically expressed the desire to add to his 'Empire of Liberty' the British-held colony of Canada.† So

---

* George Washington referred to the United States as an 'infant empire' in a letter sent on 28 July 1784 to French general and politician the Marquis de Lafayette, a leading figure in both the American and French Revolutions. In the letter, Washington expressed his hope for the US, 'this infant empire', to grow into a powerful and admired nation in the world.

† Thomas Jefferson used the phrase 'Empire of Liberty' on more than one occasion. It occurred first in a letter sent in 1780 to General and war hero George Rogers, while the American Revolution was still being fought. He wrote that his goal was the creation of an independent state that would be proactive in its foreign policy and whose interventionism and expansionism would always be perceived as benevolent. 'In the event of peace ... we shall form to the American union a barrier against the dangerous extension of the British Province of Canada and add to the Empire of Liberty an extensive and fertile Country thereby converting dangerous Enemies into valuable friends.'

while his rhetoric referred to an empire of liberty, Jefferson and other expansionists coveted an empire that would include the conquest of British-held Canada, Spanish-owned Florida and the French-owned Louisiana Territory. Indeed, Jefferson's unhappy relationship with the British would in part lead to the War of 1812, during which America would fight the British and fail miserably in its attempt to conquer Canada.* Jefferson, who also wrote the Declaration of Independence in 1776, was at pains to stress that his was not really an imperialist vision but simply a vision of an American confederation that could stand tall next to European empires. His actions would fall short of his rhetoric, as was also the case in the Declaration of Independence. In that document, Jefferson wrote these famous words: 'We hold these truths to be self-evident, that all men are created equal, that they are endowed, by their Creator with certain unalienable Rights, that among these are Life, Liberty, and the pursuit of happiness.'[1] At the time of writing that 'all men are created equal', Jefferson actually meant only white, property-owning men. One fifth of the colony's total population was enslaved in 1776, so their rights to life and liberty did not exist. In his public life, Jefferson made statements describing black people as biologically inferior and claiming that a biracial American

---

* The War of 1812 originated from the trade tensions between the young United States and the British Empire, which imposed restrictions on naval trade during its war against Napoleon. British support given to Native Americans opposed to US westward expansionism, and US territorial aims over the British colony of Canada, drove a narrow majority in the US House, under the War Hawks' pressure, to declare war on 18 June 1812. After suffering several defeats, the Americans inflicted heavy losses on the British, but the treaty ending hostilities had been signed before the news reached the battlefield. Pre-conflict situation had been restored in 1815.

society was impossible. Jefferson had 600 slaves himself and it is highly likely that he fathered six children with one of his slaves, his mistress Sally Hemings. To his credit, he freed ten of his slaves, five during his lifetime and five in his last will and testament. They were all members of the Hemings family.* Jefferson did try to insert a ban on slavery into the Declaration of Independence, but he was voted down by the majority of the Congress in Philadelphia during that sweltering summer of 1776. Later on, he would try to prevent the spread of slavery in the new western territories, but with little success. The settlers wanted the low-cost benefits of slave labour as they pushed westward, just as they wanted the lands of the indigenous peoples they came across. When it came to the treatment of Native Americans, Thomas Jefferson was ruthless. Despite his moderate rhetoric, he would lay the foundations for a century of 'Indian removal', an American form of ethnic cleansing of the original inhabitants of North America. During the Revolutionary War, Jefferson himself gave orders to exterminate a number of native tribes that were allied with the British.[2] From their point of view, they were fighting for their homeland. Little did they know that their destiny was to be near extermination of their lives and their culture and removal to reservations.

When America and Britain finally made peace, and the

---

* In 1998, a DNA analysis from a sample provided by Field Jefferson, a living descendant of Jefferson's paternal uncle, and from Easton Hemings, born in 1808, proved new biological evidence that Jefferson and Sally Hemings had at least one and probably six children between 1790 and 1808. In 2000, the Thomas Jefferson Memorial Foundation accepted the DNA-based conclusions.

Treaty of Paris was signed in September 1783, the British not only recognised the independence of the thirteen colonies but also ceded to America all land west to the Mississippi River and as far north as the Great Lakes.* This was a swathe of nearly half a million square miles that would double the size of America and eventually be divided into the states of Ohio, Indiana, Illinois, Michigan and Wisconsin. All that was needed now was to clear the land of the 'merciless Indian savages', as Jefferson described the indigenous people whose land the British had just handed them.† Jefferson's denigration of the natives showed that the war for independence from Great Britain was also a war to seize indigenous lands. From 1776 to 1783, US troops and colonial militias destroyed more than seventy Cherokee towns, fifty Haudenosaunee towns and at least ten multiethnic towns in the Ohio Valley, killing several hundred people (including civilians) and subjecting refugees to starvation, disease and death. In the decades to come, both Washington and Jefferson would call for the extermination of Native Americans who fought against dispossession. Several US armies would

---

* The treaty enshrined the end of the American War of Independence and related conflicts (the Anglo-French War, the Anglo-Spanish War and the fourth Anglo-Dutch War) and, amongst others, provided for British recognition of the independence of the thirteen colonies (which became the United States of America) and for London's relinquishment of the territories between the Allegheny Mountains and the Mississippi River, which set the new border between the US and the Spanish possessions in North America. See Peter S. Onuf, *Jefferson's Empire: The Language of American Nationhood*, University of Virginia Press, 2000.

† Jefferson referred to 'merciless Indian savages' in his twenty-seventh grievance against King George, when he accused him of encouraging 'domestic insurrection' by indigenous people against 'white colonists' (Declaration of Rights and Grievances, 14 October 1765).

try to do precisely that.* The term 'imperialism' would not be used in American politics again until a century later, in the 1890s, when the explicit promotion of the policy would enjoy a sudden and widespread political appeal.† But there can be little doubt that the original thirteen colonies had, within a few years of declaring their independence, already become the colonisers, and rebel America had begat its own continental empire. By the irony of history, the original Americans who had declared independence from the British monarchy, and thus the British Empire, would forge their very own empire. And it would be far more powerful than anything *Britannia* had ever known. In his farewell address in 1796, George Washington had been quite explicit in counselling the fledgling nation against getting involved in the affairs of warring European powers. But Thomas Jefferson was an avid diplomat and a savvy operator, and he was always looking for ways that America could benefit from Europe's Napoleonic Wars. As the President, in 1803,

---

* Jeffrey Oster, 'The Shameful Final Grievance of the Declaration of Independence', *The Atlantic*, 8 February 2020. Since the 1970s, American academics have begun to use the term 'genocide' to denounce US policies toward Native Americans. By the 1990s, works with shocking data about crimes against these peoples had been published. See David E. Stannard, *American Holocaust: The Conquest of the New World*, Oxford University Press, 1993, and Ward L. Churchill, *A Little Matter of Genocide: Holocaust and Denial in the Americas: 1492 to the Present*, City Lights Books, 1997.

† After the Civil War, several factors converge that account for America's desire to pursue an imperial policy. The economy grew rapidly – industrial and agricultural sectors produced more than the public could buy. Surpluses resulted in economic downturns that foreign markets would alleviate, and many business leaders began to cast covetous eyes overseas in a search for investment opportunities. The *Frontier Thesis* introduced in 1893 by Frederick Jackson Turner, a prominent historian of the American West, stated that westward expansion served as a 'safety valve' alleviating overpopulation by providing Americans with access to cheap or free land. Additionally, the frontier presented new economic opportunities as individuals looked for land and resources to exploit. See Ray A. Billington, *Westward Expansion: A History of the American Frontier*, New York: Macmillan, 1967

he literally doubled the size of the United States by making a deal with Napoleon Bonaparte, the self-proclaimed Emperor of France, to purchase the Louisiana Territory. Napoleon, who was warring with England, needed the money. Jefferson saw an opportunity, and he took it. He rationalised it as part of his 'Empire of Liberty' strategy.[3] In any case this was good business, and the huge territory would provide vast resources for America's westward expansion. The diplomat who had helped to negotiate the Louisiana Purchase in Paris was James Monroe; he would a few years later serve as Secretary of State under James Madison and then, starting in 1817, as the fifth President of the United States. With huge expansionary ambitions, Monroe would acquire Florida from Spain in 1819, and then four years later, in 1823, he would proclaim the famed 'Monroe Doctrine'. This declaration became a cornerstone of American foreign policy for the rest of the nineteenth century and beyond. It was a warning to European countries against any further colonisation in the western hemisphere. Any attempt by a European power to intervene or control any nation in the western hemisphere would now be viewed by the United States as a hostile act. Monroe had essentially claimed American dominion, or suzerainty, over half the globe. By the 1840s, amid the waves of westward movement of hundreds of thousands of European and American settlers, the philosophical pretext or justification for the expansion would be found in the idea of a natural right to conquer the continent, known as 'manifest destiny'. This was a right supposedly granted directly by God, by Divine Providence, by the superiority of American democratic values and institutions, by the need to spread Christianity and above all by the need for economic growth and expansion. Take your pick. All these arguments were considered valid at the time in polite society. These justifications were of course framed by the dominant white Euro-American elites. Until recently, many historians have ignored or understated the fact that America's glorious manifest destiny was achieved by a push westward that also resulted in the slaughter of millions of Native Americans, in what could be called a slow-motion and rolling genocide. They have also made little of the fact that the economy's business model was based in large part on the slave labour of millions of Africans who were being brought to America in shackles. The lure of manifest destiny, and the personal ambitions of President James K. Polk, would soon take America into war with Mexico, a war that was decried at the time by its critics as imperialistic and incompatible with democratic ideals. It was Polk, a pro-slavery firebrand from Tennessee, a man who never expected to be President, who did the dirty work. Polk was elected in 1844 on an expansionist platform that advocated the annexation of Texas and the acquisition from the British of the Oregon Territory. It was during his years in the White House that the term 'manifest destiny' became popular. Polk didn't waste any time in office. He annexed Texas in 1845. Then he wanted to lay claim to California and New Mexico, and so he started out by trying to buy the land from the Mexican government. He sent an American diplomat, John Slidell, to Mexico City, to offer $30 million for the land. When the Mexicans declined, Polk provoked an incident with Mexico and got the Congress to declare war. After two years of bloodshed, by 1848 Mexico was forced to cede to the United States the land that would become California, Nevada, Utah, Arizona, New Mexico and parts of Colorado and Wyoming. Among those opposed to the war with Mexico was a newly elected congressman named Abraham Lincoln, who declared Polk's actions as 'immoral' and as being contrary to the values of the American republic. Another critic, the author Henry David Thoreau, refused to pay taxes that would support the war with Mexico and was subsequently jailed. From prison he wrote his essay *Civil Disobedience*, in which he expressed his opposition to both the territorial expansion of the Mexican–American War and to the practice of slavery. In just one four-year term in office, the hard-driving Polk acquired more than 1 million square miles of western territory and pushed America's western boundary all the way to the Pacific Ocean. The aggressive and violent expansionary tactics of James K. Polk had fulfilled manifest destiny. It was not considered empire-building, but rather a natural and preordained outcome.

The enlargement of the United States was made possible in part by the Indian Removal Act of 1830, a law signed by President Andrew Jackson that gave rise to a dark chapter in American history. The law authorised the forced removal of Native American tribes including the Cherokee, Creek, Chickasaw, Choctaw and Seminole nations, to lands west of the Mississippi River. The main goal of the Indian Removal Act was to open up valuable lands for white settlement and to facilitate the expansion of the United States. Many white settlers coveted the fertile lands of the indigenous tribes. The removal of the Native American tribes, known as the 'Trail of Tears', was a period in the late 1830s when the United States government forcibly removed the south-eastern Native Americans from their homelands and relocated them to lands in Indian Territory (present-day Oklahoma). In 1838 and 1839, as part of Andrew Jackson's Indian removal policy, the Cherokee nation was forced to give up its lands east of the Mississippi River and to migrate away from their home. Approximately 16,000 Cherokee men, women and children were forced to leave their homes and embark on a perilous journey, covering several hundred miles on foot, with some groups travelling by boat along rivers.

The conditions during the Trail of Tears were deplorable. The Cherokee tribe faced extreme weather conditions, inadequate clothing and meagre rations. Many were ill and weakened, having been exposed to diseases such as smallpox and measles that had been introduced by European settlers. An estimated 5,000 people died of disease, exposure, malnutrition and exhaustion during this journey. This episode alas was emblematic of the times; we could call it the rotten underside of American expansionism in the nineteenth century. It has usually been treated as a footnote, alongside the issue of slavery. The fact that half of America's westward expansion was powered by slave labour is not a trivial detail. The very taking of human beings and trafficking them from Africa to North America as slaves is something, of course, that empires tended to do. But there was no talk of empire and little mention of slavery as a tool for economic growth and expansion. We were a democracy. Our narrative has been sanitised. It was in the late 1890s, as America was recovering from a major economic crisis, the Depression of 1893, that American political leaders were finally ready to speak openly about their imperial ambitions. The economy was booming by the end of the 1890s. It was the Gilded Age of American prosperity, the age of the Rockefellers and Morgans, the Astors and Vanderbilts. It was a wondrous moment of globalisation, free trade, open borders and mass immigration from Europe to the United States, and there was excitement at the newly introduced technologies, such as horseless carriages, electric streetcars, undersea communications cables, the telegraph, the telephone and other inventions, all of which provided faster communications and transportation, which in turn made the world smaller and more colonially accessible.

It was also the age of the warmongering William Randolph Hearst and other practitioners of yellow journalism. More than a century before Rupert Murdoch, Hearst was America's most unscrupulous media mogul. He teamed up with ambitious and openly imperialist politicians like

Theodore 'Teddy' Roosevelt and his best friend Henry Cabot Lodge, the hawkish senator, and together they pushed for empire-building as a top priority for the United States.

All of this occurred on the very cusp of the twentieth century, with an ambivalent President William McKinley sitting in the White House and his arch-rival William Jennings Bryan, a Democrat, accusing him of warmongering and imperialist ambition. In 1898, the idea of keeping European powers out of the western hemisphere was in vogue once more. The focus was on Cuba. There was widespread American support for the Cuban revolutionaries who had been fighting for their independence from Spanish colonial rule. Hearst was using his newspapers to whip up popular sentiment against Spain. They had been fighting for more than three years, and the Spanish had been brutal in suppressing the Cuban independence fighters, but the issue had only now become topical, as often occurs in Washington. By early 1898, tensions between the United States and Spain were running high over the Cuban situation. When the US battleship USS *Maine* suddenly exploded and sank in Havana Harbor under mysterious circumstances on 15 February 1898, Hearst, Lodge and others unfairly accused Spain of the attack. The accusation stuck, even though it was probably false. The battle cry in Hearst's newspapers became 'Remember the Maine! To hell with Spain!' The Hearst newspapers were so influential that the magnate used to brag to his dinner guests, 'This is my war.' President

McKinley, taken along by the flow of public opinion, then moved, almost reluctantly, to declare war on Spain. He justified it to the American people largely as a matter of humanitarian aid and spreading civilisation and Christianity. There would of course be no real contest. By 1898, American naval power was far superior to Spain's. Admiral George Dewey was dispatched to the Philippines and he destroyed the Spanish fleet in Manila Bay in no time at all. In Cuba, the US Navy blockaded the Spaniards and cut them off quite efficiently. After less than three months of what future Secretary of State John Hay would describe as a 'splendid little war', the Spanish were begging for peace. Hearst was meanwhile busy making his fortune and claiming credit for pushing the country into war. Roosevelt was the Assistant Secretary of the Navy but was effectively running the war much of the time.

The Spanish–American War of 1898 ended Spain's colonial empire in the western hemisphere. The US victory in the war produced a peace treaty that compelled the Spanish to relinquish claims on Cuba and to cede sovereignty over Guam, Puerto Rico and the Philippines to the United States. Alas, the question of what to do with the Philippines was a complicated matter for Washington, and in the end, President McKinley decided to annex it, which would trigger another war, this time with America's own allies against Spain, the independence fighters.

The British poet Rudyard Kipling would describe the US effort to colonise the Philippines and teach the natives about American democracy and manners as 'the white man's burden'.* Indeed that was the idea that Lodge and Roosevelt and even McKinley began preaching in public appearances, that it was America's responsibility to assist others in becoming more 'Americanised'.

Meanwhile, in 1898 the United States also annexed and Americanised the independent state of Hawaii (having previously sent the US Marines to the home of Queen Liliuokalani, to arrest at gunpoint the indigenous sovereign of Hawaii). At the time, the white population of American settlers in Hawaii amounted to 3 per cent of the inhabitants of Hawaii. The others would be, in the best imperial tradition, subjugated to the white man's will. Thus, the war with Spain and the Hawaiian and Philippine annexations enabled the United States to expand further and to establish its predominance in the Caribbean region and to pursue its strategic and economic interests in the Pacific. The Monroe Doctrine was once again vindicated. And then some.

Indeed, it was now quite politically correct and acceptable to speak openly of empire. Economists and newspaper columnists argued that it was necessary to annex new territories and open new markets for American industrial products. There was indeed a great debate about expansion across the nation, and the topic would arise during the presidential election campaign of 1900, when

---

* 'The White Man's Burden' (1899) by Rudyard Kipling emphasises the importance of the role of the white man, whose task is to civilise the colonised countries. This famous poem is considered a manifesto of colonialism and imperialism.

McKinley won re-election as a conquering hero. He defeated the Democratic candidate William Jennings Bryan, who had denounced the policy of American expansionism as wrong-minded imperialism and argued that the United States should focus instead on domestic issues. Bryan was popular with those American voters who viewed the acquisition of new colonies and protectorates like the Philippines as a wrongheaded departure from America's founding principles. He repeatedly denounced the views of Republican Teddy Roosevelt, who on 1 July 1898 created an early twentieth-century selfie by staging a photograph of himself mounted on a horse in Cuba. The headstrong Roosevelt had resigned his post as the Assistant Secretary of the Navy and was now Lieutenant Colonel Teddy Roosevelt, leading a volunteer cavalry regiment of 1,250 horsemen known as the 'Rough Riders'.

By positioning himself alongside the regular US military forces, Teddy managed to claim credit for the taking of San Juan Hill near Santiago de Cuba. He even donned a dapper blue polka-dot handkerchief and tied it to his felt cowboy hat, presumably so it could shield his neck from the hot sunshine. But the effect of the bandana streaming behind the figure of Roosevelt, mounted on his horse, proved spectacularly photogenic. The legendary photograph shows Teddy and the Rough Riders atop the conquered hill. After this premeditated stunt he became, as planned, a national war hero. The ambitious Roosevelt milked the photo for all it was worth, and he rode it all the way to the Governor's mansion in Albany, New York, just six months later. On his return from Cuba, the Republican Party bosses in New York pushed Roosevelt to run for Governor, despite their doubts about his political loyalty. Elected in November 1898, he became an energetic reformer, removing corrupt officials and enacting legislation to regulate corporations. His actions so angered the party bosses that they decided to get rid of him by drafting him for the Republican vice presidential nomination in 1900, on the assumption that this would be a largely ceremonial role where he could do no harm. Less than a month into his presidency, however, in April 1901, McKinley was assassinated by an anarchist with a pistol at close range. With Roosevelt as the new President, the battle in the Philippines quickly escalated; he pitched American forces against Filipino nationalists led by Emilio Aguinaldo, who was seeking independence for his country, as the Americans had previously promised, rather than simply a handover between colonial rulers, from Spain to the United States. Over the three years it lasted, the Philippine–American War claimed the lives of over 4,200 American and over 20,000 Filipino combatants. As many as 200,000 Filipino civilians died from violence, famine and disease. It was the first truly imperial war of the United States, at the dawn of the twentieth century. America did not acquit itself with honour or distinction; on the contrary, the US military committed multiple atrocities and massacres while they subdued the locals. Teddy Roosevelt, who was the most openly imperialist American President, was also a distant cousin of the more benevolent Franklin Delano Roosevelt, who would lead America through the Great Depression in the 1930s and throughout most of the Second World War, until 1945. But the two men came from different parties, lived at dramatically different times and rose to power in starkly different moments in American history. 'TR' was, among other things, the President who from 1901 to 1903 tried to persuade Colombia to give him the land to build what is now the Panama Canal. When they refused, he sent in the US Marines. The US military backed Panamanian rebels who took over the swathe of land between the Atlantic and Pacific coasts of what was then an isthmus of Colombia and rechristened it as Panama. The US President immediately recognised the new nation of Panama, which promptly ceded the right to construct and operate the canal to the United States. The Marines would remain deployed in Panama until 1914, when the canal was completed. In December 1904, a month after being re-elected to a full term, Roosevelt offered his most lasting contribution to the lexicon of American foreign policy: he described America as the 'world's policeman'. Historians call it the 'Roosevelt Corollary' to the Monroe Doctrine, which back in 1823 had warned European colonial powers to stay out of the western hemisphere. Now Roosevelt broadened the scope. There is condescension and glaring arrogance in Roosevelt's imperialist rhetoric: 'If a nation shows that it knows how to act with reasonable efficiency and decency in social and political matters, if it keeps order and pays its obligations, it need fear no interference from the United States,' said the man also known for his motto 'speak softly and carry a big stick'. He went on to warn, however, that

> chronic wrongdoing, or an impotence which results in a general loosening of the ties of civilized society may ... ultimately require intervention by some civilized nation, and in the western hemisphere the adherence of the United States to the Monroe Doctrine may force the United States, however reluctantly, in flagrant cases of such wrongdoing or impotence, to the exercise of an international police power.*

There it was: the first official presidential declaration of America's self-appointed role as the world's policeman, the 'exercise of international police power' to protect US interests. The Roosevelt Corollary would be used over and over again in the following decades, and in the first decade of the twentieth century alone the United States intervened to achieve regime change or to protect US economic interests no fewer than six times: in Cuba, Santo Domingo, Haiti, Nicaragua, Mexico and Colombia. The second decade of the twentieth century saw the rise of Woodrow Wilson, the historically controversial US President who was known for his utopian ('Wilsonian') vision of the League of Nations

---

* The so-called Roosevelt Corollary to the Monroe Doctrine contained a great irony: the Monroe Doctrine had been sought to prevent European intervention in the western hemisphere, but now the Roosevelt Corollary justified American intervention throughout the western hemisphere. See President Theodore Roosevelt, Annual Message to Congress, 6 December 1904.

and a world of peace and multilateral co-operation. But Wilson was actually one of America's fiercest interventionists, a man who wielded imperial power throughout his time in office, from 1913 to 1921. The morally high-minded historian from Princeton was also a fervent segregationist, whose southern upbringing had made him a racist politician who was popular with white supremacists at the time.* This is an inconvenient truth today, and it tends to clash with the rather more sanitised version of Wilson we had been spoon-fed until quite recently. When the self-righteous Wilson intervened to engage in regime change or to enforce US interests in the Caribbean, and this would be true of many American Presidents, he would always couch his reasons in the rhetoric of American moral superiority, the sense that we are the guardians of justice and democracy, of humanity itself. So when Wilson sent the US Marines into Haiti in 1915 for regime change, or into the Dominican Republic a year later for the same purpose, his language was all about 'Pan-American brotherhood', while the reality was a good deal more cynical.[4] The Marines remained in Haiti for nineteen years, and they occupied Santo Domingo for two decades. At the time of Wilson's intervention in Mexico in 1914, his advisers were urging him to 'blaze the way for a new and better code of morals than the world has yet seen'.[5]

---

* The harsh revisionism of recent years has cast a dark light on President Wilson, accused of being a racist and a white supremacist whose administration (from 1913 to 1921) set back the cause of civil rights for decades by instituting segregation and attempting to free speech. These theses have been at the centre of several academic publications. See J. W. Loewen, *Lies Across America: What Our Historic Sites Get Wrong*, New Press, 2019, and P. O'Toole, *The Moralist: Woodrow Wilson and the World He Made*, Simon & Schuster, 2019.

Wilson's Mexican adventures instead saw the US President rashly trying to take sides in the Mexican revolution and then making a hash of things. Among his other imperial adventures were the long-running 'Banana Wars', which saw US military interventions across the Caribbean and Central America, mainly to protect US business interests. Everything changed in 1914, as Europe's imperial monarchs began sending millions of young people to their deaths in defence of an archaic and crumbling world order. Enter Woodrow Wilson, who for three years had tried to keep the peace and avoid involvement in the European war. He even offered himself, unsuccessfully, as a mediator between Germany and the Allied Forces of Britain and France. Wilson got himself re-elected to the White House in 1916 with the slogan 'he kept us out of war'. But in February 1917, after the Germans declared unrestricted submarine warfare and started sinking American passenger ships, he had no choice but to enter the fray. Wilson always laced his rhetoric with moral hyperbole, and so when the President finally went before a Joint Session of Congress in April 1917 to declare war on Germany, he outlined his vision of the new world order that would emerge from the war. It would be based upon the principles of self-determination and freedom and democracy everywhere. 'The world', President Wilson informed the assembled senators and Congressmen, 'must be made safe for democracy.'

CHAPTER TWO

THE EMERGING SUPERPOWER

It was American military power that made the difference and defeated Germany, bringing an end to the world war in 1918, but Woodrow Wilson would fail to achieve his utopian vision of an internationalist League of Nations that would keep the peace. The idea was firmly rejected by the American people and voted down in the US Senate. Likewise, Wilson's clumsy and heavy-handed treatment of the losing powers in 1919 would impose a protracted period of austerity on many Europeans. Among Wilson's legacies was the punishing set of reparations that he caused his European allies to impose upon Germany in the Treaty of Versailles.[*] These austerity measures caused genuine and

---

[*] The Treaty of Versailles, signed in June 1919, officially ended the war but, despite overhauling the European state system, didn't address the root causes of the conflict. As a consequence, tensions continued to simmer beneath the surface. Berlin, judged as solely responsible for the First World War, had to accept extremely harsh conditions, both for substantial borders and army resettlements and for large sums of money to be paid to the victors as 'reparations'. Berlin called the treaty an 'imposed' peace and above all a humiliating one. Most importantly, the War Guilt Clause led Germany into an economic and social turmoil, which in turn paved the path for the rise of radical extremists like Adolf Hitler. See S. Zhu, 'The War Guilt Clause and the Rise of Adolf Hitler', *European Journal of Humanities and Social Sciences*, vol. 1, issue 3, June 2021.

widespread economic hardship and suffering in Europe, and a rising resentment that was soon exploited by the rabble rousers, nationalists, antisemitic demagogues and populist leaders who emerged in the 1920s and 1930s. The failure of austerity policies in the 1920s gave rise to extremist populism in mass politics in the 1930s. John Maynard Keynes, who was a member of the British delegation to Versailles in 1919, presciently warned that the American-imposed economic punishments for the losers of the war would ultimately prove a tragic error. In *The Economic Consequences of the Peace*, he argued that Wilson's idealistic vision for a new world order based on principles such as national self-determination and open diplomacy clashed with the harsh reparations and territorial demands imposed on Germany by the Versailles treaty.* Keynes saw Wilson's principles as lofty but impractical, at best.

The interwar decades were a period of rising anti-globalism, an early twentieth-century reaction to the previous period of globalisation and austerity. The Europeans of the 2020s have much in common with the Europeans of the 1920s. In both cases, there had been the disruption of war, a lethal pandemic and widespread economic hardship and suffering. Collective trauma. In both periods, income inequalities had been growing for decades. Then as today,

---

* As part of the British delegation to the Versailles Peace Conference after the First World War, Keynes – arguably the most influential economist of the twentieth century – had detailed knowledge of the debates about reparations that were demanded of Germany. He believed the demands on defeated Germany were too harsh. After resigning his government position, in 1920 he wrote this book explaining his reasons.

many Europeans who were angry at the austerity and hardship flocked to nationalist and extreme movements. In the 1920s and 1930s, political extremists successfully deployed their incendiary rhetoric against those they blamed for the suffering, be they foreigners, Americans, bankers, ethnic minorities, Jews or immigrants. The authoritarians were effective, and soon people would find solace in the blind promises of a Third Reich or of a new Regime Fascista.* History shows that following a collective trauma such as a war, a financial crisis or a pandemic, people tend to listen more to the demagogic harangues of populists, to those nationalist leaders who prey upon their fear and anger. The populists always offered seemingly simple solutions to complicated problems. They responded to the collective trauma that their societies were experiencing with a vivid display of national glory and pride, with unrealistic promises of prosperity and with the scapegoating of Jews and

---

* The unstable political situation and the economic crisis caused by the First World War favoured the rise of fascism in 1922, when the first Mussolini government was sworn in. The Italian liberal governments that preceded him had been unable to respond to the wave of strikes and discontent in the wake of the heavy toll the country paid to win the war. Not even the King, Victor Emmanuel III, had been willing to stop the March on Rome (1922), which paved the way for the fascist seizing of power. In the 1922 elections, Mussolini won a majority. The fascist regime decided in 1935 to transform Italy into a colonial power with the Ethiopian conquest. A year later, Mussolini signed an alliance with Hitler, the Rome–Berlin Axis, and in 1938, antisemitic racial laws were enacted. Nazism, in Germany, was also born in the wake of the dramatic economic and political crisis caused by the war, after the weak Weimar Republic was unable to stop either endemic unemployment or the devaluation of the mark, while the Germans were forced to pay exorbitant war reparations. Hitler's antisemitic and revanchist ideas, which promised to make Germany a great power again, easily won over the people. In the 1930s, Hitler organised two defence squads: the Gestapo (state secret police) and the *Schutzstaffel*, or SS, which were tasked with capturing and killing political opponents. Germany's President von Hindenburg offered Hitler the post of chancellor in 1933. In 1934, Hindenburg died and Hitler became the Führer, the 'leader' of all Germany. In 1938, Hitler's troops invaded Austria, annexing it to the German Reich. After promising not to invade any more countries, in September 1939 Hitler invaded Poland, starting the Second World War.

anyone else who could be blamed for the people's suffering. They provided visions of new empires to conquer.

In the United States, in the 1930s, this brand of fascism found its voice in the jingoist, antisemitic, isolationist and Nazi-sympathising movement known as 'America First', which was patronised by the aviator Charles Lindbergh.* So while Hitler and Mussolini were emerging in Germany and Italy, the United States was turning inward, prioritising its domestic concerns and distancing itself from global affairs. Economic troubles, mainly the Great Depression, further reinforced this isolationist stance. The Wilsonian dream of a new liberal democratic world order instead gave way to a United States that erected trade barriers and tariff laws like the Smoot–Hawley Tariff Act in 1930 and introduced new immigrant quotas. The aftermath of the First World War had left both the United States and Europe grappling with profound economic and social challenges. The combination of the slaughter of four years of war and the death count from the 'Spanish flu' influenza pandemic made for collective global post-trauma stress syndrome.

---

* Charles Lindbergh (1902–74) was the world's first aviator to fly solo across the Atlantic, from the US to Paris. His 33-hour nonstop flight was considered one of the most important feats of modern aviation and, thus, he became a popular idol and an American hero. Struck by tragedy – the kidnapping of his son, who was found dead on the side of the road after the ransom was paid – he moved with his family to Europe and Germany in 1935, where Lindbergh grew close to Hitler's Nazis regime and had been fascinated by it. After verifying the Luftwaffe's war potential and being decorated by Hitler, he returned to the United States shortly before the outbreak of the Second World War and he became a leader of the isolationist movement, America First, which was opposed to US entry into the war at any cost. Lindbergh shared the Führer's antisemitic ideology and believed that Hitler, to him the only answer to the communist threat, would win the war. After the Pearl Harbor attack, his statements made him 'persona non grata' by President Roosevelt, who in the meantime had declared war on the Axis. See Philip Roth, *The Plot Against America: A Novel*, Vintage, 2020.

The world was exhausted. The Americans were living the Depression years. In Europe there was hyper-inflation in Germany, ineffective liberal government and the rise of fascism in Italy. Apart from Mussolini, who essentially declared himself dictator in 1925, the interwar years saw a contagion of dictatorships that were taking root in Hungary (1920), Lithuania (1926), Poland and Portugal (1926), Yugoslavia (1929), Romania (1930), Germany and Austria (1933), Bulgaria and Latvia (1934) and Greece (1935). In Spain, meanwhile, in 1936 General Francisco Franco and his right-wing extremists overthrew the government, and the Spanish fascist emerged as dictator after four years of the bloody Spanish Civil War, a battle that was in many ways a microcosm of Europe's deep political divisions at the time.[1] Meanwhile, in America in the early 1920s the ineffectual President Warren Harding called for a 'return to normalcy' after the suffering of the First World War.* Harding's bland and passive management of world affairs would only be matched by that of his successors Calvin Coolidge and Herbert Hoover. It was President Hoover who took office shortly after Adolf Hitler won seats in the Reichstag in 1928. But America was not interested in foreign affairs.

---

* On 14 May 1920, Republican senator and presidential candidate Warren G. Harding of Ohio delivered his address to the Home Market Club of Boston. He outlined his hope that the United States would return to 'normalcy' after a decade of politics and foreign interventions. 'America's present need is not heroics, but healing; not nostrums, but normalcy; not revolution, but restoration; not agitation, but adjustment; not surgery, but serenity; not the dramatic, but the dispassionate; not experiment, but equipoise; not submergence in internationality, but sustainment in triumphant nationality,' he said. In November, Harding received the highest percentage of the popular vote in a presidential election up to that time. See Warren G. Harding, 'National Ideals and Policies', *The Protectionist*, 1920, pp. 71–81.

It was Hoover who watched Germany's slide toward authoritarianism and yet kept his diplomacy on permanent pause. It was President Franklin Delano Roosevelt who, throughout the 1930s, steered clear of any involvement in Europe, even though he was genuinely worried by the rise of Mussolini and Hitler. He had his hands full with the aftermath of the Great Depression and the numerous New Deal social programs he had invented. It was also politically expedient for him to avoid alienating the huge anti-war majorities across much of America. His rhetoric seemed internationalist, even Wilsonian, but for domestic reasons Roosevelt was a de facto isolationist in the 1930s. The world of the late 1930s was becoming a very dangerous place, with expansionist dictators now running the show in Germany, Japan and Italy, and with Stalin in Russia killing millions with his purges and show trials. Roosevelt reacted to Japan's rising aggression in Manchuria and elsewhere in the 1930s, but mainly with a combination of diplomatic engagement and economic measures. He made a famous speech in October 1937 condemning the aggression and calling for collective action, but he was then consumed by domestic affairs as the US had entered another recession. Roosevelt watched Mussolini's brutality as he conquered Ethiopia in 1935–36 and called for the League of Nations to impose economic sanctions on Italy. But these proved ineffectual. The US President, like everyone else, clearly saw what Hitler was doing in Austria and in the Sudetenland in 1938. But he felt his hands were tied because domestic

American political sentiment was in favour of avoiding US involvement in Europe's troubles. To his closest advisers, Roosevelt worried aloud that without American support the British and French would not be able to hold out against Hitler's forces. Austria and Czechoslovakia would soon be occupied by the Germans.[2] In 1938 Roosevelt privately regarded Neville Chamberlain with great disdain.[3] He never believed that the policy of appeasement would keep Hitler at bay. He saw American military involvement as pretty much inevitable. But in order to get himself re-elected for a third time in 1940, Roosevelt had to make it look like he would keep America out of war. He stole his strategy right out of the old Woodrow Wilson playbook, who in 1916 had promised to stay out of the First World War, and so Roosevelt disingenuously promised to stay out of the growing war in Europe. 'I have said it before and I will say it again. Your boys are not going to be sent into any foreign wars,' Roosevelt assured the crowd during a campaign address in Boston on 30 October 1940.[4] Nor did Roosevelt lift a finger to help the victims of Hitler's persecution of Jews, Catholics and members of the LGBTQ community. Millions were taken to be murdered in concentration camps because Roosevelt judged it to be politically inconvenient for him to increase the quotas for refugees from Germany and Austria in the late 1930s, and then throughout the war. Many were sent back to their deaths by an American administration that would rather turn ships around in New York Harbor than allow the refugees to be saved.[5] One notable example was the MS *St Louis*, a German ocean liner that set sail in May 1939 carrying over 900 Jewish refugees who were fleeing Nazi persecution. The ship travelled from Germany to Cuba, with the hope that the passengers would be allowed to disembark there. However, upon arrival in Cuba, the authorities denied entry to the majority of the passengers. Despite desperate pleas for help and negotiations, the ship was then denied entry by both the United States and Canada. Ultimately, the MS *St Louis* was forced to return to Europe, where the passengers were taken in by various countries, including the United Kingdom, France and Belgium. Some of these same passengers would fall victim to the Holocaust.

Roosevelt, however, was not the only cynical and flawed figure who was wielding great power at the time; his immediate peer group during and after the war included Winston Churchill and Josef Stalin. These three men, the other two of them being veteran imperialists, would begin post-war planning and the eventual carve-up of Europe and the world into spheres of influence at famous wartime meetings in Tehran in late 1943 and in Yalta in early 1945. At the Tehran Conference in 1943, Stalin, Churchill and Roosevelt had already discussed the post-war division and occupation of Germany, as well as the idea of replacing the League of Nations with a new organisation to be called 'The United Nations Organization'. At Yalta in February 1945, the leaders began creating post-war spheres of influence that would give the Soviet Union effective dominion over much of eastern Europe. This was Stalin's goal and Roosevelt deferred the matter, which to the Soviet leader meant he essentially acquiesced, also at the urging of Winston Churchill. Roosevelt saw in Stalin a member of the Grand Alliance who was defeating Hitler, and he glossed over the Soviet leader's demands for 'friendly governments' across eastern Europe. He let Churchill wax on about spheres of influence, and he let him negotiate with Stalin about the future government of Poland.[6] Roosevelt did not realise it at the time, but the American President's concessions to Stalin would pave the way for the emerging rivalry between the two great powers of the post-war period. Stalin would interpret the Yalta meeting as meaning he could engage in political machinations, probing to see if he could get away with installing puppet governments around the perimeter of the Soviet Union, and especially in places like Poland, Bulgaria and Romania. It would be Roosevelt's successor at the White House, the plainspoken and inexperienced Harry Truman, who would bring an end to the war a few months later, in August 1945. When Truman dropped atomic bombs on Hiroshima and Nagasaki, he not only ended the war; he also changed the dynamics of geopolitical power. The United States suddenly had a monopoly on atomic weapons and was immediately thrust into a position as the global leader. In 1945, America was thus in a position to shape the future of world politics; it was the greatest of the great powers and actually the only 'superpower' left standing. The institutions of future global governance would be designed by America, which was also the only nation still strong enough to shoulder the enormous cost of post-war reconstruction. What would emerge from the ashes of the Second World War was an American-designed new world order, complete with a system of American-invented and American-imposed institutions for global governance. It would become the Pax Americana. It was the dawn of what *Life* magazine publisher Henry Luce so gloriously called 'the American Century'. The United States was now the world's de facto hegemon, and even more than the world's policeman, it was emerging from the turbulence of global war as both the principal rule-setter and the guarantor and enforcer of that rules-based system.

Washington now had all the responsibilities and characteristics one would normally associate with empire. The United States was the predominant military power on the planet, having just dropped two atomic bombs on Japan. It was undoubtedly the richest nation on the planet, a major economy that had benefited enormously from the military spending and was recovering from its pre-war depression years. At a series of meetings held in 1944 in the Massachusetts enclave of Bretton Woods, the US dollar would become the world's leading reserve currency, giving the United States a huge advantage and economic dominion over international trade. In classical terms of territorial acquisitions from the war, the American empire had little to show; it was more an issue of spheres of influence at Yalta and the later Potsdam Conference. Nonetheless, as early as

December 1943, the Joint Chiefs of Staff had already drawn up a shopping list of territories and atolls to lease or occupy after the war. They were thinking ahead. By 1944, the British historian Arnold Toynbee observed that all of this preparation for the post-war period was 'the first phase of a coming American world empire'. Toynbee believed that the United States had the potential to create global harmony by promoting co-operation among nations, but he warned against the pitfalls of US arrogance and unilateralism.[7] It was in 1944, in an attempt to devise a plan to reshape and stabilise the global economy after the war, that the Bretton Woods conference in Massachusetts spawned the US-designed International Monetary Fund and the World Bank. These were the twin US-dominated financial institutions of the post-war 'rules-based' world economic order. The same people a few years later would design a set of rules for world trade called the General Agreement on Tariffs and Trades (GATT). The various new rules-based systems clearly established the United States as a *primus inter pares*, or first among equals, in all of the institutions of world governance, and with a shared veto power in the Security Council of the United Nations, which in October 1945 would be launched by Harry Truman. These institutions, formed in the 1940s, became part of the system of Western liberal democracy that is under fire today. The creation of the North Atlantic Treaty Organization (NATO) in 1949 was also a pillar of the post-war new world order. America had emerged from two world wars as a superpower, as *the* predominant superpower, and it was strong enough to dictate the rules.

Ray Dalio, the founder of the largest hedge fund in the world, has argued that over the past few centuries there has been a recurring pattern in which a new world order gets created every few generations by a concert of nations, and usually after a big war ends.[8] They get together to divide up the spoils, or to demand reparations, and they inevitably end up making geopolitical deals and redrawing the maps. Then there is a period of relative recovery, protracted prosperity and comparative peace, which exists inside the parameters of an imperial construct, a centre that dominates the periphery. And then comes the inevitable downward curve of the inverted parabola of empire, the decline that is often caused by internal domestic political or social conflict or deep divisions and inequalities in society, or even civil war. At the same time, according to Dalio's 'big cycle' theory, even as the global hegemon is losing steam, another empire is beginning to ascend the trajectory and may even soon eclipse and overtake the formerly predominant empire, which is now in decline. In 1945, the United States was the ascendant superpower; the old empires of Europe were shattered and impoverished, Japan was vanquished and traumatised by the atomic bombs that had rained down on it and China was still in the throes of a bloody civil war between the nationalists and the communists. But as the year of victory progressed, relations between the United States and Russia began to sour, and the two countries seemed increasingly mistrustful of one another.

At the Potsdam Conference in the summer of 1945, Truman became suspicious of Stalin's intentions, and the two had disagreements over key issues such as the division of Germany, the amount of reparations that Germany should pay, the setting of borders in eastern Europe, where Stalin wanted pro-Soviet puppet governments installed, and the future of Poland. Truman maintained a co-operative tone with Stalin for much of 1945. At Potsdam, he searched for common ground and tried a diplomatic approach. Some would say he was outmanoeuvred by Stalin; others would say that there was nothing Truman could do to get Stalin to budge. Truman was becoming disillusioned with Stalin's reluctance to fulfil the promises he had made at the Yalta Conference back in February 1945, particularly those concerning the holding of free and fair elections in eastern Europe. The American President was frustrated. At Potsdam, which occurred six months before the US bombing of Hiroshima and Nagasaki, Truman had decided to inform Stalin about the success of America's atomic bomb testing.* He had done so as an Allied power sharing information with a fellow leader in his normal, plainspoken manner. But from Stalin's point of view, he was being informed of a

---

* On 24 July 1945, as the Potsdam Conference entered its second week, Truman told Stalin about a 'new weapon of unusual destructive force', though he did not mention it was an atomic bomb. Stalin replied, according to Truman, that he hoped the United States would make 'good use of it against the Japanese'. The US had successfully tested their first atomic bomb on 16 July 1945. Kristine Phillips, 'He is honest – but smart as hell: When Truman met Stalin', *Washington Post*, 17 July 2018.

new super-weapon that would dramatically shift the global balance of power in America's favour. That could not have been very reassuring. So, he returned home to Moscow and gave orders to speed up the race to build his own bomb.*

Truman had been thrust into the limelight with the death of Roosevelt on 12 April 1945, less than a month before Germany surrendered to the Allies. The man was magnificently unprepared for the job. Truman would later tell his daughter Margaret that although he had served as Vice-President from 20 January to 12 April 1945, he was not kept in the loop by the President. 'I was at Cabinet meetings and saw Roosevelt once or twice in those months. But he never did talk to me confidentially about the war, or about foreign affairs, or what he had in mind for the peace after the war.'[9] And in his own diary entry on the night that Roosevelt died, Truman wrote nervously to himself:

> I knew the President had a great many meetings with Churchill and Stalin. I was not familiar with any of these things and it was really something to think about but I decided the best thing to do was to go home and get as much rest as possible and face the music.[10]

Six days after Roosevelt died, the millionaire US Ambassador in Moscow, William Averell Harriman, scion

---

* Following the Potsdam Conference, Stalin ordered that efforts to obtain a nuclear weapon be increased. By 1945, the Soviets had already managed to accumulate sufficient quantities of uranium to proceed with their nuclear program. In 1946, Moscow created its first nuclear chain reaction and on 29 August 1949, it successfully carried out the first nuclear test, codenamed RDS-1.

of the great railway and banking family, decided to fly to Washington and brief the new American President on the Soviet threat. On 18 April, Harriman arrived at the White House, bypassing entirely the Secretary of State to whom he nominally reported. He wanted to prepare the President for his meeting a week later with Soviet Foreign Minister Vyacheslav Mikhailovich Molotov, who would be calling on Truman in Washington on his way to the conference in San Francisco that was drafting the United Nations Charter. On the afternoon of 23 April 1945, as delegations were gathering in San Francisco, Molotov arrived. Until then he was the man best known for his 1939 deal with Nazi Germany, the infamous Molotov–Ribbentrop non-aggression pact. Molotov, who had been a confidant of both Lenin and Stalin, now stood before the US President. He had come to pay his respects to Roosevelt's successor, at the specific urging of Harriman. Harriman had been deeply worried that the Soviets were about to install puppet governments in every country across eastern Europe, and together with his deputy at the American Embassy, a young diplomat named George Kennan, he had plotted to schedule the Molotov–Truman meeting, because he wanted the US President to get tough with Moscow. He had briefed Truman on 18 April and he had set him up for the meeting. He would not be disappointed. Molotov turned red with anger at the undiplomatic and even harsh tongue-lashing he was now receiving from the new American President. Truman had first complained that the Yalta agreement was not being carried out and that he wanted to see a coalition government in Poland, as well as free and fair elections. Molotov demurred and promised that all difficulties could be overcome.[11] The US President then informed Molotov that all that remained was 'for Marshall Stalin to carry out the Yalta agreement in accordance with his word'. Molotov tried to change the subject, but Truman cut him off again.

'That will be all, Mr Molotov. I would appreciate it if you would transmit my views to Marshall Stalin.'

'I've never been talked to like that in my life,' protested a furious Molotov.

'Carry out your agreements,' Truman barked back at the Soviet diplomat, 'and you won't get talked to like that.'[12] Molotov, ashen-faced, then stormed out of the room.

The Yalta agreement on Poland would never be carried out, and after dithering for a few months the Soviets would eventually install a puppet communist government in Warsaw. At the time, however, Truman was actually quite pleased with his own performance during the encounter with Molotov. He told one friend that he gave the Soviet foreign minister 'the straight one-two to the jaw'.[13] The new President, in fact, was convinced that a tough stance was the only way to deal with the Soviet communists, a policy that would come to dominate American foreign policy for decades to come. Some would say that the tense meeting with Molotov marked the start of the Cold War. Others might conclude that it was merely a taste of things to come, an *amuse-bouche* before the Cold War. What is certain is that the Soviets were now being thought of less as wartime allies and more as unreliable communists with territorial ambitions. Truman himself was being increasingly surrounded by advisers, diplomats, amateur statesmen and a coterie of elite officials in the White House, State Department and Pentagon, nearly all of whom were now warning of the growing Soviet threat. Their perception was that the Soviets were bent on global domination, on the spread of communism and on surrounding their borders with puppet regimes. By the autumn of 1945, one could say that the Washington political establishment had virtually talked itself into the Cold War. Now, as 1946 dawned, the President of the United States was getting increasingly fed up with the Soviets. He was beginning to perceive them as a dangerous and unprincipled rival. This would lead him, and America, into its first post-war imperial reflex: the attempt to contain a potential rival by restricting it or by seeking to contain its power within a limited geographic territory. The goal was to spread democracy and to contain communism. The policy would become known as containment.

CHAPTER THREE

THE ACCIDENTAL EMPIRE

'I'm tired of babying the Soviets!' The President was fuming. Harry Truman sat behind the famous Resolute Desk in the Oval Office, with its tooled, brown leather surface and the small wooden plaque perched squarely in the middle, with the phrase 'the buck stops here' written on it in black lettering. It was early January of 1946. The onetime haberdasher from Missouri, now the most powerful man in the world, stared his Secretary of State in the eye. From where he sat, on the other side of the desk, Jimmy Byrnes must have realised that he was about to go through some things. Byrnes already knew he was in trouble because of the dressing down he had received a week ago when he had returned to Washington from the Moscow Conference of Foreign Ministers that was supposed to make progress on post-war order and international co-operation on atomic power. Byrnes had accepted deals that gave Stalin a clear advantage in eastern Europe and he had failed to consult Truman. Even worse, Truman learned about what Byrnes had agreed to in Moscow by reading the newspapers. The self-assured Byrnes was so pleased with himself that he had cabled home to organise a time slot for a national radio address in which he planned to tell the nation of his successes.[1] On the advice of his trusted Under-Secretary of State, Dean Acheson, Truman promptly had Byrne's radio address postponed by a week and summoned Byrnes straight off the plane. He himself departed on a cruise down the Potomac with a few presidential aides.

Byrnes landed in Washington on 29 December 1945 and was almost immediately airborne again, this time to Quantico, Virginia, where he boarded the presidential yacht, the USS *Williamsburg*. Truman took him down to the presidential cabin and gave him a piece of his mind. The President considered the 'successes' of the conference to be 'unreal' and he berated Byrnes for his failure to seek approval for his concessions in Moscow.[2] 'I have been left in the dark about the Moscow Conference,' Truman complained to Byrnes. He reminded him that he was the President after all, and he was then covered with blandishments by the sly former senator from South Carolina. Although the two men emerged an hour later smiling, their relations were becoming strained, and Byrnes's radio address had now been postponed to 7 January 1946. At dinner, Byrnes was needled by the hawkish Admiral William Leahy, Truman's Chief of Staff. Leahy later recorded in his diary that he had pressed Byrnes repeatedly 'for information as to what benefits accrue to the United States' from his deals in Moscow, but he reported, 'I was unable to get a satisfactory reply.'

After dinner, the browbeaten Secretary of State was invited to join Truman's regular poker game with the others, but he begged off and arranged to leave the yacht as soon as possible.* At the Moscow Conference, Byrnes was supposed to have pressed Stalin to respect the Yalta agreements, and above all he was supposed to reiterate the right for Poland to have its own democratically elected government. Byrnes was also supposed to have raised US concerns about Soviet machinations in still-occupied northern Iran, where Stalin was supporting rebellions by the Iranian Kurds and by ethnic Azerbaijanis, and in Turkey, where the Russian dictator wanted control of the Black Sea. He was also supposed to have ensured that the Soviets would renounce any role in post-war Japan.[3] Instead, Byrnes got nothing from the Soviets except a few cosmetic concessions that Stalin eventually offered in order to give the American something he could take home.† Byrnes desperately wanted to strike a deal, almost any deal, and so he essentially gave away Bulgaria and Romania, agreed to push Poland's borders westward and promised an international atomic agreement that

---

* James Byrnes's 'appeasement attitude' is well described by Admiral William Leahy in his diary available through the Library of Congress, Leahy Papers, Diary (pp. 2, 21 and 46) and quoted, among the others, by Walter Isaacson and Evan Thomas, *The Wise Men: Six Friends and the World They Made*, Simon & Schuster, 2012.

† The Kremlin understood well that, with the unifying factor of war gone, negotiations with the Allies would become much more difficult than before, also because the United States had a significant new lever for pressure: the atomic bomb. Nevertheless, the Kremlin did not lower its post-war ambitions and carried an extra pushy and tough stance – something made possible by Byrnes's attitude in Moscow. The conference resulted in a failure for the US post-Second World War proposals. Meanwhile, the USSR proved its strategy was able to devalue the Americans' new atomic ace. See Vladimir O. Pechatnov, '"The Allies are Pressing on you to Break your Will…" Foreign Policy Correspondence Between Stalin and Molotov and Other Politburo Members, September 1945–December 1946', Working Paper No. 26, Woodrow Wilson International Center for Scholars, September 1999.

seemed unworkable. And he let the ball drop entirely on Soviet provocations in northern Iran, which did not even get mentioned.

No wonder the Moscow meeting was seen by many as advantageous for the Soviet Union. The conference had been proposed by Byrnes himself, but at the end it not only recognised the pro-Soviet governments in Romania and Bulgaria but also granted the Soviet Union a role in postwar Japan. These were viewed as big successes by the Soviet Union.[4] This is why Truman was furious.

Veteran diplomat George Kennan, who was then serving as chargé d'affaires at the US Embassy in Moscow, observed these proceedings first-hand, and wrote in his diary a scathing commentary about Secretary of State Byrnes:

> The realities behind this agreement, since they concern only such people as Koreans, Rumanians, and Iranians, about whom he knows nothing, do not concern him. He wants an agreement for its political effect at home. The Russians know this. They will see that for this superficial success he pays a heavy price in the things that are real.[5]

Kennan was correct; Byrnes had been snookered by Stalin. A week after the dressing down aboard his yacht, on 5 January 1946, Truman summoned Byrnes a second time. This time he would read aloud from a handwritten letter. The President sat at his desk and stared across it at the former senator from South Carolina, the man who had once coveted his place as Roosevelt's running mate in 1944. The sullen Byrnes had been a good and loyal friend to Roosevelt, and he had done much to shepherd through the Senate the legislation that made possible the New Deal in the 1930s. But he had never really forgiven Truman for having had the good fortune (from his point of view) to have been named the vice-presidential candidate in July 1944, less than a year before Roosevelt died in office.

The letter that Truman read to Byrnes was harsh, and it must have been humiliating for the Secretary of State to listen to its contents. It was in some respects the edict of an emperor as read aloud to his factotum, and it reflected the posture and tone of the American President as he surveyed the post-war global landscape in early 1946. Truman began by reminding Byrnes that it was 'absolutely necessary that the President should be kept fully informed on what is taking place' and especially 'when negotiations are taking place in a foreign capital'.[6] Truman made clear that he would not approve of US recognition of the Soviet puppet governments in Romania and Bulgaria unless there was regime change. He complained about the fait accompli that he had faced in July 1945 at the Potsdam Conference: Russia's occupation of eastern Poland and eastern Germany. He regretted having pressed the Soviets to enter the war during his meetings in Potsdam less than six months before: 'The Russians have been a headache to us ever since.'[7] He told Byrnes that it was an outrage that there were still Russian troops in Iran stirring up rebellion in the north. And in case there were any doubts, Truman gave his assessment of Soviet intentions in typically blunt terms:

> There isn't a doubt in my mind that Russia intends an invasion of Turkey and the seizure of the Black Sea Straits to the Mediterranean. Unless Russia is faced with an iron fist and strong language another war is in the making. Only one language do they understand – 'How many divisions have you?' I do not think we should play compromise any longer.[8]

He then listed his goals for the post-war new world order:

> We should refuse to recognise Rumania and Bulgaria until they comply with our requirements; we should let our position on Iran be known in no uncertain terms and we should continue to insist on the internationalisation of the Kiel Canal, the Rhine–Danube waterway and the Black Sea Straits, and we should maintain complete control of Japan and the Pacific. We should rehabilitate China and create a strong central government there. We should do the same for Korea. Then we should insist on the return of our ships from Russia and force a settlement of the Lend–Lease Debt of Russia.

But it was the last sentence of the Truman letter to his Secretary of State that underscored the President's self-awareness of his own global powers and his deep frustration with a rival empire. 'I'm tired of babying the Soviets,' Truman told Jimmy Byrnes.* This was the definitive break with the Rooseveltian past, and it is something of a miracle that the Secretary of State managed to stay in his job for another twelve months. By then, Rooseveltian internationalism was out, and the national security state – with a clear policy of trying to contain the Soviet menace – was in.

The origins of the containment policy are to be found in an unusual and historic cable that was sent to the State Department in early February 1946 by George Kennan, who had been serving as Averell Harriman's deputy at the US Embassy in Moscow. Harriman had said his goodbyes to Stalin in January 1946 and had returned to Washington, keen to meet President Truman and to further his own career. Before leaving, he also said farewell to his deputy, the melancholic Kennan, who always felt that he was not being listened to. 'You're in charge now,' he told the 41-year-old Kennan. 'Now you can send all the telegrams you want.'[9] And that is precisely what Kennan would do, after a fashion.

Rather than sending lots of telegrams back to the State Department, sounding his dire warnings about the Soviets, Kennan would send one jumbo-sized telegram, an analysis

---

* Truman's famous 'babying' statement, made in January 1946, eight months after his accession to the US Presidency, is largely seen as the starting point of the new American attitude towards the unco-operative Soviet Union. After the celebrated slapping-down of Molotov and the Potsdam and Moscow Conferences, Truman's statement to his Secretary of State, James Byrnes, symbolically marked a major shift from Roosevelt's foreign policy. Seeing Russia's continued occupation of Iran and political developments in eastern Europe and the Baltic states, Truman said the time for making compromises with the Soviets was over.

that became known in the canons of Cold War history as 'the Long Telegram'. For Kennan, it was a catharsis; he let all his prejudices and fears and anger and frustration emerge, in a scathing portrait of a Soviet monster state that was hell bent on destroying America and spreading its hateful communism around the globe. The message was, to say the least, alarmist.

The strange manner in which Kennan is said to have written this historic portrait of the 'sources of Soviet conduct' is itself the stuff of a Hollywood movie. It was 22 February 1946, Washington's birthday. The embassy in Moscow was closed. Kennan was down with the flu, plus he had a toothache, and he was feeling sorry for himself in his rooms at the embassy residence. But as he reviewed cables from Washington, he came across a question from the US Treasury that wanted to know why the Soviet Union was not supporting the newly created World Bank and International Monetary Fund. George Kennan, who had complained for years that his warnings had gone unheeded, seized the opportunity to respond, but he hardly mentioned the IMF or the World Bank. Instead, he would turn his answer to this banal and technical question into a clarion call for the containment of the Soviet Union.

Even though the embassy was closed, the pompous Kennan telephoned his secretary, sent for two military attachés and gathered them all together in his bedroom. He then proceeded to dictate the entire telegram, composing his thoughts as he went along, and with his secretary and the others sitting there in his bedroom, taking notes.[10]

In Kennan's vision (or perhaps 'rantings' would be a better term), the Soviet monolith was a huge threat to the United States. He gave the Washington establishment a masterclass in Soviet history and claimed that the tradition of Marx and Lenin meant that the Soviets would always see capitalist countries as the enemy. He explained that the Russian character and world outlook was based on paranoia and insecurity and said this would always produce aggressive and expansionist policies. Only military strength could stop the Soviets, argued Kennan. The only thing Moscow understands is brute force.

The American diplomat drew a truly frightening and exaggerated picture of Soviet power and of Stalin's imperial ambitions for territorial expansion. Kennan simplified the world for his Washington audience into good and evil. The danger to America was the international spread of Soviet communism, and it had to be contained. It turned out that Kennan's timing was perfect.

The Long Telegram hit the staid corridors of the State Department like a Category 5 hurricane, and pretty soon it was being copied and circulated around the White House, the Navy Department and dozens of US diplomatic missions around the world. James Forrestal, the increasingly paranoid Navy Secretary, had hundreds of copies made. The Long Telegram was also eventually read by one Harry Truman. Truman and his advisers would take Kennan's bait, and since they were already fed up with Soviet machinations, Kennan's list of evil intentions confirmed Truman's worst fears.

Kennan became an instant celebrity, at least in policy-making circles in Washington. 'My reputation was made … my voice now carried,' he bragged to a friend.[11] A few months later, he would author a celebrated article entitled 'The Sources of Soviet Conduct', which appeared in the prestigious journal *Foreign Affairs*. In this article, which represented the collective sentiment of the American foreign policy establishment at the time, Kennan argued that 'the main element of any United States policy toward the Soviet Union must be that of a long-term, patient but firm and vigilant containment of Russian expansive tendencies'.

Less than two weeks after the Long Telegram hit Washington, another Cold Warrior stepped forward to lend a hand to Kennan, Truman, Forrestal and all the other hawks who were taking America down a more confrontational path with the Soviet Union.

In early March of 1946, Winston Churchill made a trip to Fulton, Missouri, in Truman's home state. The British leader had been humiliated and ousted as Prime Minister in the summer of 1945, but he still wanted to help Truman rouse American public opinion to take a tougher line with the Soviets. Truman had suggested that he make a speech at Westminster College, and the US President promised to personally introduce Churchill on stage. After weeks of closely co-ordinating with Truman and his advisers on the messaging, Churchill delivered his famous 'Iron Curtain' speech.

'From Stettin in the Baltic to Trieste in the Adriatic, an iron curtain has descended across the Continent,' declared Churchill.

Behind that line lie all the capitals of the ancient states of central and eastern Europe. Warsaw, Berlin, Prague, Vienna, Budapest, Belgrade, Bucharest and Sofia, all these famous cities and the populations around them lie in what I must call the Soviet sphere, and all are subject in one form or another, not only to Soviet influence but to a very high and, in many cases, increasing measure of control from Moscow.

There was truth in Churchill's statement, but it would be wildly exaggerated in Washington to reinforce those who wanted to increase military spending, search for a bigger bomb, station US troops around the world and encircle the Soviet Union with democracies. The rhetoric was all about freedom against tyranny; the self-interest of the United States was never once mentioned. In the late 1940s, Washington was full of self-righteous anti-communist ideology. A top-secret national security order called NSC-68 in 1950 proclaimed containment as the official policy of the United States. NSC-68 described the Soviet threat in wild and exaggerated terms: 'The Soviet Union, unlike previous aspirants to hegemony, is animated by a new fanatic faith, antithetical to our own, and seeks to impose its absolute authority over the rest of the world.' This focus on the ideological and geopolitical struggle between the United States and the Soviet Union left out one key element: making the world safe for Coca-Cola and IBM. The United States needed prosperous and accessible export markets, but western Europe was still in ruins, its economies devastated, its infrastructure destroyed. Kennan and the ideologues in Washington also worried about Soviet influence and about the Soviet funding of communist parties, especially in Italy, Greece and France. The Kennan sentiments, together with the Churchill fear mongering, now risked becoming a self-fulfilling prophecy, or at least a self-reinforcing mechanism of US worry and consequent escalation in the face of the perceived Soviet threat. Truman pushed forward with plans to build an even bigger bomb to outdo the Soviets: a hydrogen bomb. Stalin also raised the stakes, probing in northern Iran, causing a major crisis there in 1946 as he tried to egg on rebellious Kurds and ethnic Azerbaijanis in the north. He would eventually back down and withdraw from Iran, but only after Truman pushed through a United Nations Security Council demand that he do so.

Truman would speak of the containment policy in a March 1947 address to Congress, in which he unveiled the Truman Doctrine. 'It must be the policy of the United States to support free peoples who are resisting attempted subjugation by armed minorities or by outside pressures,' the US President announced. While the message to Stalin was clearly provocative, there was also an insidious domestic element in Truman's speech. He announced the creation of a Federal Employee Loyalty Program to ferret out subversives and communists inside the US government.* Truman's initiative unfortunately became the basis of a decade-long red scare, which gave rise to the infamous McCarthy era, in which Senator Joe McCarthy would relentlessly try to expose prominent State Department and Hollywood figures as former or current members of the Communist Party. This, alas, was also the legacy of Harry Truman.

The Truman Doctrine essentially implied that the United States had committed itself to resisting communism everywhere in the world. The need to prevent a 'domino effect' in which countries would fall one after another to communism would be an article of faith in US foreign policy for decades to follow. The wars in Korea and Vietnam would be among the most prominent examples of this imperial behaviour by Washington in the name of anti-imperialism. America would fight Soviet communist imperialism with its own crusade for democracy. Its policy would be to take preventative and proactive steps to contain the Soviet threat.

The Truman Doctrine and the containment policy were clearly imperial reflexes that were based on the US fear of a rival empire. But the Americans who surrounded Truman in 1947 did not think of themselves as an empire but as a gallant

---

* Several advisers urged Truman to launch a loyalty programme to safeguard against communist infiltration in the government. Despite initial fears that such a program could threaten the civil liberties of government workers, the rise of communism shaped Truman's decision to sign the Executive Order 9835, Prescribing Procedures for the Administration of an Employees Loyalty Program in the Executive Branch of the Government. See Joshua B. Freeman, *American Empire: The Rise of a Global Power, the Democratic Revolution at Home, 1945-2000*, Viking Presse, 2012, p. 67.

democratic great power. They were, as British historian Niall Ferguson puts it, 'an empire in denial', and the 'only one way to act imperially with a clear conscience was to combat somebody else's imperialism'. In the doctrine of containment, the United States had 'hit on the perfect ideology for its own peculiar kind of empire: the imperialism of anti-imperialism.'

* * *

The containment policy therefore created the parameters for the Cold War that would ensue, even though it was based on a wild US overestimation of Soviet strength and capabilities. One can argue endlessly about the extent to which the inexperienced and gruff Truman was at fault. One can reflect on how Stalin complained of American 'encirclement' as early as 1946, how the explicit nature of US containment policy led to the arms race, the space race and more Soviet aggression in a self-fulfilling spiral of Cold War-era hostilities. It is also worth noting that President Xi Jinping is today using the same language as Stalin did when he complains about Beijing's perception of 'American attempts at containment of China'.[*]

The greatest irony for Washington has always been the paradoxical juxtaposition of its moral superiority in defence

---

[*] On several occasions, XI Jinping complained against allegedly Western initiatives to contain China. On 6 March 2023 in his opening speech to the Parliament after receiving a historic third presidential term, Xi Jinping said, 'Western countries led by the United States have implemented all-around containment, encirclement and suppression of China, which has brought unprecedented severe challenges to our country's development.' Keith Bradsher, 'China's Leader, With Rare Bluntness, Blames U.S. Containment for Troubles', *New York Times*, 7 March 2023.

of democracy and opposition to totalitarian regimes, except when those regimes are useful to US business or military interests. And although America did not see itself as an empire, its behaviour bore all the hallmarks of an imperial power. The fight against the spread of communism led to increased US involvement in global affairs, the establishment of the Central Intelligence Agency by Truman in 1947 and the creation in 1949 of NATO, the key aim of which would be to deter Soviet expansionism.

Kennan did not like the idea of NATO; by now he had abandoned his previously hawkish position and was horrified by the genie he had let out of the bottle with his telegram. He felt that a military alliance on the borders of the Soviet Union would only provoke the Soviets. It would strike at the heart of their fears about being encircled. But it was too late.

Kennan was also a big advocate for covert operations, for intelligence gathering and for interference in European elections where needed to stop the communists in western Europe from coming to power. With James Jesus Angleton serving as CIA Station Chief in Rome, and CIA director Allen Dulles at Langley, Kennan and the team at the State Department in Washington laid the groundwork for what his friend Paul Nitze would call the 'Department of Dirty Tricks'.[12] It was a secret division created by a secret National Security Council order within the CIA and known as the 'Office of Special Projects'.[13] It was to be a directorate for overt and covert political warfare. The first efforts were relatively innocuous: dropping anti-communist propaganda leaflets from balloons in Italy and putting up posters that linked the bread supply to American aid. But in March 1948, Kennan considered the possible need to send US troops into Italy should it face a communist takeover. Angleton and many other CIA and State Department officers worked hard in early 1948 to provide cash to the Christian Democrats and their candidate, Alcide De Gasperi.

Indeed, Kennan was so worried in March 1948 that he informed Secretary of State George Marshall that there would be civil war if the communists won the Italian elections in April and that the US should be prepared to send troops in to occupy the Foggia oil fields.[14] After all, just a few months before, Secretary of Defense James Forrestal had watched with horror the situation in France and Italy, where local communist parties were trying to disrupt and bring down the governments. Forrestal asked his colleagues if the US should land troops in Italy to quell the disorders, and the reply from Under-Secretary of State Robert Lovett was, 'Not unless they ask.'[15]

While the CIA was getting involved in western European politics and channelling bags of cash to the Italian anti-communists,* back in Washington, Secretary of State George Marshall and his team were meanwhile working to create a European Recovery Plan that would shore up

---

* Studies find that the CIA notably provided an average of $5 million annually in covert aid to Italian anti-communist parties. From the late 1940s to the early 1960s, the aid went towards financially supporting centrist Italian governments; on the other hand, the Soviet Union supported activities of the Italian Communist Party, the largest communist party in Europe. See the National Security Archive, Briefing Book No. 579, 7 February 2017.

Britain, France, Germany, Italy and the rest of western Europe economically. The plan was born of the fear that unless the US helped western European countries, Stalin would keep pushing his Communist Party infiltrators and agents to destabilise their governments. The only way to keep western Europe democratic, and open to US exports, was to use Washington's considerable economic power in order to resist and counter the Soviet threat; if nations were economically stable, they would be far less vulnerable to Soviet corruption. America would be the benevolent and generous American friend and NATO ally, as long as Europe kept its markets open to American goods. The creation of the Marshall Plan from 1947 to 1948 aimed to provide economic aid to war-torn Europe, but to get the Congress to approve the commitment of an initial $6.8 billion, fully one fifth of the US annual federal budget, he had to first paint a portrait of the Soviet menace. Fortunately for Truman, the Soviet crackdown was proceeding apace across eastern Europe, and the Czech government fell in 1948 when the Communist Party used mass demonstrations, violence and a rigged election to take control.[16] Nonetheless, in order to convince Congress to authorise the funds, Truman had to use strong language. He denounced the Soviet's 'ruthless actions' and warned of a 'clear design' to take control of all 'remaining free nations of Europe'.[17]

The Marshall Plan was a game changer and a good investment for the United States. It helped keep the communists at bay in western Europe. It ensured European recovery and prosperity, integration and modernisation, and it ensured that Soviet influence in western Europe would be checked. The amount of money spent on the Marshall Plan would be the equivalent of hundreds of billions of dollars today. It helped create the new world order of the post-war with America at the helm; it made Europeans doubly grateful to America, first for having liberated them from Hitler and Mussolini and second for financing their reconstruction and creating a post-war economic boom.

This all came together in the space of less than five years after the end of the Second World War. The Kennan doctrine became the bible of the American foreign policy establishment. A massive military buildup to counter an overestimated Soviet threat began, setting off the arms race. The National Security State was created to compete with the National Security Council and the CIA, and a new Department of Defense was created, with all the services brought under one roof. In 1947, Truman asked Navy Secretary James Forrestal to become the first Secretary of Defense, and he took over in September of that year. Forrestal had been a staunch ally and promoter of Kennan, and he urged Truman to take a hard line with the Soviets nearly all the time. The combative Forrestal also strongly influenced the new Wisconsin Senator Joseph McCarthy, and not in a good way. The two men talked about their growing fears of communist infiltration of the State Department and other parts of the US government. Both had an unsettling view of politics, and both were slowly becoming more paranoid, even extremist. In the case of Forrestal, this would turn out to be clinical.

In early 1949, Truman was losing confidence in Forrestal, who was acting strangely. The punctilious and workaholic Secretary of Defense began to imagine he was being followed. He thought his phone was tapped. He had long conversations with fellow paranoid J. Edgar Hoover, the legendary head of the FBI, about subversion and communist infiltrators and the Soviet police state. And then he began meeting with Truman's rival in the 1948 presidential election, Republican Thomas Dewey, offering to stay on at the Pentagon should he be elected. Truman found out and summoned Forrestal on 28 March to demand his immediate resignation.

In the weeks that followed, Forrestal seemed mentally unstable, shouting to his friends that 'the Russians are coming' and warning that the communists and Zionists were out to get him. He told his friend Robert Lovett, 'Bob, they're after me.'[18]

Four days after resigning as Secretary of Defense, Forrestal was checked into the Walter Reed Naval Hospital in Bethesda, Maryland. He was given a VIP suite on the sixteenth floor of the building. On 22 May 1949, James Forrestal ran down the hallway and jumped out of an unguarded hospital window, plunging to his death below. On the desk in his room lay some scraps of paper, onto which

Forrestal had copied several lines from Sophocles's chorus about the warrior Ajax, a poem known as 'Worn by the Waste of Time'. It was a suicide note, of sorts.

The suicide of Forrestal was in some ways a precursor or premonition of the ultimate destiny of the American postwar hegemony, an empire that was accidentally acquired in 1945. The problem was that we Americans were really not very good at managing empire. We lived through the Korean War, which ended in a stalemate in the 1950s. We lived through the paranoia of that decade, through the McCarthy era, in which Senator Joe McCarthy and other extremists led a witch hunt against supposed Communists in Washington and Hollywood. We watched the birth of the space race. We watched the birth of the arms race. In January 1961, as America waited for its new Prince Charming (John F. Kennedy) to arrive at the White House, we heard a former soldier, President Dwight Eisenhower, warn the nation that it risked becoming 'a military-industrial complex'. Yet we paid no heed. We had sleepwalked our way into the Cold War, and now we would take on the Soviet Union with American gumption. Anywhere, everywhere, and for decades to come.

CHAPTER FOUR

THE PARABOLA OF US LEADERSHIP

The shadows lengthened in the dimly lit room of the White House, as a handful of President John F. Kennedy's advisers gathered to discuss a covert mission that would set the stage for more than a decade of global tensions. It was the summer of 1963, and the Cold War was at its peak. The buzzword of the moment in national security and intelligence circles was 'counter-insurgency'. The CIA was running something called 'Operation Switchback', a covert operation aimed at recruiting and arming mountain villagers in South Vietnam and training them to fight the Communists from the North.

The young and inexperienced President was on vacation at the Kennedy family compound in Hyannis Port on Cape Cod. Kennedy had already suffered the humiliation of his Bay of Pigs fiasco in 1961, the construction of the Berlin Wall by Khrushchev and the subsequent Cuban Missile Crisis of 1962. America had meanwhile wandered into a civil war in Laos and was now being dragged steadily deeper into the quagmire of Vietnam.

Roger Hilsman, the devious and ambitious 43-year-old Assistant Secretary of State for Far Eastern Affairs who had served as a jungle commando in Burma during the Second World War, was working with his boss, W. Averell Harriman, the grand old statesman on Kennedy's team, who was then serving as Under Secretary of State. The aristocratic millionaire diplomat had always moved at the highest levels; Harriman had carried messages for Franklin Delano Roosevelt (FDR) to Stalin and Churchill, he had been a friend and sponsor of George Kennan and a firm believer in the containment theory, and also of the domino theory.* He was a Cold War consigliere of the old school.

Back in 1954, when the French colonial masters of Vietnam had been defeated by communist insurgents at Dien Bien Phu and the country was partitioned into North and South, the hawkish Harriman had been among those urging that the US send troops into Vietnam. That did not happen, but the US effectively took over a neo-colonial or neo-imperial responsibility for Vietnam, viewing the country like Korea or Laos, as the location of yet another proxy war against the rival great power of the time, the Soviet Union. With the domino theory driving most foreign

---

* The geopolitical domino theory posits that the rise or fall in democracy in a country will have a knock-on effect in neighbouring countries. That belief was prominent during the Cold War and was used by US administrations as justification for American interventions around the world.

policy decisions, the US found itself increasingly entangled in Vietnam in the early 1960s under Kennedy.

American military advisers, present in small numbers throughout the 1950s, were introduced on a large scale beginning in 1961. When Kennedy took office in January 1961 there were 900 US military advisers on the ground in South Vietnam. By August of 1963, as the threat from the Viet Cong increased, the number had swelled to more than 16,000.[*]

The CIA, meanwhile, had unleashed numerous covert operations in the jungles of Laos and Vietnam and was now working overtime because the corrupt and dictatorial President Ngo Dinh Diem of South Vietnam had unleased havoc by shooting at peaceful Buddhist monks. There was talk of a coup plot against Diem being prepared by dissident generals.

That summer, Harriman and Hilsman were convinced that President Diem had to go; he was destabilising South Vietnam and he and his crooked brother were becoming a problem for Washington's anti-communist proxy war efforts. At White House meetings, a debate raged about

---

[*] US military advisers, present in small numbers throughout the 1950s, were introduced on a large scale beginning in 1961, and active combat units were introduced in 1965. By 1969, more than 500,000 US military personnel were stationed in Vietnam. After Radio Hanoi announced that the Viet Cong aimed at overthrowing the government to establish a regime like the communist North Vietnam, newly elected President John F. Kennedy approved on 30 January 1961 a $41 million counter-insurgency plan to help the government of South Vietnam resist communist aggression. The plan included a further 52,000 American soldiers and military advisers to assist that nation's army and civil guards. See Walter Isaacson and Evan Thomas, *The Wise Men: Six Friends and the World They Made*, Simon & Schuster, 2012, pp. 634–41. Top-secret documents uncovered in 2005 also confirmed these numbers as quoted in Brian Bender, 'Archives show JFK sought way out of Vietnam', *New York Times*, 7 June 2005.

what to do with Diem. John McCone, the CIA director, declared at one point that Diem was 'a son of a bitch, but he's our son of a bitch'. This would not be the only time an American official has referred to a bloody dictator favoured by Washington as 'our son of a bitch'. It was FDR who supposedly first made the remark about Washington's support in the 1930s for the dictator of Nicaragua, Anastasio Somoza: 'Somoza may be a son of a bitch, but he's our son of a bitch.'

Nor was it the first time the White House had sanctioned an assassination of a foreign leader by the CIA. Regime change – throughout the forty years of the Cold War, from 1949 to 1989, this was the way the United States often imposed its will on the world, when less violent means of diplomacy or persuasion had failed. The number of times this happened is literally too high to mention.[*] McNamara wanted to give Diem and his corrupt family another chance, and Kennedy considered the idea of

---

[*] CIA secret operations to facilitate or manifestly impose the establishment of a 'friendly government' abroad include, among the others, the orchestrated coup (codenamed Operation Ajax) in 1953 against Iran's democratically elected Prime Minister, Mohammad Mosaddegh, aimed at consolidating Mohammad Reza Pahlavi in power and securing US oil interests. The CIA orchestrated another military coup in 1954 (code-named Operation PBSuccess) against Guatemala's democratically elected leader, Jacobo Árbenz, quickly replacing him with dictator Carlos Castillo Armas to stop the spread of communism. The CIA helped attempts to capture (1960) then kill (1961) the first Prime Minister of newly independent Congo, Patrice Lumumba, out of fear that he would have provided fertile ground for Soviet incursion, as the Cuban Líder Maximo, Fidel Castro, already did. After backing the murder of the President of South Vietnam, Ngo Dinh Diem, the CIA notably intervened against elected Chilean socialist President Salvador Allende by supporting, on President Nixon's orders, different groups that lately, in 1973, supported military leader Augusto Pinochet. Between 1981 and 1986, President Reagan's administration secretly and illegally sold arms to Iran in order to fund Contras, a group the CIA had recruited and organised to fight the socialist Sandinista government led by Daniel Ortega. Ortega's government ended in 1990 with the election of opposition candidate Violeta Chamorro as President amid reports that the United States had provided funding to help her win.

sending a special mission to Saigon to persuade Diem to leave. Harriman preferred a simple CIA-sponsored coup by the Vietnamese generals against Diem.

In August 1963, the CIA reported to President Kennedy that there were at least three different plots being organised within the Army of the Republic of Vietnam (ARVN) against Diem. Then, on 21 August 1963, the South Vietnamese Special Forces, which were not part of the ARVN, raided Buddhist pagodas all over South Vietnam, most notably the Xa Loi pagoda in Saigon, the most sacred pagoda in South Vietnam.[1]

When this atrocity occurred, Harriman and Hilsman joined forces with an ambitious 35-year-old special assistant to the President. His name was Michael Forrestal, and he was the son of Truman's famous Secretary of Defense. President Kennedy once joked that he had hired Michael Forrestal, who was Harriman's protected protégé, 'to be my ambassador to that sovereign state known as Averell Harriman'.

The sins of the father are not always visited upon the son, but in the case of Michael Forrestal, he disgraced himself by sneaking his way around the bureaucracy to get the coup approved, and by working with Hilsman and Harriman to quickly draft and send a telegram to the US Ambassador to South Vietnam, Henry Cabot Lodge, that gave the green light for a coup against Diem. The eventual CIA-backed assassination of President Diem in November 1963, just three weeks before Kennedy was himself murdered in

Dallas, would trigger huge political turmoil and instability in South Vietnam, which in turn would drag Washington into a much more significant US military involvement under President Lyndon Johnson.

But in August 1963, Michael Forrestal was convinced it was the right thing to do. He agreed that Diem had to go, and that required the President's approval.

Forrestal was certainly under the influence of Harriman, who, in another one of history's more perverse jokes, turned out to be the young man's second father. Harriman had adopted Michael Forrestal shortly after his father had committed suicide in 1949, and he had sponsored his career from an early age. The young man received a naval commission in 1946, at the age of eighteen, while his father was Secretary of the Navy, and he was then appointed an assistant naval attaché in Moscow under his adoptive father. In Washington, in later years, Forrestal lived in the Harriman household. He was a member of the family.

The message that Forrestal and Hilsman crafted, known as Cable 243, contained a licence to kill. The US Ambassador was told quite clearly what to do: 'If in spite of all your efforts, Diem remains obdurate and refuses, *we must face the possibility that Diem himself cannot be preserved*,' the cable said. The US Ambassador, it continued, 'should urgently examine all possible alternative leadership and *make detailed plans as to how we might bring about Diem's replacement if this becomes necessary* [author's italics].'

The cable was drafted in a deserted Washington on Saturday 24 August, while Vice President Lyndon Johnson, the Secretary of State Dean Rusk, the Secretary of Defense Robert S. McNamara, and CIA director John McCone were all out of town. The President was up at the Kennedy family compound in Hyannis Port on Cape Cod. He was spending a two-week vacation at the luxurious beachfront estate on Nantucket Sound, with Jackie and the kids.

Amid the torpor of Washington, Forrestal, Harriman and Hilsman raced around the nation's capital, tracking down the deputy Secretary of State and other officials to get them to sign off on the instructions. Forrestal called Kennedy in Hyannis Port that Saturday evening to get his approval for the cable. The historians may debate whether Kennedy was negligent, distracted or just cautious, but the President gave his authorisation, on condition that the Secretaries of State and Defense both agreed. The Secretary of State, Dean Rusk, was telephoned by Hilsman and Harriman and gave his approval, while Secretary of Defense Bob McNamara could not be reached (he was hiking in Wyoming). But the cable was sent anyway, and in the following days all hell broke loose at the White House, with angry generals and Cabinet members claiming they had been tricked into agreeing. Nearly all of them, however, would later endorse the idea that Washington should not stand in the way of the coup.

As for Forrestal, Kennedy was furious with the young

man, but when he offered to resign, Kennedy replied, 'You're not worth firing. You owe me something, so you stick around.'²

Forrestal stayed on another year, but Lyndon Johnson never liked him, and he eventually forced him out in 1965. The escalation in Vietnam, meanwhile, roared ahead under Johnson, who would always blame his predecessor for America's descent into the quagmire. Indeed, recently released White House tapes and transcripts show just how much both Johnson and Richard Nixon would blame Kennedy for their Vietnam troubles. 'We went in and killed Diem, we got a goddamn bunch of thugs and we went in and assassinated him. Now we've had no political stability since then,' President Johnson complained to Senator Eugene McCarthy during a conversation in early 1966.*

'I'm putting all of the blame for this whole thing on Kennedy,' Richard Nixon told the Reverend Billy Graham in 1971 in a private telephone conversation. 'He started the whole damn thing, and he killed Diem, and he sent the first 16,000 combat people there himself.'†

According to declassified tapes of a secret 29 August

---

* The conversation took place on 1 February 1966, after the US had resumed bombing North Vietnam. As Senator McCarthy, belonging to the anti-Vietnam War Democratic platform, raised questions about this policy, President Johnson showed increasing anger at the mess that the Kennedy administration left him. Johnson blamed the previous administration for the Diem coup, which he felt was a bad idea at the time and continued to feel that it was a bad idea. See American Public Media, Vietnam and the Presidency, transcripts (americanradioworks.publicradio.org).

† On 7 April 1971, President Richard Nixon spoke for three minutes on the telephone from the Oval Office to the Rev. Billy Graham. The telephone tapes of this conversation, released in 2011 from the Nixon Presidential Library, confirm Graham's behind-the-scenes role as political counsellor to the President. The transcript of the conversation is also available at the Presidential Recordings Digital Edition, Miller Center, University of Virginia, https://prde.upress.virginia.edu/conversations/4001630

1963 White House meeting, Kennedy himself was clearly not averse to the coup against Diem. Recognising that some in Congress might get 'mad' at him for supporting coup-minded Vietnamese generals, Kennedy said that '[they] will be madder if Vietnam goes down the drain'. Nor did Kennedy disagree when Secretary of Defense Robert McNamara said that the US needed to 'plan how we make this thing work'.

* * *

The American war in Vietnam would of course end with a humiliating withdrawal from Saigon on 30 April 1975. It can be better understood if we see it in the context of an accidental empire that had begun by default after the end of the Second World War in 1945 and which by the 1960s had morphed into a hegemonic Pax Americana that was under constant threat from the Soviet Union and was now fighting various proxy wars and backing counter-insurgencies. And it was all being managed by some of the 'best and the brightest' Cold War statesmen and advisers, who were often more clumsy than brilliant. After Kennedy had allowed America to drift into more and more military involvement, the war in Vietnam was then disastrously prosecuted by the blundering Lyndon Johnson, and later still by President Richard Nixon and his Rasputin-like national security adviser, the redoubtable Dr Henry Kissinger.

Vietnam can probably best be seen as the first large-scale

case of American imperial overreach in the post-war period. A failure. It is also a prime example of genuinely incompetent management of empire over a protracted period of time, for more than a decade, from 1961 until 1975.

The final death count following the US defeat in Vietnam in 1975 was 58,220 American lives, 250,000 South Vietnamese soldiers, more than 1 million North Vietnamese and Viet Cong fighters, and 2 million civilians in both the North and South.*

The top White House policy advisers in the 1960s and early 1970s were nearly all middle-aged white men who had been schooled in the Cold War. For decades, they were convinced that their superior military strength would prevent the spread of communism in south-east Asia. They were happy to intervene in elections and to use covert methods to both seat and to unseat Washington's preferred leaders in numerous cases across Europe, Latin America, Africa, the Middle East and south-east Asia. They believed in regime change, partitions, proxy wars and covert operations as their default policy mix. At some point, the Cold War against communism had transformed America into a neo-imperial military hegemon that was not afraid to use crude methods to achieve its goals. In the 1960s, the 'best

---

* The Vietnam Veterans Memorial in Washington DC was in 1982 inscribed with the names of 57,939 members of US armed forces who had died or were missing because of the war. Over the following years, additions to the list have brought the total past 58,200. (At least 100 names on the memorial are those of servicemen who were Canadian citizens.) Vietnam released its official numbers much later, in 1995, and estimated that as many as 2 million civilians on both sides and some 1.1 million North Vietnamese, including the Viet Cong fighters, died in the war. The US military has estimated that between 200,000 and 250,000 South Vietnamese soldiers died in the conflict.

and the brightest' of the presidential advisers often showed frighteningly little cultural sensitivity or sophistication.*

During this time, the power elite that was supposed to represent the eastern establishment of the United States frequently made matters worse with an arrogant and often naive and simplistic approach to their task, the defeat and containment of Soviet communism.

The Vietnam War can thus be seen as part of a longer-term problem of US leadership, or perhaps the beginning of a phase in which America began to lose its collective innocence. Vietnam and the turbulent years which ensued the war's end were indeed among the main reasons for the formation of the inverted parabola shape of American influence: it was not malevolent intentions but mismanagement of empire and domestic divisions that weakened America's will and for a time its self-confidence. America's declared goals appeared to be noble, at least that was the rhetoric, but its covert methods were often squalid, and the blowback from repeated US failures would ultimately lead to widespread animosity toward Washington from many in the Global South. The victims of American foreign policy mistakes are scattered across Asia, Latin America, the Middle East and Africa.

As for John F. Kennedy, he was truly a Cold Warrior of his time, a man who was actually less modern than he

---

* These adjectives – 'best and brightest' – ironically refer to the title of David Halberstam's masterpiece about the history of the Vietnam tragedy. See David Halberstam, *The Best and the Brightest*, Ballantine Books, 1993.

appeared. He had been schooled in the politics of the 1950s. He was headstrong, and he was rich. Surprisingly, at the age of seventy-six, in 1960, Harry Truman became Kennedy's greatest critic. Truman was firmly against the idea of Kennedy being the Democratic Party's candidate. He told JFK to step aside, saying that America needed someone 'more mature'. He felt that Kennedy was a bounder, a dandy, too young, too inexperienced and perhaps also too Catholic. But his main objection had nothing to do with any of these. The main problem was that he was Joe Kennedy's son, and Truman hated the one-time bootlegger, who as US Ambassador to London had been a Nazi sympathiser. 'It's not the Pope I'm afraid of,' Truman once famously cracked, 'it's the pop.'[3]

Sadly, John F. Kennedy's inexperience, combined with the hawkish advisers he chose to listen to, had produced the early humiliation at the Bay of Pigs. It was this disaster, many historians believe, that led to the Soviet installation of nuclear missiles in Cuba and the subsequent Cuban Missile Crisis of 1962. Kennedy is hailed for his management of this game of nuclear brinksmanship, but his real legacy in Indochina is a much darker chapter in history. He allowed America to be dragged into a war that would continue for many years, and it would be the first war that the United States would lose.

When the war ended in the spring of 1975, President Gerald Ford was in the White House, having taken over eight months earlier from Nixon, who had been pardoned following the Watergate scandal and was now sulking at his home in California with his wife, Pat.

Henry Kissinger had been promoted to Secretary of State by Nixon in September 1973, but he kept his White House job at the same time for another two years. He became the first person ever to serve as both Secretary of State and national security adviser. With Nixon he had either racked up an impressive set of achievements or a collection of mistakes and war crimes, depending on whether you listen to his admirers or his critics.

Together with Nixon, Kissinger had plotted the 1972 Christmas bombing of Hanoi, which was much criticised, and Operation Linebacker, an extremely intense and massive bombing of North Vietnam that led to numerous civilian deaths.[*]

Kissinger was also the main architect of a series of 'secret wars' in Cambodia and Laos that would ultimately unleash the terror of Pol Pot and the Khmer Rouge, resulting in the death of 2 million innocent Cambodian civilians in the infamous 'killing fields' reign of terror that would follow.[†]

The secret bombing campaign in Cambodia from 1969 to 1973 was known as Operation Menu. It was conducted without informing Congress or the American public, and it aimed

---

[*] The Christmas bombing was the final bombing raid on North Vietnam, and it is generally known as the one that brought peace. The eleven-day US air offensive planned and conducted by the US Air Force and the US Navy Task Force began on the night of 18 December 1972 and targeted strategic interests but also civilians.

[†] In 2005, new findings demonstrated that the death toll was approximately 2.2 million, about a half million higher than commonly believed. See Craig Etcheson, *After the Killing Fields: Lessons from the Cambodian Genocide*, Texas Tech University Press, 2006.

to destroy North Vietnamese supply routes that ran along the border, in and out of Cambodia. Apart from the numerous civilian casualties caused by the bombings, Kissinger's war effectively destabilised Cambodia. It fuelled anti-American sentiment, helping to radicalise Cambodians, which brought to power in 1975 the notorious and brutal dictator Pol Pot and his Khmer Rouge regime, which placed millions of Cambodians in forced labour, saw mass executions, forced mass relocations and led to widespread suffering and the death of 2 million people out of a population of 7 million.

The secret war would end in 1973; the dead would remain dead. The war in Vietnam would continue for nearly another two years. Yet Henry Kissinger would soon fly to Oslo to pick up a Nobel Peace Prize. His 'achievement' for the Nobel Committee was having negotiated a ceasefire and the withdrawal of all US troops from Vietnam, together with Le Duc Tho, the North Vietnamese negotiator (who declined the controversial prize). The Paris deal was then dressed up in fancy diplomatic wrapping paper and called 'the Paris Peace Accords' of January 1973. But Kissinger didn't get to attend his own public awards ceremony in Norway at the end of 1973. There were too many anti-American protesters in the streets, calling Kissinger a war criminal and carrying placards saying that he did not deserve the prize. With an eye on his personal security, Kissinger chose to receive the Nobel Peace Prize in a private ceremony at the US Ambassador's residence in Oslo rather than at the usual public ceremony in the Norwegian capital.

While Henry Kissinger got his Nobel prize, Nixon was trumpeting the idea that the US withdrawal from Vietnam could be called 'Peace with Honor'. Nixon actually managed to convince half of America that the words meant something. It was fifteen months later, on 30 April 1975, with Nixon already retired to California, that the last American helicopters would finally hover above the US Embassy in Saigon, as desperate crowds raced up wobbly ladders to the roof, waving their passports, shouting, begging to be taken away. On that day, the BBC reported the facts in London:

> The war in Indochina is over. The US has withdrawn in defeat from Saigon, amidst frantic crowds demanding to be evacuated. The US helicopters flew to a waiting aircraft carrier in the South China Sea, where the choppers were frantically landed and then pushed off the carrier and into the sea.

Richard Nixon and Henry Kissinger called it 'peace with honour'.

* * *

If we were to measure some of the most powerful collective trauma, shock and deep divisions to afflict American society in the second half of the twentieth century, Vietnam would be a good case study. The American empire had until now seemed invincible. Now it had lost a war, having been unable to use American military might to defeat guerilla warfare in the jungle. Vietnam was a trauma, a knock to the empire, but there was more to come as the 1970s played out.

The mid-to-late 1970s was a time of great upheaval and crisis for America, and not just because of Vietnam and Watergate and Nixon's resignation, but also in the Middle East. After the Israeli victory in the Yom Kippur War of 1973, the Arab nations were still angry with America and seeking leverage against the American hegemon. Washington suddenly found itself facing the appearance of a new global oil producers cartel called OPEC, the Organization of Petroleum Exporting Countries. For the first time, a strange assortment of Arab desert kingdoms with unheard-of names like Qatar and Oman and Abu Dhabi were joining with Iran and Saudi Arabia to create a cartel that for a time would control global energy prices. Even worse, in October 1973 OPEC would impose an oil embargo on oil exports to the United States, Canada, European nations and others who supported Israel. The oil price would soon quadruple, leading to record US inflation levels and then recession, and thus the worst of both worlds: a condition of simultaneously soaring prices and economic contraction known as 'stagflation'.

Taken together, the Vietnam defeat, the Watergate scandal, the first-ever resignation of an American President, the OPEC embargo, the energy crisis and the sharp recession all comprised a painful set of asymmetric shocks for America and for the American-designed world order. There was more turbulence on the horizon, especially toward the end of the decade, when events in the Middle East would once again challenge the standing of the Pax Americana.

In December 1978, one of the world's most arrogant dictators, the Shah of Iran, Mohammad Reza Pahlavi, would be told by his staunch ally the United States that his time was up. As the Iranian Revolution of 1978–79 saw violent protests and political turmoil, it became clear that the Shah was not going to survive as ruler. In December, the US Ambassador in Tehran, William Sullivan, was dispatched by President Jimmy Carter to advise the Shah that he should probably leave the country. This was not the first time the Shah had been exiled from his Persian Empire. Back in 1953, the CIA had sent him abroad for a few months while it orchestrated regime change in Tehran, but a strong and independent Prime Minister named Mohammad Mossadegh came to power and threatened to nationalise US and British oil concessions, so the Shah had to be plucked from exile and reinstated on the Peacock Throne. That was 1953. But this time was different, because Ayatollah Ruhollah Khomeini was about to arrive from his exile in France, and the Shah did not have a chance of surviving after that.

So on 16 January 1979, the Shah and his third wife and his entourage bundled everything they could carry into two Boeing 707s and took off for a wild ride that would see them going first to Egypt and then to Morocco. But when in March 1979 the Shah asked the White House to allow him to settle in the United States, the answer was no.[4] Jimmy Carter had been a harsh critic of the Shah's reliance on the SAVAK secret police, which specialised in brutality toward dissidents, torture chambers and other human rights abuses. And back home, the Shah was seen by the Iranian revolutionaries as a puppet of Washington and a symbol of tyranny and oppression. He was indeed all of these things.

In an eerie prelude to what would happen later in the same year, in February 1979, with the Shah by now visiting with café society in exile in Marrakech, the US Embassy in Tehran was attacked by a group of Islamist militants. Remarkably, there were no fatalities, and no hostages were taken, and the militants eventually left the embassy. But it was clear to the White House that if the Shah were allowed into the United States, things would get a great deal worse. In late February it fell to Zbigniew Brzeziński, the President's national security adviser, to inform the Shah's emissaries that it would be difficult to welcome him into the United States. Brzeziński tried to get Carter to reconsider, while his predecessor Henry Kissinger was fuming that it was wrong that such 'an old friend of the United States' would be treated so badly. But an angry and prescient Carter said no again. He told his advisers that he did not want the Shah playing tennis in the United States while Americans in Iran were being kidnapped or killed.*

---

* Despite Henry Kissinger advocating to relocate the Shah to the United States, President Carter thought that this was not the time for him to be allowed into the US. By late July 1979, Carter wrote in his diary that he didn't see any benefit in the Shah's moving to the US: 'I don't have any feelings that the shah or we would be better off with him playing tennis several hours a day in California instead of Acapulco, with Americans in Tehran being killed or kidnapped,' he wrote. See William J. Daugherty, 'Jimmy Carter and the 1979 Decision to Admit the Shah into the United States', American Diplomacy, April 2003.

Kissinger teamed up with David Rockefeller to lobby Carter, arguing that since the Shah had cancer, he should at least be admitted into the United States to have medical treatment. The Kissinger–Rockefeller team got the Shah a temporary respite in the Bahamas, and then in Mexico, then in Panama and finally, in October 1979, Carter relented and agreed to allow the Shah to enter the US for the treatment of his cancer.

On 22 October 1979, the Shah flew into Andrews Air Force Base near Washington. In Tehran, all hell broke loose as the Islamic revolutionaries poured into the streets. The Great Satan had given refuge to their puppet. They denounced what they perceived as decades-long US support for the authoritarian regime, at the expense of the Iranian people. Thirteen days later, on 4 November 1979, and just as Carter had feared, the militants stormed the US Embassy in Tehran. This time they took fifty-two hostages and they would proceed for 444 days, until January 1981, to humiliate Jimmy Carter and the United States of America. As if to emphasise the case of imperial impotence that had now stricken America, the Carter White House was further humiliated by its aborted attempt in April 1980 to send the elite Delta Force soldiers to stage a rescue mission for the hostages. The mission, called Operation Eagle Claw, ended as US helicopters crashed into the desert and eight US servicemen lost their lives.

These events marked a death knell for Jimmy Carter's presidency, and six months later he was soundly defeated by Ronald Reagan in the November 1980 vote. Ayatollah Khomeini would keep the hostages imprisoned in the embassy in Tehran until 20 January 1981. They were released just moments after Reagan was sworn in as the fortieth President of the United States.

The most extraordinary aspect of the Iranian hostage crisis, apart from the way it brought down a President and caused a lengthy and collective trauma for the nation, was that it was another textbook case of imperial malfunction. The Shah had been 'our son of a bitch' for a long time, since the Second World War. He had been an imperial proxy for the United States, a recalcitrant, foppish and brutal strongman who was propped up for decades.

What happened was a remarkable humiliation of American power, in this case at the hands of Iran's ayatollahs. What extraordinary decades the 1960s and 1970s had been for the American empire, bookended by the war in Vietnam and the Iran hostage crisis and buffeted by assassinations, a failed war, a national nightmare of presidential scandal, a breakdown of social cohesion in a divided nation and then the humiliation imposed by the ayatollahs on the Shah's imperial overlords.

By the time Reagan arrived at the White House, the parabola of American leadership appeared to be truly tilting in a downward trajectory. The story of how he turned things around in the 1980s is a remarkable case study of the fullest possible exercise of imperial power. Reagan outspent the Russians on arms, and by the end of the decade he had won the Cold War. He also played a key role in shaping the contours of a more interconnected and interdependent world economy. With his neoliberal economic policies in the 1980s, Reagan would accelerate the early stages of a process that would later become known as globalisation.

CHAPTER FIVE

THE EMPIRE STRIKES BACK

The decline of the American empire has been foretold many times, over and over again, and for many years mainly by intellectuals on the fringes of academia. Until recently, all of those making the prediction have been wrong.

Pundits, politicians, historians, critics and foreign observers have pronounced the death knell of the Pax Americana on numerous occasions, as an almost Pavlovian reflex, each time the United States suffers a setback, is challenged by terrorists or gets entangled in lengthy and seemingly unwinnable wars that are conducted halfway across the world. This was as true in the 1970s as it would be a half century later.

But sometimes, the empire strikes back. America has a way of surprising, of defying expectations. Just when it seems to be sinking in failure, when one of Washington's regime change or nation-building plans has gone badly wrong, America stages a comeback. There is some hidden spark in the dynamic of the huge economy, combined with the superpower confidence, the frontier spirit and the capacity for innovation and for using technology to achieve huge productivity gains that makes America the superpower it is. Rather than its exceptionalism, it is innovation that makes America great. Put it all together and you have the extraordinary energy of America, the sense of uniqueness and manifest destiny, but in a good way. This, fortunately, is also America.

And so, in the 1980s, after a decade of humiliation, scandal and war, the arrival of an optimistic cheerleader like Ronald Reagan stirred something deep in the American psyche. Reagan, with his showman's ebullience and his Hollywood smile, essentially seduced the American electorate. He positively thrashed poor old Jimmy Carter in the election of November 1980, winning 489 electoral votes to Carter's measly forty-nine.[*]

After Carter's debacle of a presidency, the Americans were looking for reasons to be cheerful, and the booming 1980s under Ronald Reagan provided what they wanted. The economy roared ahead, yuppies proliferated throughout America, stock markets soared and people had money to spend. Reagan came with all sorts of neoliberal economic policies and 'trickle-down economics' and massive tax cuts that seemed to favour the rich but that he promised would eventually create new wealth that would trickle down to the

---

[*] The failure to resolve the hostage crisis severely affected both the campaign and the outcome of the 4 November 1980 presidential election won by then Republican Governor of California, Ronald Reagan. After decades, revelations from Reagan's closest entourage made it clear what was behind Carter's electoral failure: not only the handling of the hostage crisis but also a well-conceived plan to sabotage his re-election. See Peter Baker, 'A Four-Decades Secret: One Man's Story of Sabotaging Carter's Re-election', *New York Times*, 18 March 2023.

middle classes. Reagan emphasised free-market principles, and he played a key role in the early stages of the globalisation process. His administration made deregulation, tax cuts and the promotion of free trade the hallmarks of what would be called 'Reaganomics'.

Reagan's policies would indeed spur economic growth, but they also laid the groundwork for the creation of a new American *lumpenproletariat* of underpaid service industry workers, the working poor. Reagan essentially cut taxes on the rich while at the same time slashing welfare for the poor. This process widened income inequalities and caused large-scale job displacement of workers and a growing wealth gap in American society. Reagan's free-trade promotion was meanwhile clear in his advocacy of the North American Free Trade Agreement (NAFTA), a new free-trade zone that would include Canada, the US and Mexico. Rather than practising economic imperialism, Reagan integrated and in some ways incorporated the Canadian and Mexican economies in a free-trade zone.

Reagan's time in office was full of controversy and scandal, the biggest one being the Iran–Contra scandal, in which the White House secretly sold arms to Iran from 1981 to 1986, violating the US arms embargo, and then tried to use the proceeds to finance the 'Contras', an extreme right-wing rebel group in Nicaragua that was opposing the left-wing government of Sandinistas. Together with Colonel Oliver North, a colourful cast of arms dealers and tales of drug runners and CIA pilots, the Iran–Contra scandal revealed the dark underside of Reagan's management of regime change. Actually, very little had changed since President William Taft had intervened in Nicaragua in 1912, at the time to protect US business interests in the 'banana wars'. For much of the twentieth century, the de facto American empire tended to interfere with Latin American countries at will, a process that would very often have disastrous and unintended consequences.

The other big scandal during the Reagan years was related to the funnelling of more than $5 billion of secret US government-guaranteed loans to Saddam Hussein through the Atlanta, Georgia branch of a big Italian state bank that was called Banca Nazionale del Lavoro. An obscure local banker was allowed to send the billions as letters of credit and other financing, even though the CIA, together with British and Italian intelligence services, were aware that the money was not being used for the stated purpose of financing Iraqi purchases of US grains but to ship arms and missile parts to Iraq, which was then at war with Iran. For years, cluster bomb materials that originated in Pennsylvania, as well as all sorts of US and British technology, was sent to Saddam in a program that allegedly involved then Vice President George Herbert Walker Bush, a former CIA chief who was Reagan's deputy. Bush issued a denial and he had the Iraqgate scandal closed down by his Attorney General at the time, the servile William Barr (yes, the same man who pops up later as Attorney General in the Trump administration). There is even documentary evidence that Bush participated in the cover-up of the Iraqgate affair.*

Both the Iran–Contra scandal and the Iraqgate affair were prime examples of covert operations run by rogue operators in collusion with US intelligence services and with the secret approval of the White House. Such imperial adventures have, of course, been part and parcel of US foreign policy since 1945.

During his two terms in office, Reagan's imperial approach to managing American leadership was almost constantly on show, whether it was a small invasion of the Caribbean island of Grenada in 1983 or the bombing of Colonel Muammar Gaddafi's home in Tripoli in 1986. Reagan didn't mind throwing American military weight around, and by the time he left office, the United States had more than 900 military bases scattered around the globe.†

The 1980s was nonetheless a period of regained confidence; there was a sense of America coming back, of an *empire redux*. What had appeared to all to be the decline of

---

* Multiple findings point at the fact that the Bush administration pursued a secret policy in cooperation with Iraq to pervert US agricultural assistance programs to help Saddam Hussein obtain weapons. In fact, newspapers like the *New York Times* kept telling their readers that through these programs 'George Bush continued to provide billions of dollars in loans to Saddam Hussein after the war with Iran ended in 1988 ... Iraqi agents [stole] some of the money and used it to buy and build biological, chemical and nuclear weapons'. David Shaw, 'Iraqgate. A Case Study of a Big Story with Little Impact', *Los Angeles Times*, 27 October 1992. See also Alan G. Friedman, *Spider's Web: The Secret History of How the White House Illegally Armed Iraq*, Bantam, 1993.
† As to the latest available Pentagon documents based on 2020–2021 data, the US controlled approximately 750 military bases outside the fifty US states and Washington D.C. The poor Pentagon data reporting practices and the notoriously difficult definition of the term 'base' make a fully comprehensive list impossible to create.

American leadership and power was now being reversed. It was visible. Whether you liked the cowboy-President or not, Reagan's management of empire ultimately proved successful in maintaining and expanding American influence. Over his two terms as President, he would outspend the Soviets (doubling the Pentagon's annual budget from $150 billion to $300 billion), trigger a new arms race and announce a new Hollywood-sounding missile defence system called the 'Star Wars' project, or as it was known in the corridors of the Pentagon, the Strategic Defense Initiative (SDI).

He would also use his considerable acting skills (and a good team of speechwriters) to reach epiphanies of rhetoric such as his 'evil empire' speech in March 1983, before the National Association of Evangelicals meeting in Orlando, Florida. It was here that Reagan first described the Soviet Union as an 'evil empire' and as 'the focus of evil in the modern world'. There was no sense of irony here: the President of a de facto empire was sounding his anti-imperialist trumpet in denouncing a rival great power as an evil empire. The slogan struck a chord with many Americans; it alarmed and angered the Russians.

By the second half of the 1980s, Washington was winning the arms race. The Soviet Union was creaking. Mikhail Gorbachev had launched the most ambitious, sweeping and, from the West's point of view, promising program of reform in the history of the Soviet Union. It was called glasnost. Reagan presented himself as the stern but willing partner of the declining Soviet Union.

In June 1987, Reagan stood in front of thousands of cheering fans at the Brandenburg Gate in Berlin and reminded the crowd of the previous visit to Berlin, twenty-four years before, in June 1963 by President John F. Kennedy, when he had stood before the Berlin Wall and famously declared, in support of the struggle of Berlin's residents against oppression and division, 'Ich bin ein Berliner.'

Now, in an equally historic speech, Reagan stood before the wall and called for the reunification of the divided city. 'Mr Gorbachev, tear down this wall!' declared the American President, who by now had almost won the Cold War.

In Moscow, Mikhail Gorbachev was releasing political prisoners, allowing new press freedoms and preaching the gospel of perestroika and glasnost. It was a moment of bold actions, of bold rhetoric. For Reagan it was all about America's moral superiority and the exporting of the American model of democracy. 'We in the West must resist Soviet expansion,' Reagan reminded Chancellor Helmut Kohl and the crowd in Berlin, 'and so we must remain strong, we must maintain defences of unassailable strength.'

Although Gorbachev would eventually be consumed by his revolution, he was certainly the boldest leader the Soviet Union had ever had. Reagan was bold as well, but more importantly he was the leader who designed and executed the most expensive and winning strategy. By the time the Berlin Wall actually came tumbling down in November 1989, to be rapidly followed two years later by the dissolution of the Soviet Union, America was becoming once again, for the second time since 1945, the only surviving superpower in a suddenly unipolar world. With a quiescent China turned inward on its own massive economic reform program, and the imploding Soviet Union posing no threat, America would become a 'hyperpower'. Sadly, the man who took over from Reagan was not really up to the task. During four years in office George Herbert Walker Bush would fail to design a grand strategy for the new post-Cold War world order. His critics used to say that he lacked vision.

As news of the Berlin Wall being dismantled reached Washington on the afternoon of 9 November 1989, Brent Scowcroft, the national security adviser, walked into the Oval Office to tell President Bush that it seemed that the wall had been opened. But Bush did not betray any reaction to the news. He had been a silent Vice President for many years and before that a silent director of the Central Intelligence Agency. The man was cautious, prudent. As Bush biographer Jon Meacham recounts in *Destiny and Power*, Bush was determined not to 'gloat'.[2]

When he met with reporters in the Oval Office, Bush struck a tone so subdued that CBS reporter Lesley Stahl asked, 'This is a sort of great victory for our side in the big East–West battle, but you don't seem elated.'

'I'm not an emotional kind of guy,' replied Bush. When pressed further, he added laconically that he was 'very pleased'.*

In fact, Bush was worried that an overreaction might antagonise the Soviets or create a boomerang. The previous day, he had written in his diary, 'If we mishandle [the dramatic changes occurring in eastern Europe] and get way out looking like [promoting dissent] is an American project, you would invite crackdown, and ... that could result in bloodshed.'

With similar concerns, Gorbachev had cabled Bush the day that the Wall opened, urging him not to overreact. In appreciation of Bush's muted response to the situation, a Soviet spokesman told the press, 'I think he's handling it as a real statesman.'[3]

Bush, however, was not thinking ahead. When he met Gorbachev just a few weeks after the Berlin Wall came down in December 1989 in Malta, Bush was his usual restrained and cautious self. Other men might have used such an obviously historic meeting to say a few words for posterity and thus symbolically ratify the end of the Cold War. But Bush's words were muted. He did not rise to the occasion, although he would later argue that this

---

* Journalist and writer Walter Shapiro remembers President Bush's response at this turning point in history in '1989–2001: America's Lost Long Weekend', *New Republic*, 27 June 2022. See also 'President Bush Comments on the Relaxation of East German Border Controls', in World History Commons, https://worldhistorycommons.org/president-bush-comments-relaxation-east-german-border-controls

was intentional. For years after the Malta meeting, Bush maintained his benign neglect, failing to come up with any vision of the future at all.

As the Wall came down, and in the months that followed, borders were reopened, people flowed freely for the first time in generations and free elections were held across eastern Europe, ousting communist regimes nearly everywhere. Even the Soviet Duma voted itself out of existence in 1991, and an unsuccessful coup against Gorbachev would result in failure, but it brought to power one of the most amiable and sublimely drunken leaders ever to grace the world stage: Boris Yeltsin.

Amid all this turmoil, Bush and his friend James Baker, a wily Texan lawyer who served as Secretary of State, did not grasp the mantle of history. They both seemed magnificently unprepared for the collapse of the Soviet Union and the need for a minimum of strategic vision. Instead, they promised Gorbachev that there would be no expansion of NATO, which meant that Germany would be reunified as one country, and after that they practised a form of benign neglect.[*]

Bush and Baker devoted more time to the Iraqi invasion of Kuwait in 1990, and the first US war in the Persian Gulf

---

[*] According to the Russians, the agreement on non-expansion of NATO to eastern Europe took place orally while the leaders of the Alliance claimed that no such promise was made. Soviet President Gorbachev, who participated in the 1990 negotiations, subsequently mentioned the existence of a 'guarantee of non-expansion of NATO to the east', confirming its existence in some interviews and refuting it in others. See Adrian Blomfield and Mike Smith, 'Gorbachev: US could start new Cold War', *Daily Telegraph*, 6 May 2008, and Peter Baker, 'In Ukraine Conflict, Putin Relies on a Promise That Ultimately Wasn't', *New York Times*, 9 January 2022.

that ensued in 1991. The Bush administration's handling of Operation Desert Storm was ultimately successful, but it demonstrated a reactive rather than a proactive approach by Bush. While successfully repelling Iraq's invasion, Bush and Baker did not articulate a broader vision for the Middle East. They simply secured the oil supplies in Kuwait, contained Saddam and left the thorny issues of regional stability largely unaddressed. As a result of this mismanagement of the end of the war, problems in the region would fester.

Likewise, the administration's response to the dissolution of the Soviet Union and the reunification of Germany lacked a clear roadmap. The absence of a well-defined strategy for integrating former Soviet states into the global community and managing the geopolitical implications of German reunification would contribute to uncertainties in the region.

Bush and Baker were not long-term planners or visionaries; they did not attempt to imagine how US policy should adapt to changed international conditions. They were Texan dealmakers committed to preserving the status quo. Their time in government represented a huge and historic missed opportunity and thus a crucial flaw in the post-Cold War management of America's growing imperial commitments and responsibilities.

This is not to say that the Bush presidency was a failure. Between 1989 and 1992, the Berlin Wall fell, Soviet forces withdrew from Afghanistan, Germany reunified peacefully, the Warsaw Pact dissolved, the Soviet Union crumbled and the Cold War ended. The American military ejected the dictator Manuel Noriega from Panama and liberated Kuwait from Saddam Hussein, protecting US strategic interests in the Middle East. And the United States emerged as the world's pre-eminent hegemon after four decades of a superpower standoff, after numerous proxy wars, covert interventions and a nuclear confrontation in Cuba.

The prudent management of empire under Bush, in sharp contrast to the muscular and noisy policies of Reagan, had by now lulled Washington into a false sense of security and to some degree a sense of self-satisfied comfort. In November 1992, Bush would lose his bid for re-election. His bland patrician demeanour and his lack of charisma would eventually make him a one-term President. Bush was beaten badly by a rising new political rockstar from the state of Arkansas, a man who was running as a Democrat but who would embrace and promote Republican policies. He was a fast-talking former Rhodes Scholar at Oxford from a poor family in Arkansas, and his name was William Jefferson Clinton. He was more popularly known as Bill.

Bill Clinton was a generation younger than Bush, and he was a great deal more energetic. But the former Governor of Arkansas had no foreign policy experience, and he was very much a creature of domestic politics. His campaign manager used to stress the importance of his domestic policies by joking, 'It's the economy, stupid!'

When Clinton entered the White House in January 1993, he had no particular international agenda in mind.

Since there was no longer a threat from the now dissolved Soviet Union, the new President could indulge his domestic priorities, which tended to be to continue the Reagan welfare cuts, introduce tougher 'workfare' laws, continue tax breaks for the affluent, increase spending on technology and innovation. He would also pursue an unbridled and irresponsible deregulation of Wall Street, and in particular the derivatives market, that would contribute to an environment that later fostered the financial crisis of 2008.

Indeed the Clinton years, perhaps the height of the post-Cold War era, were all about deregulation. The President appointed a former Goldman Sachs banker named Bob Rubin as the Secretary of the Treasury, and he nominated Alan Greenspan for a third term as President of the Federal Reserve Board, the central bank. Greenspan, a Republican who had once consulted for a controversial savings and loan bank, would later team up with Rubin's successor as Treasury Secretary, an ambitious and sharp-elbowed economist named Larry Summers. Together, Greenspan and Summers actively and explicitly campaigned for the deregulation of the highly leveraged and increasingly dangerous derivatives market, complete with its securitisation of subprime mortgages. More than anyone else, these two men were responsible for the lax regulation and negligence that led to the collapse of Lehman Brothers.[4]

In the absence of any real strategy for America's role in the post-Cold War order, Bill Clinton did latch on to one idea that would guide his foreign policy and management of the American hyperpower he had inherited. The idea was globalisation: the increasing interconnectedness of economies, the idea of 'inter-dependence' among nations, the free cross-border flows of goods and services and capital, in combination with technological innovation, especially in communications and transportation.[5]

Globalisation soon became the rallying cry at the annual meetings of CEOs and billionaires and world leaders that were held at the Davos World Economic Forum, the networking event in the Alpine ski resort. Clinton would gleefully attend this summit, fraternising with Bill Gates, Bono and a bevy of admirers. He loved to speak of globalisation as the ushering in of a new age of wonder. Globalisation was the centrepiece of Clinton's foreign policy, his main approach to managing the American empire. As far as Clinton was concerned, globalisation was an unequivocal force for good in the world that would bring prosperity, peace and democracy. It was the new religion, and Clinton, the consummate schmoozer with his contrived and folksy approach, would become its High Priest.

When he delivered his State of the Union speech before a Joint Session of the Congress in February 1997, Clinton sang the praises of globalisation. Three years earlier he had signed into law the new North American Free Trade Agreement (NAFTA) that Reagan had promoted. In 1995 Clinton pushed through the establishment of the World Trade Organization. The President was convinced that globalisation was a panacea for the world; as for the dark underside of the phenomenon, he either did not perceive it or chose to ignore it.

'By expanding trade,' Clinton declared to Congress, 'we can advance the cause of freedom and democracy around the world.'[6]

Indeed, if one had to sum up Clinton's management of empire, it would be that he was determined to make the world safe for 'market democracies'.

To provide an intellectual framework for the globalising 1990s, Clinton and nearly all of the US foreign policy establishment had seized upon the ideas of an obscure official in the State Department named Francis Fukuyama. An article written by Fukuyama and entitled 'The End of History?' had been published in the summer issue of the *National Interest*, a neoconservative journal published in Washington.[7] The author was unknown to the public, but his thinking would condition a generation of US leaders as much as George Kennan's article in *Foreign Affairs* had birthed the policy of containment.

What was Fukuyama saying?

That the end of history was a good news story. That the Cold War had been won by the good guys. That what was happening in the world was nothing less than 'the triumph of the West' and the final moment in human evolution into a peaceful and capitalist world that was based on the American-designed world order. After all, there had been free elections in Poland and Hungary. An economic reform movement was underway in China. And the Berlin Wall had come down. So it was game over. We won.

'What we may be witnessing is not just the end of the Cold War, or the passing of a particular period of post-war history,' wrote Fukuyama, 'but the end of history as such: that is, the endpoint of mankind's ideological evolution and the universalisation of Western liberal democracy as the final form of human government.'[8]

Fukuyama had been a protégé of Paul D. Wolfowitz, one of the Pentagon's most notorious warmongers, and in 1989 he was serving as the deputy director of the State Department's policy planning staff under James Baker. After the article's publication, he became an instant celebrity. In 1992, he published a book-length version of his simplistic argument that Western liberal democracy would now become the norm for ever. Washington loved it. Bill Clinton considered it to be his bible.

Not everyone was convinced, however, that the American hyperpower could just rest on its laurels and enter a new and utopian era. 'I don't believe a word of it,' said the publisher of the *National Interest*, Irving Kristol. Strobe Talbott, editor at large for *Time* magazine, said 'The End of History' was actually 'The Beginning of Nonsense'.[9]

But for Clinton, Fukuyama was his intellectual beacon.

Another happy troubadour of globalisation was the *New York Times* journalist Tom Friedman [no relation]. His bestselling book was called *The World is Flat*, and in it he celebrated globalisation in every way. Friedman did not, however, analyse the downside. Neither did Fukuyama nor Clinton; all three failed to devote energy or column inches to the consequences of globalisation. Neither did they examine the consequences of past globalisation phases in world history. Had they done so, had they thought about the huge income and social inequalities and wealth gaps that came with the Gilded Age (1870–1914) in America, they might have tempered their troubadour enthusiasm.

The lack of vision about the long-term effects of globalisation produced a narrative in which globalisation became an unequivocal force for good, a value unto itself. This, together with the technology boom and the birth of Silicon Valley, would in time lead to the famed irrational exuberance of the stock markets, to the just-in-time global supply chains that were becoming the norm, and to the availability of the internet in 1996. On the downside, the result of globalisation would also be a huge economic and social displacement, and dislocation of millions of workers around the world that would lead to widespread suffering and austerity a decade later.

Clinton's cheerleading for the Western liberal world order was not really the problem; it was the blind trust in market forces, the way Clinton over-embraced the neoliberal theories of Reagan and Bush, as if to prove that he was really a Republican rather than a Democrat. Clinton once mockingly described himself as an 'Eisenhower

Republican', and indeed there was something of a 1950s feel to the Clinton years of the 1990s.*

On the home front, America under Clinton was flirting with a new form of laissez-faire capitalism and massive deregulation that would later lead to financial crisis, bankruptcies, recession and austerity. In the 1990s, however, it brought widespread economic growth and job creation. The promise of globalisation was still golden.

Internationally, by the end of the 1990s America had squandered more than a decade of post-Cold War opportunity. Few in Washington were thinking about the new world order that could emerge; it was taken for granted that the world would now be governed by Western liberal democracy everywhere and that globalisation would guarantee peace and prosperity. The managers of the American empire had been sleepwalking through a field of squandered opportunities, reacting to world events, managing occasional crises where needed but largely basking in the victory over the Soviet Union. Such was the self-contented atmosphere in Washington at the start of the new millennium. It seemed that the post-Cold War glow and the dream of globalisation would last for ever, with America continuing as an unchallenged hyperpower. The Fukuyama illusion of the end of history had persisted throughout this

---

* 'Where are all the Democrats?' Clinton cried out at a White House meeting early in his administration, according to *The Agenda*, Bob Woodward's account of the first part of the Clinton presidency. 'I hope you're all aware we're all Eisenhower Republicans. We're Eisenhower Republicans here, and we are fighting the Reagan Republicans. We stand for lower deficits and free trade and the bond market. Isn't that great?' Conversation quoted by E. J. Dionne Jr, 'Clinton Swipes the Gop's Lyric', *Washington Post*, 20 July 1996.

period, from the fall of the Wall in 1989 to the end of Bill Clinton's two terms in the White House in early 2001. Critics of Clinton would say that it was as though Washington took a long weekend, a twelve-year-long after-party or celebration of the reaffirmation of America's idea of world order following the collapse of the Wall. Globalisation was underway, America seemed strong, and while there were always challenges, the empire was on the rise again.

On 20 January 2001, Clinton handed power over to his successor, the newly elected son of former President George H. W. Bush. This jaunty Texan cowboy, a former dilettante businessman and Governor of Texas who had beaten his alcohol and drugs problems, was named George W. Bush. He would now inherit the mantle of American power, the responsibility of empire. But neither he nor the American people would be in any way prepared for the ugly new world that they would wake up to on the morning of 11 September 2001.

CHAPTER SIX

IMPERIAL OVERREACH: THE FAILED WARS OF GEORGE W. BUSH

The destruction of the World Trade Center in New York on 11 September 2001 was a seismic event for the American empire. It was a bitter and unexpected bookend to the long and complacent post-Cold War period that had begun in 1989 with the collapse of the Berlin Wall.

For the stewards of American power, the 9/11 attacks were more than a mere assault on a pair of iconic towers – they were a profound challenge to the very essence of American exceptionalism.

The attacks would send shockwaves across the nation and around the world, and the ensuing first decade of the twenty-first century would prove to be a critical inflection point in the broader story of American leadership. It was the start of a new period of uncertainty and of a renewed decline in the big cycle of US leadership. It was the beginning of the end of Pax Americana, which Ronald Reagan had worked so meticulously to restore in the 1980s.

The successful attacks launched by Osama bin Laden also marked the end of the 'Fukuyama era' of post-Cold War complacency. This was no longer the end of history, a peaceful and globalising world based on the supremacy of the institutions of the Western liberal world order. This was the end of the post-Cold War illusion that all would be well.

The West had not won; it may have beaten the Soviet Union in the Cold War, but it was now being confronted with the harsh reality of new and menacing challenges to the world order from a new kind of enemy, non-state actors, terrorists, who were being financed by the Arab world, by Iran and Saudi Arabia, and even more discreetly by some of the emirates in the Persian Gulf. Al-Qaeda was the first of these barbaric groups to band together and challenge America, but Washington's reactions to the 9/11 attacks would be followed by the emergence of ISIS, the return of the Taliban and the rise of Hezbollah, Hamas and numerous other jihadists.[1] Like their predecessors in the jungles of Vietnam, these terrorists were well armed, well financed and well trained, but they now knew how to conduct asymmetric warfare and terrorism with such skill that they were able to successfully attack the American hegemon even from inside its borders.

George W. Bush was in a state of shock. It was apparent from the moment he was first informed of the 9/11 attacks. He was fuming, and he vowed revenge. Nine days after the attacks, on 20 September 2001, Bush went before a joint session of Congress to announce the commencement of the so-called global 'War on Terror'.* He called on world leaders to join the US in its response to al-Qaeda, putting things in characteristically blunt terms.

'Every nation in every region now has a decision to make,' he said. 'Either you are with us, or you are with the terrorists.' This 'with-us-or-against-us' formulation used by Bush was a Texan spin on classic imperialist rhetoric, with a distinctly menacing tone.

Two weeks later, in early October 2001, the first airstrikes by the United States and Great Britain were launched in Afghanistan against Taliban and al-Qaeda training camps. The war in Afghanistan had begun, a war that would see another failure of American power and that would cost US taxpayers more than $2 trillion. It would of course then end in a disastrous US defeat in 2021, with Washington humiliated, the Taliban back in power and a wide array of terrorists, including ISIS, still operating out of Afghanistan.

Between 2001 and 2021, Bush's failed war in Afghanistan would cost the lives of 2,324 US military personnel, 3,917 US contractors and 1,144 allied troops. For Afghans, the numbers were far worse: some 70,000 Afghan military and police deaths, nearly 50,000 Afghan civilians and some 53,000 opposition fighters killed. Almost 67,000 other

---

* On 20 September 2001, Bush announced to a joint session of Congress the commencement of the global 'War on Terror'. 'Our war on terror', he said, 'begins with al-Qaeda, but it does not end there. It will not end until every terrorist group of global reach has been found, stopped, and defeated.' His speech is available on https://georgewbush whitehouse.archives.gov/news/releases/2001/09/20010920-8.html

people were killed in neighbouring Pakistan in relation to the Afghan war.[2] The failed war would also sap American energy, causing a decline in US influence.

When it all came to an end with the horrendous American withdrawal from Kabul Airport in August 2021, the scenes were just as traumatic as had been the images of those scrambling up the ladders and onto the roof of the US Embassy, begging to be taken away by helicopters during the collapse of Saigon on 30 April 1975.

Bush's war in Afghanistan was a case study in the mismanagement of empire, a case of imperial overreach. It was marked by extraordinarily incompetent, and at times dishonest, decision making. But the Texan cowboy, less astute than his father, was only just getting started.

For Bush, the 9/11 attacks were a call to arms, an imperative to assert American strength and root out and destroy the forces that dared to challenge the Pax Americana. He soon approved a raft of laws that allowed American citizens to be spied upon and wiretapped and that curtailed numerous civil rights.

During a press conference on 16 September, the gaffe-prone President made the mistake of using the word 'crusade' in describing his intentions toward Islamic terrorists. 'This is a new kind of evil,' Bush declared. 'And we understand. And the American people are beginning to understand. This crusade, this war on terrorism, is going to take a while.'[3]

Muslims around the world were immediately incensed. But the Bush administration was on a holy mission to root out the architects of the 9/11 attacks and, for that matter, as many Islamic terrorists as could be found. They didn't care if they inflamed Arab opinion. Their goal was retribution.

The bevy of hawks around Bush saw an excellent opportunity to use American military might in a war zone. They were war lovers, as gung-ho for battle as had been Teddy Roosevelt 100 years before when he pushed for war with Spain. The hawks were led by Vice President Dick Cheney, by Secretary of Defense Donald Rumsfeld, and by the zealot Paul Wolfowitz. These three men, to the displeasure of then Secretary of State Colin Powell, seized the opportunity to push their agenda with Bush, and with great success.

After starting the war in Afghanistan in October 2001, they quickly moved on to consider Iraq, still under the tyrannical rule of Saddam Hussein. The Iraqi leader had once plotted to assassinate George W. Bush's father, former President George H. W. Bush.[*] Iraq had not attacked the US or its allies. In fact, there was no real proof that Saddam was harbouring terrorists connected to the 9/11 attacks. But this was not merely another war launched by Washington to root out terrorists. This was also a personal vendetta for the younger Bush, to avenge his father. The hawks goaded him on.

---

[*] According to independent CIA reports and other sources of intelligence, there was a strong case that Iraqi leader Saddam Hussein directed a plot to kill President George H. W. Bush while visiting Kuwait on 14–16 April 1993. Also see David Von Drehle and R. Jeffrey Smith, 'U.S. Strikes Iraq for Plot to Kill Bush', *Washington Post*, 26 June 1993.

In June 2002, Bush first spoke of the possibility of 'pre-emptive war' as a way of keeping the world safe for democracy. Bush was really thinking about how best to justify an attack on Iraq, even though there was no *casus belli*, no obvious reason to launch an invasion. In a commencement address to graduating cadets at West Point, Bush repeated the Fukuyama theory about the end of history to justify America's self-righteousness: 'The twentieth century ended with a single surviving model of human progress based on non-negotiable demands of human dignity, the rule of law, limits on the power of the state, respect for women and private property and free speech and equal justice and religious tolerance.'[4]

In order to preserve this liberal world order, Bush had now decided that unilateral action was needed, first in Afghanistan and now also in Iraq. By September 2002, the White House had formalised the Bush Doctrine, which took the form of a document called 'the National Security Strategy of the United States'.[*]

It essentially said that where a country had been judged malignant or a danger to global security, the US would

---

[*] The new strategic approach assumed that 'today the task [of defending the US against its enemies] has changed dramatically ... Enemies in the past needed great armies and great industrial capabilities to endanger America but now, shadowy networks of individuals can bring great chaos and suffering to our shores for less than it costs to purchase a single tank.' According to this approach, the US must use 'every tool in our arsenal' to defeat these new threats. 'Our enemies have openly declared that they are seeking weapons of mass destruction, and evidence indicates that they are doing so with determination [...] The United States will not allow these efforts to succeed [...] and will act against such emerging threats before they are fully formed.' See The White House, 'The National Security Strategy of the United States of America', 17 September 2002, https://georgewbush-whitehouse.archives.gov/ and Max Boot, 'The New American Way of War', *Foreign Affairs*, 1 July 2003.

be justified in taking unilateral action. The idea of 'pre-emptive war' against Iraq emerged in the heart of the document: 'There are few greater threats than a terrorist attack with weapons of mass destruction. To forestall or prevent such hostile acts by our adversaries, the United States will, if necessary, act pre-emptively in exercising our inherent right of self-defense.'

The Bush Doctrine was as imperial an edict as was possible; its twisting of facts and reality to suit the President's personal preferences represented a pure and unadulterated form of imperialism. It was a decree from an American neo-imperial ruler who would use it to justify America's invasion of Iraq and its general vocation of being the world's policeman.

Dick Cheney, the conniving Rasputin who often operated behind the President's back, now teamed up with Wolfowitz and Rumsfeld to come up with reasons to justify an invasion of Iraq. They revved up their friends in the CIA and other intelligence agencies and had them cook up reports warning of the presence of weapons of mass destruction in Iraq. They would topple the dictator based on this dishonest and politically fashioned intelligence. America would use its overwhelming power to smite a dictator, and then, the neoconservatives around Bush believed, a new and perfectly functioning Western-style democracy would grow up in place of Saddam in Iraq. In retrospect, it was idiocy.

In the summer of 2002, as Bush was laying the

groundwork for his unilateral invasion of Iraq, one of his own top White House advisers blurted out the way that the Bush administration truly perceived the world. In an interview with the *New York Times*, this anonymous senior Bush adviser said quite plainly, and without a sliver of irony:

> We're an empire now, and when we act, we create our own reality. And while you're studying that reality – judiciously, as you will – we'll act again, creating other new realities, which you can study too, and that's how things will sort out. We're history's actors ... and you, all of you, will be left to just study what we do.*

The phrase 'drunk with power' comes to mind, but George W. Bush was beyond drunk; he was sincerely convinced that the use of American military power to engineer regime change was a good idea. The hawks around him either never studied the fraught relations and conflicts between the Sunni minority and the Shia majority in Iraq or they never bothered to study the history of the country they were about to take over.

By the autumn of 2002, Bush had already told the United Nations General Assembly that Iraq posed a grave threat to global security and insisted that the international community must come together to disarm Saddam Hussein,

---

* Ron Suskind's article about the presidency of George W. Bush included this famous quote from someone described only as a 'senior adviser to Bush'. See Ron Suskind, 'Faith, Certainty and the Presidency of George W. Bush', *New York Times*, 17 October 2004.

whom he accused of having weapons of mass destruction. This latter statement, of course, turned out to be a lie.*

Then, in February 2003, the White House sent Secretary of State Colin Powell to go before the United Nations Security Council and famously hold up to the cameras a vial of what he claimed to be anthrax. This was proof of WMDs, he said, along with satellite imagery that he presented. This would serve as the administration's justification for the impending invasion of the country. His presentation, however, later proved to be based on flawed or manipulated intelligence and unreliable sources.

In the aftermath of the invasion of Iraq in March 2003, it became increasingly clear that the justifications presented by the Bush administration were flawed. No substantial evidence of weapons of mass destruction was ever found in Iraq, and the alleged ties between Saddam Hussein and terrorist groups were not substantiated.

The US invasion, codenamed 'Operation Iraqi Freedom', saw Bush charging ahead in the face of harsh criticism from America's traditional allies, including France and

---

* In one of his most controversial addresses to the UN General Assembly, on 12 September 2002, President George W. Bush reminded that since the Iraqi invasion of Kuwait (1990), Saddam Hussein had never proved he was complying with international obligations. 'He has proven instead only his contempt for the United Nations, and for all his pledges. By breaking every pledge – by his deceptions, and by his cruelties – Saddam Hussein has made the case against himself,' stated President Bush at that time. Later, US Secretary of State Colin Powell warned the Security Council in his briefing on 5 February 2003, aimed at convincing members that Iraq had failed to disarm. 'Clearly, Saddam Hussein and his regime will stop at nothing until something stops him', he said. In fact, on 6 October 2004, the head of the Iraqi Survey Group, Charles A. Duelfer, announced to the US Senate Armed Services Committee that the group found no evidence on stockpiled mass destruction weapons since 1991, when UN sanctions were imposed. See Jeremy Pressman, 'Power without Influence: The Bush Administration's Foreign Policy Failure in the Middle East', *International Security*, vol. 33, issue. 4, Spring 2009.

Germany. The leaders of these countries, French President Jacques Chirac and German Chancellor Gerhard Schröder, expressed strong reservations about the military intervention and opposed the invasion.

In the case of France, President Chirac made it clear that France would not support a UN Security Council resolution authorising the use of force against Iraq. France, along with Russia and Germany, opposed the resolution proposed by the United States and the United Kingdom.

Tony Blair, the British Prime Minister, was instead known to critics as 'Bush's poodle' because of the way he slavishly followed the American President and acquiesced to all of his demands.[5] Despite significant domestic opposition, Blair was a faithful follower of the warmongers in the White House and Pentagon in the war against Iraq.[*]

The war in Iraq would be over in two months, but the United States would be stuck in Iraq for years, unable to leave and by 2007 needing to escalate troop levels in order to prevent the country from becoming a failed nation. Perhaps the worst decision made by Bush was to appoint an American proconsul in Baghdad, whose prerogative it was to administer the post-war country and presumably put it on the path to becoming a functioning democracy

---

[*] 'We should remain the closest ally of the US,' the Prime Minister told Britain's ambassadors and senior diplomats in January 2003, 'and as allies influence them to continue broadening their agenda. The price of influence is that we do not leave the US to face the tricky issues alone.' Mr Blair is only the latest in a long line of British Prime Ministers, going back at least to the Suez Crisis nearly five decades ago, to believe that only by standing with Washington in public could London hope to influence it in private. See Ivo H. Daalder, 'Why Blair Took the Risk of Making War to Iraq', Brookings Institution, 20 November 2003.

and citizen in good standing of the American-designed, American-managed world order. Bush picked Lewis Paul Bremer III, a former counterterrorism expert from the State Department who now worked for Henry Kissinger at his consulting firm on Park Avenue, Kissinger Associates. Bremer was used to using Kissinger's star power to make money off corporate clients, but he knew nothing about governing Iraq.

In May 2003, Bremer was appointed as the Administrator of the Coalition Provisional Authority (CPA) in Iraq. Bremer was supposed to oversee the reconstruction and governance of post-war Iraq. But his year-long reign in Baghdad, until June 2004, was marred by a series of decisions that contributed to instability, heightened sectarian tensions and the eventual rise of ISIS. Bremer's mismanagement and ill-conceived policies created a combustible environment that fuelled discontent and set the stage for prolonged conflict.*

Bremer's implementation of a sweeping de-Ba'athification policy, which aimed to remove members of the Ba'ath Party from positions of influence in the government and security apparatus, was a disaster. While the intent was to eradicate the remnants of Saddam Hussein's regime, the

---

* Paul Bremer, who governed Iraq's Coalition Provisional Authority (CPA) for thirteen months after President Saddam Hussein was toppled, argued there had been a serious miscalculation by those responsible for planning the invasion. In effect, his order to dissolve the entire Iraqi Ground Forces and put 400,000 former soldiers out of work has been widely criticised for creating a 'large pool' of young people armed for the insurgency. See Kenneth M. Pollack, 'The Seven Deadly Sins of Failure in Iraq: A Retrospective Analysis of the Reconstruction', Brookings Institution, 1 December 2006.

policy was implemented too broadly and indiscriminately. Thousands of experienced administrators, teachers and military officers were dismissed, creating a void of skilled professionals and exacerbating the challenge of rebuilding the country. This move alienated a significant portion of the Sunni population, contributing to their disenfranchisement and fostering a sense of marginalisation.

Likewise, the disbanding of the Iraqi military created misery, violence and further conflict, giving rise to sectarian tensions and paving the way for the emergence of groups like ISIS.

Bremer struggled to navigate the complexities of a fractured nation and therefore inadvertently sowed the seeds of future chaos. His failure would leave America weakened, and this was the real legacy of George W. Bush's failed war in Iraq, another case of imperial overreach, of America getting bogged down in a foreign war, of the American people eventually tiring of the war and the President of the day withdrawing American troops in failure, disguised as compromise or 'peace with honour'. This was the pattern, the sequence, in the cases of Vietnam, Afghanistan and Iraq.

These wars had a far more damaging long-term effect on the idea of Pax Americana. Sadly, the mismanagement of the war in Afghanistan, coupled with the costly misadventure in Iraq, severely strained relationships with traditional allies in Europe and contributed to a decline in US leadership and influence on the global stage. The perception of the United States under Bush as an aggressor, acting unilaterally without sufficient international support, damaged diplomatic ties with many countries. The erosion of American soft power became evident as the world now questioned the wisdom and efficacy of US foreign policy decisions. The decline of the American empire was underway.

CHAPTER SEVEN

OBAMA'S MISMANAGEMENT OF THE ARAB SPRING

On the afternoon of 4 June 2009, Cairo University's hallowed grounds became the setting for an extraordinary convergence of time, place and the indomitable spirit of Barack Obama. The new US President, who had taken office less than six months ago, bounded onto the stage at the university's Reception Hall. Speaking from a lectern set against the backdrop of plush red curtains, with Egypt's President in the front row, he delivered what the White House had billed as 'a major speech to the Muslim world'.

The address was Obama's attempt to launch what he called 'a new beginning between the United States and Muslims around the world'. The auspicious initiative came towards the end of the first decade of the twenty-first century, a decade that had begun with the toxic legacy of the 9/11 attacks. George W. Bush's controversial wars in Afghanistan and Iraq had inflamed Arab opinion, and Obama was here to extend an olive branch.

The 55-minute speech was widely praised for its eloquence and ambition. As the atmosphere crackled with significance, President Obama, an emblem of grace and composure, issued a form of apology for past US behaviour in the region and promised a new era of friendship and co-operation with the Muslim world.

'I have come to Cairo to seek a new beginning between the United States and Muslims around the world, one based on mutual interest and mutual respect, and one based upon the truth that America and Islam are not exclusive and need not be in competition,' Obama told the captivated audience in Cairo. 'Instead, they overlap and share common principles – principles of justice and progress; tolerance and the dignity of all human beings.'

With lofty rhetoric, he spoke of mutual respect, of shared values and of a commitment to addressing the grievances that had fuelled tensions for decades. The entire world listened, and in the Arab world hope surged. The Oslo Nobel Committee would a few months later recognise this audacious vision, rather controversially awarding Obama the Nobel Peace Prize later that year. For many, Obama's mishandling of the Arab Spring, and the subsequent rapid reshaping of the political landscape of the Middle East and north Africa, would make a mockery of that decision.

The Arab Spring, a series of pro-democracy uprisings that swept across the Middle East and North Africa over a two-year period, marked a pivotal chapter in the decline of the American empire. As nations sought political transformation, Obama grappled with the harsh reality of trying to balance his democratic ideals and America's geopolitical and economic interests.

It all began in Tunisia on 17 December 2010, when a fruit vendor named Mohamed Bouazizi set himself on fire in protest against his mistreatment by corrupt local officials. This triggered a spontaneous wave of protests against government corruption and authoritarian rule. Less than a month later, in January 2011, President Ben Ali, the notorious dictator who had been in power for twenty-three years, was forced to flee into exile to Saudi Arabia.* Sadly, the events that would follow in rapid succession would expose the inadequacies of Obama's foreign policy apparatus.

Accelerated by the rapid connection of protesters via Twitter, Facebook and other newly introduced social media, Tunisia's turmoil set off a domino effect that swept throughout the region, catching the Obama administration off guard. In quick succession, protests erupted in Egypt, Saudi Arabia, Morocco, Algeria, Libya, Yemen, Bahrain and Syria, each with its unique set of challenges and demands. The White House scrambled to respond to fast-moving events.

The Obama administration, however well-intentioned,

---

* Ben Ali led Tunisia as President from 1987 to 2011, mostly disappointing the expectations that Western countries had placed onto him and his program to gradually reform the country. After he fled to Saudi Arabia, a Tunisian court sentenced him in absentia for unlawful possession of cash and jewellery, for inciting violence and for violent repression of protests. Interpol also issued an international arrest warrant, charging him with money laundering and drug trafficking. Ben Ali served none of those sentences (including a life sentence) but died in exile, in Jeddah, on 19 September 2019.

seemed unprepared and ill-equipped to navigate this complex web of uprisings. At first, Obama cautiously welcomed the developments in Tunisia. Later on, he would acknowledge the significance of the pro-democracy revolution. 'The United States', he would tell the UN General Assembly, 'continues to support those who seek dignity, opportunity and a voice in their government. The Tunisian people have forged a new path, and we applaud their courage.'*

As protests spread from Tunisia to Algeria, Bahrain, Morocco, Yemen and Saudi Arabia, Obama's response remained cautious, reflecting a delicate balance between endorsing democratic aspirations and maintaining strategic alliances with dictators.

Obama was very, very careful about what he said of Saudi Arabia, the traditional US ally and oil supplier: 'We recognise that change ultimately comes from within, and our support will be measured, but we stand ready to assist in fostering inclusive political dialogue.'[1]

In Morocco, similar calls for political reform were met with Obama's feeble acknowledgement of the complexities involved in such processes: 'We support the steps taken by the King of Morocco to bring about positive change.'

---

* President Barack Obama on several occasions has publicly recalled how the United States, in keeping with the founding spirit of the nation, will always defend peoples around the world who harbour aspirations for freedom and self-determination. Prior to his address to the UN General Assembly, on 25 September 2012, President Obama stated that the Middle East and north Africa were facing 'a historic opportunity'. 'We have the chance to show that America welcomes change that advances self determination. Yes, there will be perils that accompany this moment of promise, but after decades of accepting as it is in the region, we have a chance to pursue the world as it should be,' he said in a speech delivered on 19 May 2011, while repeating that 'it is not America that put people into the streets of Tunis or Cairo ... and it's the people themselves that must ultimately determine their outcome.'

It was wishy-washy stuff. It was milquetoast policy, and it was policy that was being made on the hop. Once again, America was preaching on the basis of a principled belief in the moral superiority of democracy, but it was not practising what it preached. On the one hand, Obama was raising expectations of a new and democratic Arab world; at the same time the US President was loathe to criticise the dictators of Saudi Arabia, Morocco or Bahrain, and so he turned a blind eye to their brutal repression of pro-democracy movements.

The greatest two examples of Obama's erratic policies and his haphazard management of the Arab Spring were to be found in Egypt and Libya.

In January 2011, protests erupted in Cairo against Egypt's long-serving dictator Hosni Mubarak. Washington had provided billions of dollars of aid to Mubarak, who in turn relied on his military to prop up his government. Egypt was a staunch ally of the United States, but it was also a totalitarian state that was ripe for revolution. Although initially hesitant, Obama eventually decided that he would support the revolutionaries who were occupying Tahrir Square to protest against decades of oppressive rule under President Mubarak. This meant breaking with Mubarak, and it would allow the previously banned Muslim Brotherhood to come to power in Egypt. Several of Obama's advisers counselled against this, on the grounds that Mubarak might be a dictator, but he was 'our guy'. They also warned of the prospect of post-Mubarak Egypt being governed by the Muslim

Brotherhood, a group whose spiritual leader liked to quote Hitler and support terrorists.[2]

But Obama, who just eighteen months ago had spoken at Cairo University, had made his decision. With Wilsonian idealism and fervour (that turned out to be tragically misplaced in 21st-century Egypt), the US President decided to go with his gut. On the evening of 1 February 2011, Obama had a very tense telephone call with Mubarak. He told him that his latest speech, broadcast to hundreds of thousands of protesters in Tahrir Square, had not gone far enough. He told Mubarak that he had to step down.[3]

Minutes later, Obama appeared before hastily summoned cameras in the Grand Foyer of the White House. The end of Mr Mubarak's thirty-year rule, Mr Obama proclaimed, 'must begin now'. With these words, the US President decreed the end of Mubarak's regime. It was an imperial gesture, a Roman thumbs down.

Ten days later, on 11 February 2011, Mubarak resigned.

Unfortunately, as the CIA and Pentagon had warned, the overthrow of Mubarak led quickly to the rise of the Muslim Brotherhood, a fundamentalist Islamic group with deep ties to jihadists that would also help create, as an affiliate, the terrorist group Hamas in the Gaza Strip. The previously banned Muslim Brotherhood was thus legalised in 2011 and promptly won the next presidential election, when its candidate, Mohamed Morsi, became Egypt's first President to gain power through a democratic election. He did not last long. Egypt was divided. In the summer of 2013, the Muslim Brotherhood government was ousted in a coup led by Egyptian General Abdel Fattah al-Sisi. On 3 July 2013, General al-Sisi appeared on television to announce that Morsi had been removed from office, the constitution suspended and an interim government installed. Muslim Brotherhood supporters and others opposed to the military's actions held protests throughout Egypt, but security groups confronted them with deadly force.

Once again, Obama was caught off guard, and his first reaction was to say that he was 'deeply concerned' and to call on the Egyptian military to move 'quickly and responsibly to return full authority back to a democratically elected civilian government as soon as possible through an inclusive and transparent process and to avoid any arbitrary arrests of President Morsi and his supporters'.[4] He was not listened to. General al-Sisi would proceed to arrest and imprison his predecessor, who would die eight years later in prison, and no free elections would ever be held.*

The official White House position at the time was the quintessence of ambiguity: 'We're on neither side,' said spokesperson Jen Psaki. 'We're on the side of the Egyptian people.'

Meanwhile, as the Arab Spring spread to Libya, Obama was zigging and zagging his way through a series

---

* In the aftermath of the de facto coup, Mohamed Morsi supporters were silenced in blood (the army made over 800 kills). Egyptian prosecutors charged Morsi with various crimes and sentenced him with the death penalty, a sentence that was overturned in November 2016. Morsi died during trial on 17 June 2019 amid claims that he was being denied appropriate medical care while in custody.

of case-by-case decisions. The Leader of the Free World, the well-intentioned but ineffectual US President, would change his Arab Spring policies more often than one changes a shirt. His decision-making was erratic, his advisers were divided, his NATO allies were befuddled and the result was disastrous.

Libya is a prime example of what happened when Washington took a step back and decided to 'lead from behind'. By March 2011, as protests spread across the country, the flamboyant and unhinged Colonel Gaddafi ordered his security forces to open fire on protesters in Benghazi. The revolt soon escalated into an armed conflict involving local tribal militias, genuine pro-democracy rebels and Islamic extremists and jihadists. When Gaddafi ordered airstrikes on the rebels, even his staunchest defenders like Italy's Prime Minister Silvio Berlusconi were embarrassed. When he vowed to hunt down and kill the protesters like 'rats', the tide in favour of military action in Libya began to turn. President Nicolas Sarkozy of France led the charge; he wanted a no-fly zone, he wanted to bomb Gaddafi's forces and he wanted action. With his own poll numbers floundering, and the need to make himself look important rising, Sarkozy convened a special international summit on Libya that was to be held at the Élysée Palace on the afternoon of 19 March 2011.

Sarkozy had already rushed to recognise some of the Libyan rebel leaders as the legitimate new government of Libya. The French President had been very embarrassed when Saif al-Islam, Gaddafi's son, threatened to reveal a 'grave secret' if France recognised a rival government. On 16 March, in an interview with Euronews, Saif made good on his threat and claimed that Libya had secretly financed Sarkozy's 2007 presidential election campaign. The revelation seemed as surreal as everything else that was going on in the Arab Spring, and Sarkozy dispatched his spokesman to issue a prompt denial. But Saif Gaddafi's claims would lead to French prosecutors opening a case file, investigating for years and finding what were purportedly documents showing the secret agreement for €50 million. In 2025, Sarkozy is scheduled to go on trial, accused of illegally taking the money from Gaddafi to fund his 2007 campaign.

In March 2011, however, Sarkozy was keen to showcase his leadership, and he was a volcano of activity. He started by co-opting the new British Prime Minister, David Cameron, and making him part of his plan to bomb Gaddafi's forces in Libya. As soon as Cameron arrived in Paris, he was given a private mini-summit with Sarkozy, who told him of his plans to run sorties over Libya.

If, in Washington, the Obama administration was happy to 'lead from behind' and to allow the Europeans to decide what to do about Libya, Sarkozy was keen to lead.[*] The

---

[*] The recurring 'leading from behind' phrase was supposedly coined in 2011 by a White House official to describe President Obama's Libyan policy. The GOP quickly seized on that way of saying to negatively characterise the President's approach in foreign policy. As mentioned by Josh Rogin, 'leading from behind' originated from Ryan Lizza's *New Yorker* article that quoted a presidential adviser using the phrase to characterise Obama's thinking leading up to the US involvement in the war in Libya. See Josh Rogin, 'Who Really Said Obama was "leading from behind"?', Foreign Policy, 27 October 2011, and Charles Krauthammer, 'The Obama Doctrine: Leading from behind', *Washington Post*, 28 April 2011.

inexperienced Cameron deferred to the voluble French President.

Hillary Clinton, then serving as Secretary of State under Obama, arrived in Paris for the meeting after a week of shuttle diplomacy and a G7 meeting of Foreign Ministers. She had been to Cairo to show her solidarity with the protesters in Tahrir Square, and she had even found the time to give a light wrist-slap to the ruler of the strategically important Gulf emirate of Bahrain, a country that was also using force to put down Arab Spring protests.

Obama thought about coming to Paris himself for the Libya summit, and history shows that he should have done so. But he decided to embark instead upon a long-planned, five-day visit to Brazil, Chile and El Salvador. The trip was aimed at building markets for US exports and extending US influence. There was plenty of controversy in political Washington over whether Obama should have really departed for Latin America. Defensive White House officials claimed that Obama could monitor the Libya crisis and the decision over whether to take military action while he visited Brasília and Rio de Janeiro. Many of his key national security officials, including Thomas E. Donilon, the national security adviser, were travelling with him in South America. So were his wife, Michelle, his daughters, Sasha and Malia, and his mother-in-law, Marian Robinson. They landed in sunny Brasília on 19 March.

Back in Paris, Hillary Clinton was arriving at almost the same time at the Élysée Palace. Obama had delegated authority to his Secretary of State to handle the summit on Libya. Others on the guest list included Angela Merkel, Silvio Berlusconi, Spain's José Luis Rodríguez Zapatero, Britain's Cameron, Amr Moussa from the Arab League, UN Secretary-General Ban Ki-moon, as well as the Prime Ministers of Qatar and the United Arab Emirates.[5]

Just before he welcomed his guests, Sarkozy held a private mini-summit with David Cameron and Hillary Clinton. Like her boss, Clinton had changed her mind about Libya; until a couple of days ago, she had been cautious, but now she was happy to press ahead with plans for military intervention in which France and Britain would get out in front. Some of the wags at CNN were referring to Hillary as 'the acting President'. Her mantra was 'no boots on the ground', although to European leaders it seemed more like 'no visible US leadership'.

The US Secretary of State sat at the oversized table in the Salle des Fêtes in the Élysée Palace alongside thirty world leaders. The Prime Minister of Spain said Sarkozy seemed to be in a hurry: 'Sarkozy started immediately by saying that Gaddafi was nearing Benghazi and that we had to stop him or there would be a massacre,' recalled Prime Minister Zapatero. 'Sarkozy then announced that his planes had started their engines and were on their way to Libya.'

Italy's Berlusconi, who was proud of having befriended the Libyan leader, was furious. But he was outnumbered. Hillary Clinton gave America's approval and thus began the actions that would turn Libya into a failed state. In

October 2011, seven months later, as the war raged, the world was treated to the images of a bloodstained and shaken Muammar Gaddafi being dragged out of a culvert where he had been hiding, in his home town of Sirte. He would meet the same fate as Saddam Hussein, when he was dragged out of a hole in his home town of Tikrit, in Iraq. Gaddafi was dragged off the hood of a car and pulled to the ground by his hair. Gunshots rang out and the Libyan dictator was dead.

In Paris, Sarkozy was jubilant. In Rome, Berlusconi was livid. As for Hillary Clinton, who was in Kabul that day, she reacted to the news of Gaddafi's death in a most peculiar manner. She was preparing for a softball CBS News television interview when an aide handed her a Blackberry with the first news that Gaddafi had been killed.

'We came, we saw, he died,' she joked in a sing-songy voice to the startled CBS TV reporter, and then she threw her head back in a raucous outburst of laughter.[*]

Apart from Hillary's cheap and tasteless behaviour, the entire Libyan chapter of the Arab Spring, and what came afterwards, underscored the erosion of American influence and the emergence of a power vacuum in the region. The carving up of Libya by militias and rival factions, Turkish soldiers and Russian mercenaries would come a decade later, but these were the roots of Libya's descent into failed nation

---

[*] On 20 October 2011, Secretary of State Hillary Clinton had six consecutive television interviews: she joked in between formal interviews when told about an early, still unconfirmed, report of Gaddafi's death. See https://www.cbsnews.com/news/clinton-on-qaddafi-we-came-we-saw-he-died/

status, courtesy of an over-active French President and Washington's de facto abdication of any real responsibility.

The abdication of American leadership in Libya was followed by the December 2011 withdrawal of US troops from Iraq. Obama had always been opposed to the Bush administration's war in Iraq. Now he intended to stick to his timetable for getting out of Iraq. Unfortunately, it was not as easy as he may have (naively) imagined. Not only did his withdrawal appear messy and a sign of US weakness, but it also created a power vacuum that would eventually hand real power and influence over Iraq's destiny to the neighbouring jihadist ayatollahs of Tehran. It would also attract Sunni Islamist groups from Syria who had trained with al-Qaeda. The terrorists who were still dreaming of a caliphate said they had created the Islamic State in Iraq and Syria (ISIS). Their grisly executions and bloody tactics seemed to go beyond the horrors of al-Qaeda, but they would not have been able to spread and grow had Barack Obama not pulled US troops out of Baghdad. In the event, Obama was forced to send US soldiers back into Iraq three years later, in 2014, in order to try and fight the new terrorist groups that his withdrawal had helped create. At this point, the US management of its politico-military responsibilities in the Middle East could be accurately described as a disaster. Obama was a feeble and erratic leader of an American empire that he neither wanted nor believed in. His time at the White House, in which he appeared to be weak and indecisive, would thus accelerate its decline.

Perhaps Obama's gravest mistake came in 2013, by which time the Arab Spring uprisings in Syria had turned into a bloody civil war. Syrian dictator Bashar al-Assad had turned his guns upon his own people, and he had done so with the backing of the Islamic Republic of Iran. Russia's Vladimir Putin also saw an opportunity to challenge US interests in the Middle East by backing the Syrian dictator. The Syrian civil war would see more than 350,000 people killed in the decade after 2011 and saw more than 5 million people flee the country.

In 2012, Obama turned down his advisers when they suggested the US should help train and arm Syrian resistance fighters. But he used strong words to warn Assad that he would not tolerate the Syrian dictator using chemical weapons against his own people. That, proclaimed Obama, would constitute the crossing of a 'red line' and Washington would take action in such a case.*

Assad duly proceeded to use chemical weapons against his own people. He used the devastating sarin gas attack in the Damascus suburb of Ghouta in August 2013. Obama's response was notably indecisive. Despite the violation of his clearly stated red line, the administration ultimately refrained from taking direct military action, a decision that fuelled criticism and raised questions about the credibility of US commitments on the international stage.

---

* President Obama's 'red line' statement is one of the most famous of his presidency. It was prompted by a question taken at a White House Press Corps on 20 August 2012. Glenn Kessler, 'President Obama and the "red line" on Syria's Chemical Weapons', *Washington Post*, 6 September 2013.

Obama considered bombing Syria. He even put the British and French on standby to support US action. But then he changed his mind. It was then that Vladimir Putin, whose cynical backing of Assad should have alarmed the White House, offered to broker a deal in Syria to eliminate the chemical weapons stockpile. A naive President Barack Obama agreed to Putin's proposal.[6]

In the Kremlin, Putin must have been laughing at his good fortune. The United States lost decades of credibility, Obama was deemed by many a weakling, and the Russian dictator would soon expand his ties with the ayatollahs in Tehran and with the Syrian dictator. He would also scale up his interventions in Libya and elsewhere in Africa.

In the shifting sands of the Middle East, then, the decline of the American empire was no longer a distant prophecy but a palpable reality. The threat of Putin's revanchist and expansionist tendencies was somehow not on Obama's radar screen. The White House was flying blind. The lack of decisive action contributed to a perception of a diminished American influence. Washington had faltered. Wobbled. And Vladimir Putin, from Moscow, was watching events carefully, with a KGB colonel's eye for detail.

Eighteen months after Obama's mishandling of the Syrian chemical weapons matter in 2013, the Syria crisis was worsening. By now, 300,000 were dead, and Syria was in the hands of ISIS combatants, Assad loyalists, anti-Assad resistance fighters, Russian advisers and soldiers and Iran's Revolutionary Guard. Yet even as Syria dominated global attention, in the autumn of 2014, events unfolded in Ukraine that would test the mettle of Obama once again. Pro-European protests erupted in Kyiv's Maidan Square, setting the stage for a tug-of-war between the West and Russia over Ukraine's future. Viktor Yanukovych, the Ukrainian President, faced mounting opposition as protesters called for closer ties with the European Union. All hell broke loose, and 100 protesters were gunned down by the security forces before the President fled to Moscow and the Ukrainian people were free of the dictatorship of a pro-Russian ruler.

Amid the chaos in Ukraine, Putin capitalised on what he perceived as Western distraction and indecisiveness. In February 2014, Russian forces, without insignias but nonetheless Russian military personnel, swiftly invaded and occupied Crimea. Within thirty days, Putin had annexed Crimea.

Barack Obama, meanwhile, reacted to the news of Putin's invasion of Crimea with the same style he had used in Syria. He condemned the invasion, had a tense telephone call with Putin, agreed a few weeks later to impose sanctions on Russia and generally threw his hands up in despair. Based on the way events would proceed in Crimea and in Ukraine, seen from today, Obama's remarks about the annexation of Putin look incredibly naive.[*]

Just days after Vladimir Putin's well-choreographed

---

[*] President Obama made several remarks on the ongoing situation in Crimea at PBS NewsHour on 3 March 2014. https://www.youtube.com/watch?v=cjlcGrgtM90

'referendum' in Crimea, and after the formalities of annexation had been completed, Obama spoke up. During a visit to Brussels, he devoted most of a forty-minute speech to Putin's invasion of Crimea.

'Ukraine, of course, is not a member of NATO, in part because of its close and complex history with Russia,' declared the US President, as he explained why US and NATO military power would not be used against the Russians in Crimea. 'Nor will Russia be dislodged from Crimea nor deterred from further escalation by military force,' said Obama, as though he wanted to recognise publicly that he felt Crimea could not be reconquered.[7]

But 'with time', said the American President, now sounding like a hopeful high school student who is reading an essay to a school assembly, 'so long as we remain united, the Russian people will recognise that they cannot achieve the security, prosperity and the status that they seek through brute force'.

How reassuring. Although he delivered this utopian scenario with smooth Lincolnesque intonation, it was more tragic than laughable. There is a reason why the American political scientist William Appleman Williams wrote a book called *The Tragedy of American Diplomacy*. There is a healthy dose of Shakespearean tragedy, or perhaps tragicomedy, in Obama's handling of the invasion and annexation of Crimea in 2014. Once again, the leader of the global hegemon appeared weak, even embarrassingly so.

The foreign policy of Barack Obama between 2008 and

2016 could be characterised as 'declinist', but it might better be described as awkward, naive and frequently incompetent. Even if this was the farthest thing from his mind, there is no doubt that Obama's time in the White House helped to accelerate the decline of the American empire, which had already begun after 9/11 and during the Bush years at the start of the century. Obama was an honest, intelligent and well-intentioned President, whereas Bush was a more simple-minded, trigger-happy cowboy. Yet neither was up to the job of managing America's global responsibilities, and what they shared was not ideology but a general lack of competence in international affairs.

Obama's erratic approach to the Arab Spring showcased a lack of strategic vision. His failure to act decisively in Syria and respond effectively to Russian aggression in Crimea signalled a waning American influence. It was a self-inflicted wound.

And then came Trump.

CHAPTER EIGHT

TRUMP AND OTHER MISCREANTS

It was a cold and grey Friday afternoon in January 2017 when the newly inaugurated President Donald Trump, draped in a sombre black overcoat, stared down from the Capitol steps at the thousands of people gathered below on the National Mall. Ominous clouds overhead accentuated the gloomy day. Many of those who had come to watch Trump's swearing-in started putting on ponchos and covering their heads from the drizzle and rain that began just minutes after Trump had been sworn in as President.

With harsh and aggressive language, Trump now painted a dystopian picture of the country that had just elected him. In the second row, across the aisle from the Trump family, the television cameras showed a grimace on Hillary Clinton's face. In front of her, and seated next to the outgoing President, Michelle Obama could not hide her revulsion. Barack Obama looked tense, as if he were finding it hard to maintain his aplomb.

Trump broke with the American presidential tradition

of calling for national unity, or healing. He threw aside any pretence of being bipartisan. He did not try to be presidential at all. Instead, he went for the shock effect, attacking the Washington establishment and then going into a protectionist and ultra-nationalist diatribe. It was a long and ugly litany about mothers trapped in poverty and rusted-out factories and violent crime and the gangs and the drugs and immigrants that had stolen American lives and jobs.

Then, with the kind of rhetoric one would more normally associate with a strongman or dictator than with a democratically elected President of the United States, Trump pronounced the words of rage that will go down in history for their crude and authoritarian tone.

'This American carnage stops right here, and stops right now,' said Trump, as his predecessors seated behind him cringed.

'From this day forward, a new vision will govern our land,' shouted the xenophobic new American President. 'From this day forward, it's going to be only America First, America First! Every decision on trade, on taxes, on immigration, on foreign affairs, will be made to benefit American workers and American families.'[1]

With those words, it became clear that this would never be a normal or even a presidential President. This President had lifted his slogans from the isolationist and anti-semitic 'America First' movement of the 1930s, popularised by controversial aviator Charles Lindbergh and a motley crew of Nazi sympathisers.* Trump had appropriated the language of the worst of America's 1930s anti-immigrant populists and extremists. Now, he put the whole world on notice that things were about to change, as he repudiated the long-standing bipartisan Washington consensus under which the United States would shoulder its responsibilities as Leader of the Free World. Not anymore. Gone was any talk of promoting democracy. America, Trump proclaimed, would no longer seek 'to impose our way of life on anyone'. Instead, everything would become transactional; everything would be case by case. This, as the world would soon learn, meant the spectacle of a new American President who repeatedly attacked his democratic allies in Europe and cosied up to some of the world's most brutal dictators.

Four years later, by the end of his term in the White House, Trump had wrought unprecedented damage to the fabric of American society, to the international standing of the United States and ultimately to the very functioning of American democracy. Indeed, the final act of Trump's presidency was a unique form of what we might call 'American carnage'.

The carnage came to Washington on 6 January at Trump's invitation, when Trump incited the mobs and betrayed the constitution that he had sworn to uphold. Here was an American President who had no qualms about inciting armed rioters to engage in a violent insurrection rampage

---

* See Chapter 2.

that was aimed at stopping the certification, in the US Senate, of the 2020 electoral victory of Joe Biden.

Four years after taking office, Trump had become the first American President in history who had tried to halt the peaceful transfer of power. He failed in this enterprise, and he would face impeachment and multiple criminal trials as a result.

Where Trump was more successful, sadly, was in actively working to dismantle the Western liberal world order that had kept the peace for more than seventy-five years, since the end of the Second World War. He succeeded in diminishing American power and influence, in accelerating the decline of the American empire and in doing irreparable harm to America's credibility. Above all, Trump's actions ultimately gave comfort to America's enemies and helped them to flourish and prosper. There should be a special place in Dante's Inferno for a man like that.

Trump's disdain for established norms and institutions became evident early on. He moved quickly to withdraw the United States from a number of multilateral agreements, and he mocked and challenged the system of US alliances that had preserved the Pax Americana.

In his first week in office, he withdrew the United States from the Comprehensive and Progressive Agreement for Trans-Pacific Partnership, hurting US economic interests, leaving America's allies in the lurch and effectively handing a victory to China, which would now eagerly expand its influence across Asia. Soon after he took office, he pulled the United States out of the Paris Agreement, signalling a US shift away from international efforts to combat climate change. He also denied the science of global warming, siding with the fossil fuels lobby and with assorted conspiracy theorists.

Trump then began work on the infamous wall along the border with Mexico. His draconian anti-immigrant measures set a standard for cruelty that had never been seen. He ordered children to be separated from their parents at the border; many of them ended up literally in cages. He tried to impose a complete ban on Muslims entering the United States. He repeatedly attacked and demeaned the United Nations. He withdrew the United States from the United Nations Educational, Scientific and Cultural Organization (UNESCO) and from the UN's Human Rights Council, claiming these organisations had an anti-Israeli bias.

In 2018, he pulled the US out of the historic Intermediate-Range Nuclear Forces (INF) Treaty, a move that pleased Vladimir Putin, the Russian dictator whom Trump had always admired. Putin now felt free to expand his own arsenal, and he was encouraged further when Trump also withdrew the US from other arms-control agreements such as the Treaty on the Prohibition of Nuclear Weapons, where the US formally requested the removal of its signature, and the UN Arms Trade Treaty, where the US cited newly developed concerns about national sovereignty.

Trump, who by the second year of his presidency was surrounding himself with yes men and extremist zealots, fulfilled his campaign promise to withdraw the United States from the landmark Iran Nuclear Deal that had been reached by his predecessor Barack Obama and by key European allies. This would further energise the ayatollahs to challenge US interests. It would also please Vladimir Putin, who saw a new opportunity to befriend an enemy of Washington.

Even before he became President, Donald Trump had shocked his NATO allies by calling into question Article 5, NATO's founding principle. Article 5, NATO's common defence clause, states that an attack on one member is an attack on all member states. At a disastrous NATO summit in Brussels, Trump left his NATO allies aghast. Nicholas Burns, who had served as the US ambassador to NATO after the 9/11 attacks, wrote on Twitter, 'Trump sows further doubt whether the US under his leadership would defend our allies. Another gift to Putin.'

In 2018 Trump meanwhile declared a trade war on Europe, imposing new tariffs that were soon the highest in post-war history. He threatened tariffs on imported European automobiles in the name of US national security. He imposed a 25 per cent tariff on steel imports from Europe, and tweeted that 'trade wars are good, and easy to win'.*

The Trump administration used an obscure provision of the Trade Expansion Act of 1962 – a Cold War relic

---

* On 2 March 2018, the day after announcing steep tariffs on imports of steel and aluminium, President Trump noticed that 'when a country [the US] is losing many billions of dollars on trade with virtually every country it does business with, trade wars are good, and easy to win'.

seldom used before it became the President's weapon of choice – that allowed the US to impose tariffs or other trade restrictions on trading partners on national security grounds. Trump said the EU's 'unfair' trade policies were jeopardising the existence of critical US industries, and he threatened duties on the European auto industry on similar grounds. Had it not been real, it would have seemed ridiculous.

Trump's four years in the White House therefore represented a systematic and continuing attack not only on democratic values at home but on America's international obligations. By the end of his first year in office, using the incendiary anti-immigrant rhetoric that would become a model for illiberal democrats in Europe, Trump pulled out of the United Nations' ambitious plans to create a more humane global strategy on migration, the Global Compact for Migration. He sent Nikki Haley, the inexperienced former Governor of South Carolina and US ambassador to the United Nations to parrot his xenophobic and anti-immigrant tropes: Haley would announce America's hostility to the migration pact, saying it interfered with American sovereignty and ran counter to US immigration policies.[*]

A year later, Haley, by now a willing lackey and Trump accomplice in the dismantling of America's commitment to

---

[*] On 4 December 2017, Haley pointed out that a global approach to the immigration issue was 'simply not compatible with US sovereignty'. 'No country has done more than the United States, and our generosity will continue,' said Haley, 'but our decisions on immigration policies must always be made by Americans and Americans alone.' A statement previously released by the US mission to the UN noted that President Donald Trump made the decision.

the UN system and to the liberal world order, announced that Washington was slashing aid for Palestinian refugees by cutting funding of the UN Relief and Works Agency for Palestinian Refugees (UNRWA).

While constantly criticising Angela Merkel, the German Chancellor, and praising Viktor Orbán, the pro-Putin Prime Minister of Hungary, Trump also took a swipe at the Helsinki Commission, proposing significant budget cuts to the Organization for Security and Co-operation in Europe (OSCE), which had been a pillar of post-war stability.

When he famously met Vladimir Putin in Helsinki in July 2018, Trump became the first and only US President in history to defend Russia and to belittle the CIA at the same time. He excluded all note-takers and assistants from the summit and emerged after two hours with a curious smile on his face, as though he had just impressed his boss.

At a press conference, Trump was asked if he had told Putin that the CIA and sixteen other US intelligence agencies had concluded that Russia was behind a massive effort to tip the scale of the US election against Hillary Clinton, with a Moscow-run campaign of cyber attacks and fake news stories planted on social media.

Trump, who by now no longer sought to hide his admiration for Putin, promptly contradicted the CIA, sided with Putin and said there had been no reason for Russia to meddle in the vote.

'President Putin says it's not Russia. I don't see any reason why it would be,' said Trump. Putin beamed with pleasure. He was only too happy to repeat that Russia had never interfered in US affairs.

Even Trump's Republican allies were shocked. The Speaker of the House of Representatives, Paul Ryan, a man who rarely criticised Trump, released a strongly worded statement in which he reminded the US President that he 'must appreciate that Russia is not our ally'.[*]

'There is no moral equivalence between the United States and Russia, which remains hostile to our most basic values and ideals,' said Ryan, adding that there was 'no question' Moscow had interfered in the 2016 election.

Senior Republican Senator John McCain described Trump's craven behaviour in Helsinki as a 'disgraceful performance' by a US President. 'No prior President has ever abased himself more abjectly before a tyrant,' said McCain.

But over the next few years, the Republicans in Congress would get used to being more pro-Putin, as Trump turned the party into a cult following and proceeded to purge all the moderates, forcing them into retirement or defeating them with Make America Great Again (MAGA) candidates who had been certified by Trump. This is how Trump transformed the Republican Party into an extremist and anti-democratic organisation, filled with conspiracy theorists, racists and white supremacists, and most of them were prepared to do whatever the Master of Mar-a-Lago

---

[*] President Trump's answer on 16 July 2018, at the joint news conference after the summit, came a few days after special counsel Robert Mueller indicted twelve Russian intelligence officials for meddling in the US election. Therefore, Trump came under widespread, bipartisan condemnation. On 17 July, he tried to clarify his widely criticised comments.

commanded. The Republican Party, once the most anti-communist and anti-Soviet manifestation of American politics, was now a shadow of its former self.

In June 2020, as he prepared to run for re-election, Trump continued his retreat from US commitments in world affairs. He made the International Criminal Court (ICC) the next target of his contempt for the global rule of law. He signed an executive order imposing sanctions on prosecutors and visa bans against ICC officials who were investigating allegations of US misconduct in Afghanistan and Israeli officials in Palestine. Trump was essentially telling the international court to get lost.

Later that same year, while more than a million Americans were dying of the Covid virus, and Trump was recommending that people try drinking disinfectants, the US President began insulting the World Health Organization and accusing it of being pro-China. In July 2020, he announced that the US would be withdrawing from the UN body. As a result, US financial contributions to the WHO fell by 25 per cent during the worst years of the global coronavirus pandemic.[2]

Trump also managed to paralyse the World Trade Organization, the only international trade body that was committed to a rules-based system of global commerce. But Trump was not interested in the traditional Republican mantra of 'free trade'. *That* Republican Party was dead, and in its place was a protectionist and populist rabble.

Over the years, each of Trump's decisions weakened the

United States, further diminishing its role as a global leader. The 'America First' doctrine had become a thinly veiled excuse for isolationism, for challenging traditional alliances and for a new form of neo-authoritarian democracy.

Trump's affinity for dictators and strongman leaders upended decades of US foreign policy and caused multiple ruptures in international relations. From Russia's Vladimir Putin to Saudi Arabia's Mohammed bin Salman, Trump's willingness to turn a blind eye to human rights abuses completely undermined America's moral authority. His obsequious behaviour toward the dictator in oil-rich Saudi Arabia might be considered realpolitik by some, but he behaved as though he saw the Saudis and the entire galaxy of Gulf Arab rulers as potential billionaire clients of the Trump Tower in New York or the Trump Hotel in Washington. (They were, of both.)[3]

Trump's controversial son-in-law, Jared Kushner, who served in the White House, was dispatched to make friends with MBS, and the two soon became good friends, just as the Saudi prince had wanted. The Saudi prince is undoubtedly a modernising influence with a sophisticated vision of the kingdom's future, but he is also a ruthless dictator.

After the murder of Jamal Khashoggi, a *Washington Post* columnist and critic of MBS, who was killed inside the Saudi Consulate in Istanbul, Turkey, the Saudi government washed its hands of any responsibility and called it a 'rogue operation'. Despite overwhelming evidence implicating the Saudi Crown Prince in the murder, Trump hesitated. He would not hold MBS accountable. In fact, just as he had defended Putin from accusations of election interference, the US President now defended the Saudi leader. Once again, he trashed the findings of US intelligence agencies. Once more he weakened the leadership of the United States; he essentially gave license to authoritarians everywhere to behave as they wished. Trump was an opportunist, a narcissist and a grifter, but as President he behaved as though his mission in life was to betray his own country, its values and its history. In the name of some half-baked reiteration of 'America First', this President did great harm to his country.

Amid the Khashoggi affair, allegations surfaced that Jared Kushner had co-ordinated efforts to shield MBS from international condemnation. Subsequent revelations about a $2 billion private equity investment Kushner received from the Saudi sovereign fund, controlled by MBS, raised further questions. Kushner has always denied any wrongdoing, but just six months after he left the White House in 2021, he did receive a cheque for $2 billion. It was publicly revealed that the entire board of Saudi directors voted against giving the money to Kushner, who had no experience in private equity investments. But MBS overruled the board and told them to give Trump's son-in-law the money. The Emir of Qatar chipped in $200 million on the side, and soon Kushner, who had been serving as the President's Middle East peace envoy, was filling his basket with another $800 million of foreign contributions, including another $200 million from the Emir of Dubai.*

* * *

Vladimir Putin, Mohammed bin Salman and Hungarian autocrat Viktor Orbán are just three examples of the kind of leaders that Trump has embraced over the years. He has inspired other strongmen and spawned various imitators who have pushed illiberal democracy even further than Trump. In this nefarious group of like-minded leaders, alongside Trump, Putin, MBS and Orbán, one must not forget Recep Tayyip Erdoğan of Turkey, Jair Bolsonaro of Brazil, Rodrigo Duterte of the Philippines, Narendra Modi of India and Benjamin Netanyahu of Israel, to name but a few of Trump's favourites.

Together, they constitute a group of miscreants, leaders who take away civil rights, who do not care about human rights, who use populist nationalism and xenophobia as tools to control an angry and frightened electorate. The most striking thing is that, apart from thoroughbred dictators like Putin and China's Xi Jinping, most of the Trump

---

* According to several reports, Affinity Partners had raised $2 billion by the end of November 2022. Afterwards the firm updated the filing to reflect additional commitments, which exceed $3 billion, according to additional reporting. See Jonathan Swan, Kate Kelly, Maggie Haberman and Mark Mazzetti, 'Kushner Firm Got Hundreds of Millions From 2 Persian Gulf Nations', *New York Times*, 30 March 2023, and Kushner's Middle East Shakedown Affinity Partners https://americasbestpics.com/picture/kushner-s-middle-east-shakedown-affinity-partners-aum-us-investors-RQZUksKkA?s=cl

Club of Miscreants are authoritarians who have all been legally and democratically elected. Just like Trump.

They are all part of a group of nationalist demagogues who flourished in the years following the 2008 financial crisis, partly because of the failings of globalisation and the social divisions caused by severe income inequalities throughout much of the Western world. Trump was not the cause of this wave of far-right nationalist populism; he was merely a symptom, a manifestation.

Like the extremists of the 1930s, Trump and these other strongmen were ready and willing to shatter the norms and customs of democracy. Each leader developed a militant, often violent, cult following. Each leader seemed bent on bending the independence of the judiciary in their country to meet their personal needs. Each of these leaders tried in one way or another to crack down on dissent, especially with curbs on press freedoms, attacks on the media and the use of social media to spread disinformation. Each of these leaders tended to be anti-immigrant, anti-abortion and anti-LGBT. What all of them clearly had in common was a disregard for the rule of law.

Trump therefore became the first US President in history to treat his traditional European and NATO allies with animosity and to favour dealings instead with the world's most despotic leaders and extreme right-wing politicians who had trampled on democratic values.

Trump enjoyed a warm relationship with Recep Tayyip Erdoğan, the authoritarian President of Turkey who has governed since 2003. Erdoğan changed the constitution so that he could remain in office until 2029, expanded his presidential powers, arrested journalists and rivals, manipulated the courts and helped to finance terrorist organisations like Hezbollah and Hamas. He has, over the years, transformed Turkey, a NATO member, into a more Islamic and dictatorial regime.[4]

Jair Bolsonaro was known as the 'Trump of the Tropics', and he was a copycat strongman if ever there was one. The far-right former army captain has mimicked Trump's nationalism, his policies on law and order and his flair for often violent rhetoric. The firebrand former Brazilian President has praised Brazil's former dictatorship and attacked political correctness. He has insulted women and homosexuals, ridiculed the Covid vaccine, denied the science of climate change, made war on the environmentalists and helped destroy part of the Amazon rainforest during his time in office.[5]

In January 2023, Bolsonaro even copied Trump's 6 January insurrection plot, launching his own violent version of an attempt to stop the peaceful transfer of power to his democratically elected successor, President Luiz Inácio Lula da Silva.[6] This is the kind of legacy that Trump's presidency would bestow on the world: the legitimisation by the White House of miscreant leaders who were and are standing enemies of democracy.

In the case of Rodrigo Duterte, Trump was also legitimising mass murder, in the form of extrajudicial killings.

The foul-mouthed Duterte, the President of the Philippines from 2016 to 2022, literally ran his election campaign promising to murder all the drug dealers in his country. He bragged that he had killed a large number of criminals himself, with his own two hands. Duterte's 'war on drugs' unleashed the Philippine National Police and other violent para-military groups to instigate and incite the killings of more than 12,000 Filipinos.[7] No arrest, no trial. Just a death sentence.

When Barack Obama criticised Duterte's violation of human rights and his bloody and extrajudicial killing spree in 2016, Duterte replied by calling Obama the 'son of a whore'.[8]

Trump instead praised Duterte for doing an 'unbelievable job' in combating the illicit drug trade, and when he met the Filippino President during an Asian summit in late 2017, he refused to comment on human rights violations. 'We've had a great relationship,' proclaimed Trump, lifting his glass to toast his buddy, Rodrigo.[9] He then heaped more praise on the Filipino strongman.

President Duterte may have been crude, but he also knew how to play the game with Trump. Just weeks before Trump's election, he appointed as a special envoy to Washington a businessman named Jose Antonio, whose company Century Properties had developed the Trump Tower in Manila. Duterte and Trump would both deny there was any conflict of interest because, technically speaking, Trump had been paid a royalty and had not taken a shareholding in the business.* This is the way the world works, if ethics are tossed out of the window. This was the world that Trump embraced.

Narendra Modi is even more similar to Trump than Duterte or Erdoğan. Modi is an authoritarian Hindu-supremacist politician who has won repeated re-elections in India since 2014, even as he has progressively dismantled the institutions of what was once the world's largest democracy.

As Chief Minister of the Indian state of Gujarat, Modi was accused of allowing many Muslims to die. In 2002, anti-Muslim carnage engulfed the Indian state, killing at least 1,000 people. Most of the victims were Muslims. Modi, a lifelong member of Hindu extremist groups, ordered the police not to stop the massacres.[10]

As Prime Minister, Modi has led his nationalist Bharatiya Janata Party to electoral success, espousing an intolerant Hindu supremacist approach and often causing violence against India's Muslim population.† Modi and his allies have used partisan mobs to silence critics; they have fanned social divisions and systematically violated civil liberties. Modi has clamped down on press freedoms, taken major steps to erode the independence of the judiciary, especially

---

* In 2011, Trump struck a deal with Century Properties Group Inc. to build a $150 million branded luxury housing tower located in Manila's premier business district, Makati. The deal for the 57-storey tower is a licensing agreement under which President Donald Trump provides the use of his name in exchange for royalties. See Carolyn Kenney and John Norris, 'Trump's Conflicts of Interests in the Philippines' (part of 'Trump's Conflicts of Interest'), Center for American Progress, 14 June 2017

† India's population is 1.3 billion, of which 195 million are currently Muslims, or about 14 per cent of the total. Source PLFS data, 2022 report.

by manipulating the Supreme Court, and pursued harsh and discriminatory measures against the LGBT community.

It is not hard to see why Trump has repeatedly said he admires Modi, just as he has said that he admires President Xi Jinping of China, calling him smart and intelligent and noting on more than one occasion that he controls over a billion people 'with an iron fist'.[11]

Benjamin Netanyahu is another crony of Trump's, as close as the Middle East comes to offering its own version of a Mini-Me to Trump's Dr Evil. Another ultra-nationalist, another authoritarian and anti-democratic leader who has been repeatedly re-elected by an increasingly right-wing electorate. Netanyahu has openly tried to curb the powers of Israel's Supreme Court by introducing legislation that would neuter the court's power to judge on his own personal criminal corruption trials. And he succeeded, until the Israeli people took to the streets and protested until their action was eclipsed by the Hamas terrorist attack of 7 October 2023. That the same Supreme Court should have rejected the Netanyahu law even during the war in Gaza shows how much the court viewed Netanyahu as a threat to democracy.

So these were a few of the honorary members of the Club of Bad Actors, that exclusive group of potentates who have been enemies of democracy for decades. In 2024, they are stronger than ever, emboldened in no small part thanks to the negligence and opportunism practised by the Trump administration in place of a coherent US foreign policy.

None of Trump's authoritarian friends felt more emboldened than Vladimir Putin. He had invested a lot of money and time in cultivating Trump, in playing Trump, in observing Trump. The former KGB colonel had built a substantial personality profile on Trump, and he was too smart not to factor his observations into his strategic equation and vision for Russia. With Trump there was no unipolar world, there was no post-Cold War moment, nor was there any attempt at containment of Russia. Putin had been watching; he had seen the reaction of Obama to his annexation of Crimea in 2014. He had seen how Trump pulled the US out of Syria in 2018, allowing Russian troops to take over US military bases in the country, to literally move right in after the Americans left.

Putin had watched the first impeachment of Donald Trump, in 2019, when Trump was accused of trying to threaten and extort the President of Ukraine, Volodymyr Zelensky, in a July 2019 telephone call. Trump asked Zelensky to do him a favour: Washington would send valuable Javelin missiles in a $200 million military aid package for Ukraine, if Zelensky would 'look into' the Biden family.[12] No dirt on Biden, no Javelins. For this, Trump was impeached by the House of Representatives. But the Republican Trump followers in the Senate voted to acquit Trump, a lesson not lost on Putin.

Putin was also watching in February 2020 when Trump made a deal with the Taliban, brokered in Doha, Qatar, the city of spies, businessmen and billionaire terrorists. Trump sent Mike Pompeo, his Secretary of State, to witness the signing of the deal, which Trump's national security adviser, H. R. McMaster, would later call 'a surrender agreement with the Taliban'.[13] In many ways, it resembled Henry Kissinger's famous 'Peace with Honor' 1973 deal with North Vietnam. In that deal, the US agreed to withdraw all its troops and got nothing in return.

The terms of Trump's deal with the Taliban were simple: the United States was to withdraw all its troops from Afghanistan within fourteen months, by 1 May 2021, while the Taliban would promise not to let Afghanistan become a haven for terrorists and would stop attacking US service members. What could the value of a promise from terrorists be? Sadly, the Taliban were soon back in power in Afghanistan, and the deal went through various iterations, and Trump kept withdrawing US troops throughout 2020, so that by the time Joe Biden was inaugurated as President in January 2021 there were only 2,500 US troops left in the country.

This was the grim situation inherited by Biden, who had a political sense that he needed to get American troops out of Afghanistan in 2021, but who was also warned repeatedly by the CIA and the Pentagon that he was risking a bloodbath.[14]

Top military officials were furious at Biden's national security team because they wanted to start evacuating vulnerable Afghans as early as May but were not allowed to do so. After their advice not to pull out was disregarded, Pentagon brass sought to exit as soon as possible in the interest of troop safety and planned to get all troops out by as early as 4 July. But as the July date approached, the White House grew concerned and ordered the military to delay and keep troops until 31 August.

American spy agencies over the summer of 2021 painted an increasingly grim picture of the prospect of a Taliban takeover of Afghanistan and warned of the rapid collapse of the Afghan military, even as Biden and his advisers said publicly they thought that this was unlikely to happen as quickly. NATO allies complained that they were not being consulted, and European governments began getting their people out throughout the summer.

And then came the Fall of Kabul, the total victory for the Taliban, which now controlled all of Afghanistan. Twenty years after the start of George W. Bush's failed war, that same war had ended in US defeat. The Taliban, whom Bush had started the war to remove from power, were now firmly back in power. The United States had been humiliated into making a deal and accepting the promises of good behaviour from the same terrorists who had harboured Osama bin Laden and the nomenclature of al-Qaeda.

Afghanistan is a story not merely of imperial overreach but of extreme incompetence in diplomacy, as one might expect from Team Trump. It must be said that Team Biden did little to distinguish itself either, and if anything they took a bad situation and made it worse. Kabul was Biden's biggest foreign policy disaster.

The debacle of Kabul is an image still seared into our

collective consciousness. No one can unsee the image of that Afghan man falling from the under-carriage of a cargo jet. No one can forget the terrorist attacks that blew up Afghans and American soldiers at Kabul Airport. Nor can we ignore the way America betrayed thousands of local Afghani contractors and loyalists, who would now face death, prison or worse under the Taliban.[15] This is the legacy. This is what happened.

Kabul was perhaps the worst humiliation of America in half a century, since 30 April 1975, when the helicopters were touching down on the roof of the US Embassy in Saigon as crowds waved their passports and clambered up ladders to escape the fall of the city.

Meanwhile, in Moscow, Vladimir Putin was watching. He observed what Trump had wrought. He observed the attempts by the new American President, Biden, to turn things around, to return America to its traditional relationships and friendship with its European allies. Putin observed above all the weakness of American leadership, the confusion and chaos of the disaster in Afghanistan.

A few weeks after the Kabul fiasco, Vladimir Putin began mobilising the Russian Army, and by the end of the year he had dispatched nearly 150,000 troops.* Together

---

* Despite Russian officials' assurances between November 2021 and February 2022 that no invasion of Ukraine was being planned, satellite images showed, by April 2021, progressive Russian military buildup along the three sides of Ukraine's borders. Ukrainian authorities confirmed that the number of Russian troops increased from 100,000 to 120,000 by mid-April, which was accepted in the West as an accurate number. See Mykola Bielieskov, 'The Russian and Ukrainian Spring 2021 War Scare', the Center for Strategic and International Studies, 21 September 2021.

with the Russian Navy hovering in the Black Sea, the Russian military would soon encircle the neighbouring country of Ukraine.

CHAPTER NINE

PUTIN'S WAR ON WESTERN DEMOCRACY

Vladimir Putin is not the most relaxed person you could ever hope to meet. At 8 p.m. on the evening of 25 July 2015, after spending a few hours sipping tea, munching biscuits and waiting in the anterooms of Putin's grandiose offices on the second floor of Building No. 1 in the Kremlin, I get my chance.

The clock mounted high on the Spasskaya Tower has marked 4.20 p.m. by the time I enter the Kremlin complex. I am led through a long and narrow white corridor with high ceilings on the ground floor of Building No. 1. Then we go up to the executive suite, a sumptuously decorated string of state rooms that Putin has renovated in neoclassical style. Everything looks polished to perfection. The walls in some rooms are adorned with golden damask and red velvet; in others with pure white walls hang depictions of Red Square and the Kremlin. I think that this is the same set of offices from which Lenin and Stalin have ruled. Finally, I am brought to the Chimney Room, the large and baroque chamber that has been chosen for my meeting with Vladimir Putin. Two empty chairs stand in front of a marble fireplace that is often featured in TV news reports of Putin's meetings with foreign leaders. Atop the fireplace sits a neo-classical, gold clock that is covered with tiny angels.

After only three and a half hours of waiting for him to appear, I watch the white double doors of Putin's office finally swing open in the distance; the inner sanctum is four rooms away from the Chimney Room. Putin has emerged and is walking toward me. He has that determined see-saw stride. I am standing – with a dozen security people, press handlers, video camera technicians and interpreters down the hall – at the door to the Chimney Room. The arrival of the Russian President is like a Siberian breeze. He is followed by his aide Dmitry Peskov, members of his staff and still more security men trailing behind.

When we finally sit down, in the chairs in front of the fireplace, I notice that it is taking a while for him to feel at ease. The poker face remains the same, the piercing blue eyes and his body language are tight, almost a martial-arts type of posture, with both legs planted firmly in front of him. But he fiddles a lot with his tie, often twisting it around, and he plays with his earpiece. He seems quite tense, until after a few minutes I finally begin mentioning the name of his friend Silvio Berlusconi, who has organised the interview. Suddenly, Putin relaxes. Now the Russian dictator is smiling, and a minute later I can hear the interpreters in my earphone report how he recalls with pleasure the exquisite tagliolini with white truffles that Berlusconi's cook Michele had once served him in Milano. Now, he looks hungry.

Putin was hungry, but not for Silvio's white truffles; he wanted land, he wanted to redraw the map of Europe. He had a revanchist vision in which he would restore the rightful territorial possessions of what had once been the Soviet Union. Or perhaps even better, of the Czars. He wanted expansion, and he thought the West was weak. By 2021, he had seen Joe Biden make a mess of things in Kabul. He had seen how Trump had played into his hands, almost as though it had been planned: the weakening of American power, the creation of regional power vacuums and the rising doubts about US leadership. He had taken Crimea and eastern Ukraine in 2014 and the world had let him get away with it. He had sent his troops into Syria in 2018 to support Assad. He had sent his Wagner Group mercenaries into Libya over the years to take a piece of the country. What possible reason was there to stop now? This, at least, was the likely thought process of the Russian dictator, as evinced by his actions.

When I asked Putin about his intentions toward Ukraine back in July 2015, he assured me that Russia would not allow the differences it had with the West over Ukraine to drag it back into another Cold War. 'There are some people who want to drive a wedge between Europe and Russia, or Ukraine and Russia. We understand this very well,' said Putin. 'And at times those who pursue such goals succeed. But this only suggests that our work is not efficient enough. We will not let anyone drag us into a new Cold War of any kind.'[1]

That was back in 2015, at a time when the revanchist Russian leader had perhaps not yet formulated his plan to invade Ukraine. He was still busy digesting Crimea.

Four years after I interviewed Putin, in the spring of 2019, I found myself congratulating my friend Lionel Barber, who was then the editor of the *Financial Times*, for a scoop that he had achieved, a big interview, in the Kremlin, in the Chimney Room, with Vladimir Putin.[*] But when I reread Lionel's interview and thought about Putin's pronouncement of the death of Western values, I wondered who had really benefitted more from the interview: the *FT* because it was an exclusive? Or Putin, because he used the front page of one of the world's most authoritative newspapers to launch a malevolent prophecy? The answer was undoubtedly both.

The substance of what Putin said to the *Financial Times* on 19 June 2019 is, however, of historic importance, mainly because he effectively declared war on Western values in that interview.

Putin praised the far-right national populist movements in Europe and America, and he announced that 'the liberal idea' had 'outlived its purpose' as the public turned against immigrants, open borders and multiculturalism. As the *Financial Times* observed at the time, 'Mr Putin's evisceration of liberalism – the dominant western ideology since the end of the second world war – chimes with anti-establishment leaders

---

[*] On the eve of the G20 summit (27–29 June 2019), President Vladimir Putin spoke with the *Financial Times* editor Lionel Barber and Moscow Bureau Chief Henry Foy. The transcript of the conversation was published by the newspaper on 27 June 2019, and it is available on www.ft.com.

from US President Donald Trump to Hungary's Viktor Orban, Matteo Salvini in Italy, and the Brexit insurgency in the UK.'[2]

Putin had not only captured the zeitgeist of the seismic shift toward the right side of the political spectrum that was occurring in both America and Europe; he had also launched a manifesto for a world that no longer believed in liberal democracy. It was a declaration of war against the West, an argumentation wrapped in KGB double bluffs and twisted half-truths.

Putin would then proceed to do whatever it took to make his prediction into a self-fulfilling prophecy. He would also return to the theme of the end of Western values over and over again. This was also a classic tactic of disinformation campaigns that make use of a 'big lie': if you repeat a falsehood enough times, some people will think it is a fact. Putin's megaphone-like announcement of the death of liberal democracy, from the front page of the *FT*, was essentially a 'psy-op'. He proclaimed the Western liberal world order to be obsolete. He railed against the globalist elites who ruled America and Europe, crying that they had lost contact with the people. He supported the anti-elitist populists with money and election interference on their behalf. Add to this a few conspiracy theories produced by a troll farm in Saint Petersburg and a well-coordinated clandestine cyber-war across the world's social media and voilà: the decline of Western liberal democracy would soon go viral, become a meme, a mantra, a slogan. Putin's war on the West was always a hybrid war, from the very beginning.

By the end of 2021, Putin was ready for his biggest move; he began deploying long columns of Russian tanks and artillery that would soon see more than 100,000 troops on the borders of Ukraine.

Putin had been encouraged and emboldened by his observation of the decline of American influence and leadership since the start of the twenty-first century. He had probed and probed and found no resistance. Even before he annexed Crimea in 2014, he had already over the years managed to take control of various sovereign territories. One such example was the Transnistria region of Moldova, where Russian troops today prop up a puppet government.*

In 2008, Putin backed the separatists in the Georgian province of South Ossetia and the Abkhazia region. These regions are today phoney and unrecognised 'independent states' – in reality, they are the pro-Russian protectorates that resulted from Putin's brutal intervention in Georgia. Georgia's staunchly pro-West leader at the time, Mikheil Saakashvili, became a political prisoner in his own country, poisoned, imprisoned and then kept for years in a hospital in downtown Tbilisi.†

In 2015, Putin began taking control of the government in Syria when he intervened to support dictator Bashar

---

* The Russian military presence in Transnistria dates back to 1992, when Moscow intervened in support of Transnistrian separatists. In the aftermath of that war, the Russian forces stayed in the region under an alleged 'peacekeeping mission'. The presence of Russian troops in Moldova is considered illegitimate by Chișinău.
† Since the poisoning attempt with arsenic and mercury in 2022, Saakashvili lives under 'aggravated risk' of death, according to US experts. See Shaun Walker, 'Gaunt and ghostly, Georgia's jailed ex-President nears death in hospital', *The Guardian*, 16 April 2023.

al-Assad and established a formidable Russian military presence there. In 2018, he was able to move some Russian troops directly into abandoned US bases in Syria, thanks to Trump's unilateral withdrawal from the battered country.* Today, Putin remains a major player in the region, and more recently he has become the staunch ally of the ayatollahs of Iran, who in turn have supplied drones and other armaments for Putin to deploy against Ukraine.[3] With Iran, Putin has also forged a mutually beneficial understanding on the price of oil inside the expanded oil producers' cartel, OPEC Plus.

Putin has also established an important military presence in Libya, which after the death of Gaddafi in 2011 became a failed state that would be worn down by intermittent civil wars involving a variety of militias, jihadi groups, the UN-recognised Government of National Accord (GNA) in Tripoli and the opposing Libyan National Army (LNA), with its stronghold in Eastern Libya, led by General Khalifa Haftar.

Haftar's abortive 2019 assault on the seat of the UN-backed government in Tripoli relied heavily on Wagner mercenaries that Putin had sent to Libya but failed to overcome the Turkish-backed armed forces who were supporting Tripoli. Haftar still relies heavily on Russian mercenary

---

* In December 2018, President Trump ordered via Twitter the withdrawal of 2,000 American troops from Syria, de facto ceding a strategically vital country to Russia and Iran. See Mark Landler, Helene Cooper and Eric Schmitt, 'Trump to Withdraw U.S. Forces From Syria, Declaring "We Have Won Against ISIS"', *New York Times*, 19 December 2018, and Tom Vanden Brook, 'Russia takes over key U.S. outposts in Syria, filling vacuum left by American withdrawal', USA Today, 15 October 2019.

group Wagner for military support. The involvement of external actors, including Russia and Turkey, has further complicated the Libyan conflict.

The United States has been nearly silent on the issue, even under Joe Biden. When Turkey's President Erdoğan, Egypt's President el-Sisi and others asked Trump to get involved in the conflict and counter Putin's forces, Trump told those leaders that he'd rather not. Italy, France and the rest of Europe have meanwhile launched multiple failed efforts to improve the situation.

By slowly increasing its involvement in Libya, Russia has managed to secure the bulk of its tactical and strategic objectives without much interference from the West. For now, Putin is the dominant foreign actor in Libya.*

* * *

In October 2021, President Joe Biden was shown a highly classified intelligence report, complete with satellite images, intercepted communications and human source information, that concluded that Vladimir Putin was about to launch a full-scale invasion of Ukraine. Gathered around the coffee table in the Oval Office were Secretary of State Tony Blinken, Vice President Kamala Harris, General Mark Milley, the chairman of the Joint Chiefs of Staff, plus

---

* Thomas D. Arnold, 'Exploiting Chaos: Russia in Libya', Center for Strategic and International Studies, 23 September 2020.

Jake Sullivan, national security adviser and Avril Haines, director of national intelligence.* A few weeks later, in early December, Biden told Putin during a two-hour video conference that there would be severe consequences if Russia were to invade Ukraine. He told Putin directly that if Russia further invaded Ukraine, the United States and its European allies would fortify their allies on the eastern flank of NATO, impose strong economic sanctions and provide additional defensive materiel to Ukraine.

Putin didn't care. He might even have begun to believe some of his own propaganda about the death of Western liberal democracy. He certainly believed that he could divide the Europeans and outmanoeuvre the lethargic Joe Biden, who had presided over the disastrous US withdrawal from Afghanistan just six months before. NATO was still licking its wounds after four years of maltreatment by Trump. And Putin had meanwhile managed to make Germany and much of the continent dependent on Russian energy, which allowed him to play upon European fears of a disruption in energy supply with great skill and success.

In any case, Putin had his plan for his massive and rapid invasion, a quick regime change and the complete surrender of Ukraine, which would soon be restored to its

---

* Shane Harris, Karen DeYoung, Isabelle Khurshudyan, Ashley Parker and Liz Sly extensively describe the urgent meeting in the Oval Office that took place in October 2021 in 'Road to war: U.S. struggled to convince allies, and Zelensky, of risk of invasion', an exclusive report published by the *Washington Post* on 16 August 2022.

rightful place and reunited with Mother Russia. He even had picked a puppet figure to replace President Volodymyr Zelensky, and his tanks were filled with dress uniforms so that the Russian troops could drive into downtown Kiev, take over the city, quickly change out of their battle gear and then participate in a victory parade. According to the plan, it would all be over in three days.

Putin badly underestimated Joe Biden, NATO, the European Union and the capability of his own military machine, and he badly underestimated the will of the Ukrainian people to defend themselves. Today, the horrific result of Putin's miscalculations is still before our very eyes, in real-time war and suffering, in the atrocities and war crimes and hundreds of thousands of dead soldiers on both sides. But the Russian dictator is not a man to be easily cowed, by a situation or circumstance, by a war or by history. Putin is also, to a large degree, an anti-historical figure. He looks backwards, into the past, for inspiration. In the third decade of the twenty-first century, he launched a Second World War-style tank invasion that became a First World War-style trench conflict, and all this in his quest to turn back time and recreate the Russian empire of the Tsars.

But the war against Ukraine launched by Putin is more than just a misguided nostalgia trip for a brutal dictator; it is also a war against Europe, against NATO, against the United States, against Western democracy, and against Western cultural values. For Putin it has also become an existential matter; he knows from reading history that Russian leaders who lose wars do not generally fare well.

Putin has also been counting on public opinion in Europe and the United States to sour on continuing military support for Ukraine. The calculation has been correct; indeed this kind of 'Ukraine fatigue' was even alluded to during a leaked telephone conversation in 2023 with the Prime Minister of Italy, during a hoax call by pranksters.[*] With Trump in the White House, Putin is counting on getting what he wants in Ukraine, by hook or by crook.

Putin and his surrogates and proxies and sympathisers have meanwhile forged strong ties with the nationalist far-right populists in Europe, most notably Viktor Orbán, who behaves like a Putin pawn. In the United States, the Russian disinformation campaign continues, and thanks to Trump's continuing lapdog admiration, Putin is now extremely popular with far-right Trumpist members of the Republican Party. Trump's people have delivered for Putin, including Mike Johnson, the Republican Speaker of the US House of Representatives who blocked and then delayed aid for Ukraine for four months, and who, it has been revealed, received controversial Russian funds during

---

[*] European leaders are 'tired' of the war in Ukraine, Italian Prime Minister Giorgia Meloni told two Russian pranksters in a call, thinking she was speaking with officials with the African Union. The telephone conversation took place on 18 September 2023, but the audio of the call has been released by the comedy duo on 1 November 2023.

his last election campaign from an oligarch close to Putin.[*] In the Senate, meanwhile, the opportunistic Senator James David 'JD' Vance was towing the Trump line and became a vehement critic of Ukraine and a big fan of Putin. Vance even called the autocratic Viktor Orbán of Hungary a model for the United States. This is the man who would become Donald Trump's 2024 running mate.

It is worth recalling that Donald Trump himself has been a Putin admirer for a very long time. Since the 1980s, Trump and his family members have made numerous trips to Moscow in search of business opportunities, and Trump has bragged about meeting all the top Russian oligarchs. Russian investors, including friends of Putin's, have spent heavily to buy in to Trump properties around the world.[†]

'Russians make up a pretty disproportionate cross-section of a lot of our assets,' Trump's son, Donald Jr, told a real estate conference in 2008. 'We see a lot of money pouring in from Russia.'[‡]

In 2013, Trump fawned over the Russian dictator during a visit to Moscow to celebrate the Miss Universe beauty

---

[*] FEC investigations into suspicious campaign contributions to US Representative Mike Johnson revealed that he received donations totalling nearly $10,000 from Robert Houghtaling, CEO of American Ethane, whose main stakeholder was Konstantin Nikolaev, an oligarch close to Vladimir Putin. See Ewan Palmer, 'Mike Johnson's Campaign Contributions from Company Tied to Russia', *Newsweek*, 27 October 2023.

[†] See Luke Harding, *Collusion: Secret Meetings, Dirty Money, and How Russia Helped Donald Trump Win*, Vintage Books, 2017. The author, who's also foreign correspondent at *The Guardian*, carefully reconstructs the many ties between Trump and Moscow, starting with his early business travels as a young real estate developer to the Soviet Union in the 1980s.

[‡] Trump's son comments as posted by Turbonews, a multi-daily online bulletin reporting on market trends, travel, and tourism. See also Glenn Kessler, 'Trump's claim that "I have nothing to do with Russia"', *Washington Post*, 27 July 2016.

pageant. The Trump Organization company would later try to lobby Dmitry Peskov to get authorisation to build a Trump Tower in Moscow.[4] Trump has always seen Russia as a business opportunity.

Think about how much Putin has to be grateful for.

In December 2023, Trump, Speaker Johnson, and their far-right followers in the US House of Representatives worked to block $61 billion of military aid for Ukraine.[*] Finally, in April 2024, Biden had the CIA brief Johnson on how close to defeat Ukraine really was without aid, and the House Speaker changed his mind. Congress approved the aid. Nonetheless, Trump made clear that if he was made President again, he would cut off all aid to Ukraine.[†] This, of course, is precisely what Putin has been counting on.

Meanwhile, in Europe, Viktor Orbán, the authoritarian leader of Hungary, has carved himself an unusual niche in modern history. Orbán will go down as a quintessential Fifth Columnist, as a man who betrayed European democracy and the rule of law and who instead befriended Putin; he helped Putin by blocking €50 billion of military aid for

---

[*] On 6 December, the Republican majority in the Senate blocked the emergency spending bill to fund war in Ukraine, demanding strict new border restrictions in exchange. Negotiations with Democrats in the Congress are ongoing at the time of writing, but as many fear, it will become even harder to reach a deal ahead of the 2024 election season.

[†] After six months of public pressure exerted by the White House, on 24 April the Senate approved new military aid for Ukraine. In the meanwhile, Donald Trump repeatedly asserted that the conflict would never have happened under his watch, suggesting he was not in favour of helping Ukraine defend itself against Russia. This statement was also confirmed by Hungary's leader, Viktor Orbán, who claimed in an interview that Trump's plan 'is not [to] give a penny' to Kyiv. See Vaughn Hillyard and Rebecca Shabad, 'Hungary's leader claims Trump told him he would cut off U.S. military aid to Ukraine', NBC News, 12 March 2024, and Max Boot, 'Why U.S. aid to Ukraine is still in jeopardy', *Washington Post*, 29 April 2024.

Ukraine in December 2023. It would take the EU another three months of wrangling in order to get military aid to Ukraine.*

Orbán's actions against Ukraine came at the same time as the Republican Party's similar actions in Washington. The far right was united across the Atlantic.

What has been happening in the United States is deeply connected with the internal divisions in American society. The 2024 presidential election campaign saw one of the ugliest demonstrations of democracy in action, a violent rivalry between two alternate realities: one United States that has respect for the rule of law, the constitution and the norms of democracy; the other, a populist rabble-rousing Trump, who promised 'revenge' and 'retribution' against his enemies while swearing that once he was back in power, he would end the war in Ukraine in twenty-four hours. Trump's relationship with Putin will, presumably, be the subject of debate among historians for decades to come.

Putin's war against the West is also predicated on the important changes in international power structures that are currently underway. He has moved to embrace not only the ayatollahs of Tehran but also His Majesty Prince Mohammed bin Salman of Saudi Arabia, a fellow dictator.

---

* On 14 March 2024, the EU member states in Brussels agreed on 5 billion euros in urgent military aid to Kyiv in the framework of the Ukraine Assistance Fund (UAF), which is financed through the European Peace Facility (EPF). The UAF also envisions the possibility of covering the costs of purchasing weapons in the international market to be delivered to the Ukrainian military. The EU and its member states have mobilised about €30 billion in military support to Kyiv since the beginning of the war.

This helps Russia to co-ordinate oil prices as a member of OPEC Plus, but it goes well beyond just that.

With the arrival of war in the Middle East in October 2023, Putin gained multiple advantages in his hybrid war against the American empire. He was able to welcome both the ayatollahs and the terrorist leaders of Hamas to the Kremlin.* He would travel to Saudi Arabia. He would forge new business ties with Prime Minister Narendra Modi of India, mainly based on discounted energy for India and the authoritarian Modi's neutrality over Ukraine. Modi was one of several leaders from the emerging Global South to appear ambiguous over Putin's invasion of Ukraine. The other prominent figure is President Lula of Brazil, who has repeatedly snubbed Zelensky and cosied up to Putin. With Turkey's Erdoğan, there is much business to discuss, including the co-ordination of grain shipments from the Black Sea, the situation in Syria and a shared sympathy for Hamas and Hezbollah.

Putin indeed is nurturing a variety of relationships with terrorists and fellow travellers in the world that emerged after the immediate post-Cold War period. The unipolar world of American predominance has ended, almost before our very eyes, and a fundamental realignment is underway. Yet perhaps because America still remains so powerful a

---

* Pictures released by Hamas showed Bassem Naeem, its head of international relations, and Mousa Abu Marzouk, a senior member of the Hamas politburo, together in Moscow on 26 October 2023. Mikhail Bogdanov, Putin's special envoy to the Middle East, was also present, and Ali Bagheri Kani, the deputy Foreign Minister of Iran, who is known as a sponsor of Hamas, was also in Moscow for talks.

nation, and still the world's military hyperpower, we do not even notice what is happening. A set of tectonic changes and transformations in power equilibria are underway in trade and military alliances, new medium-sized regional players are emerging and the system of Western liberal institutions that was designed by the United States in 1945 is being upended.

With this backdrop, the war in Gaza was a godsend for Putin, and the distraction from Ukraine covered over a period of impasse on the battlefield. It also afforded him new opportunities to work with Iran, which by 2024 had become a key supplier of arms to Moscow. The hugely disproportionate retaliation launched by Benjamin Netanyahu for the 7 October Hamas terrorist attacks would become a major problem for Joe Biden. Biden's approval ratings and America's reputation both suffered greatly as thousands of young people spilled onto the streets of world capitals to show their solidarity with Palestinians. America was beset by the greatest and most violent period of student unrest since 1968, and on 5 November, the hapless Kamala Harris lost much of the youth vote as a result of the Biden administration appearing unable or unwilling to restrain Netanyahu.

At the same time, the internal divisions in American society during the presidential campaign season would sharpen. America was a polarised and broken society. Most striking, for a nation plagued by almost weekly school shootings and massacres, the propensity for violence in political life was growing. In January 2024, one in four Americans, and one in three Republicans, said they believe that violence is justifiable in the pursuit of political goals. This was the America that saw the failed assassination attempt against Trump in July 2024, by a shooter who was a registered Republican and supporter of Trump himself. Other assassination attempts followed. Political violence in America is now a reality, a part of life.

Many thoughtful Americans believe that the coming years will see a rising low-density form of social conflict, with various manifestations of violence that could be characterised as civil war. Indeed, just over half of all Americans believe that a civil war is possible or likely in the next few years.[5]

We should remember that Trumpism is not the cause of America's breakdown in social cohesion; it can more accurately be described as a manifestation of the problem or a symptom of widespread malcontent. Trumpism is the pus that oozes out of the wound; it is not the cause of the wound.

Such domestic strife and conflict in contemporary America does not bode well for its ability to salvage its role as the world's only superpower. Domestic divisions have accelerated the decline of the American empire. In the history of empire, be it the Roman Empire or the Ming Dynasty, whenever civil wars occur, or whenever deep societal conflicts or divisions happen, the empire is inevitably weakened, and in a trajectory of inexorable decline.[6]

So Putin's war in Ukraine can be seen as just one part

of his attempt not only to expand Russia's borders but to supplant the Western liberal order with chaos and disorder, posing multiple challenges that exist on too many fronts at the same time for the West to remain cohesive. That is the essence of Putin's hybrid war on the West, in Ukraine, Libya, Syria, Gaza and in his multiple interferences, coups and election rigging across more than twenty countries in Africa. It is a shotgun aimed at the heart of Western democracy, capable of causing multiple wounds.

As for Putin, he can get himself re-elected as many times as he can maintain the regime in Moscow. But in the process of waging war on Ukraine and the West he has also been forced to compromise, if only for economic reasons. He may have dreamed of a high-profile alliance with China that would allow Russia to stand tall again, but in the end he has transformed himself into a vassal of President Xi Jinping.

Russia, by 2024, had become a discount gas station for Beijing.

CHAPTER TEN

THE CHINESE CENTURY

For the better part of 2,000 years, and up until the 1800s, China was the world's biggest economy.

While Europe was still in the Dark Ages, in the tenth and eleventh centuries, the emperors of the Song Dynasty were governing vast expanses of territory, made up of advanced civilisations, great wealth and knowledge and huge scientific achievement. Long before Europe experienced the Renaissance, China boasted an advanced economy that featured sophisticated trading networks, rich cultural achievements, urbanisation and the development of a market economy.

It was only in the 1800s, just 200 years ago, that Europe really took off. While this was mainly because of the Industrial Revolution, it was also the result of the way European empires subjugated China throughout the century. At the start of the nineteenth century, China was still the world leader, accounting for around 30 per cent of global

GDP.* China's position as the world's largest economy would shrink dramatically as a result of it being exploited by foreign powers. By the end of the nineteenth century, it represented less than 10 per cent of global GDP.

As Europe and America raced ahead with the steam engine and railroads and the telegraph, China was left as the eternal object of imperial desires. It was often referred to in the 1800s as 'the grand prize' for ambitious European imperialists.[1] It was a huge and rich market of potential customers, a perfect destination for surplus investment capital, cheap labour and abundance of raw materials. Tea, silk, porcelain, spices, precious metals and more. China was the perfect model for European mercantilist policies, a prize to be fought over, a country to be plundered, a market for the sale of opium that was made in India and a cheap manufacturing hub.

As the nineteenth century unfolded, China was whittled away by Western imperialism. The Opium Wars in the 1840s and 1850s saw the British fighting to force open Chinese markets for opium trade. The White House, under the leadership of President John Tyler during the first Opium War, and President James Buchanan during the second, was

---

* It is widely recognised that China was the largest economy in the world between the sixteenth and the nineteenth century, when it accounted for 25–30 per cent of the global economy. At the beginning of the 1800s, the increasingly tight control of the Chinese imperial government and the development of the Western Industrial Revolution eventually weakened the Qing Dynasty (the last imperial dynasty, which lasted until 1912) and made the country's output shrink in relative terms. See Helena Holodny, 'The rise, fall, and comeback of the Chinese economy over the last 800 years', Business Insider India, 9 January 2017, which includes charts on changes in China's output over the past 800 years elaborated by Viktor Shvets of Macquarie Research.

wary of taking sides in what was seen as a foreign conflict. At least in public.

Put another way, the US maintained a neutral stance officially, but American merchants and missionaries were deeply involved in the trade and had a keen interest in the outcome. This period set the stage for future diplomatic conflicts with China, which were almost always about access to the Chinese market for American-made products.

In 1899, while President William McKinley was still fighting an imperial war for control of the Philippines, the issue of China came up again. At the time, China was experiencing a bloody uprising, fuelled by anti-foreign sentiment, and even the taking of foreign legations in Beijing as hostages. It was known as the Boxer Rebellion. The United States, which was going through its only uncloseted imperialist period in history, ended up siding with the European imperialists, who had no intention of allowing China to close its markets to Western goods. President McKinley supported US participation in the so-called Eight-Nation Alliance against China. In August of 1900 this alliance, consisting of the United States, the United Kingdom, Germany, France, Russia, Japan, Italy, and Austria–Hungary, sent 20,000 soldiers overland to capture Beijing and to march right up to the Forbidden City. An American occupying force, together with the Europeans, then suppressed the Boxer Rebellion and imposed harsh penalties on the rebels. There were American troops occupying the streets of Beijing in 1900.

In 1901, the US Secretary of State John Hay created what was called the 'Open Door Policy', which ostensibly aimed to prevent further colonisation of China but in reality was meant to keep China's door open to US exports. It was a contract aimed at safeguarding US economic and commercial interests. The imposition of unequal treaties, economic subjugation and territorial acquisitions by Western powers including the United States altered the trajectory of China in the 1800s, contributing to its economic decline and making its leaders increasingly resentful victims of colonial exploitation.

In the early days of the twentieth century, while China was being forced to pay millions of dollars of penalties and reparations to the United States and the European conquering powers, there were some who saw into the future, some who could imagine what an unleashed and revanchist China might one day become. Oddly enough, it was a Marxist economist named John Hobson who was the greatest of all prophets. In 1902, he published a study of imperialism that contained these prescient words about China's destiny:

> It is at least conceivable that China might turn the tables on the Western industrial nations, and, either by adapting their capital and organizers or, as is more probable, by substituting her own, might flood their markets with her cheaper manufactures, and refusing their imports in exchange might take her payment in liens upon their capital, reversing the earlier process of investment until

she gradually obtained financial control over her quondam patrons and civilisers.*

China, wrote Hobson in 1902, might someday 'launch herself upon the world market as the biggest and most effective competitor, taking to herself first the trade of Asia and the Pacific, and then swamping the free markets of the West and driving the closed markets of the West to an ever more rigorous Protection'.[2]

Fast forward to today, and here we are. Hobson got it right. Little more than a hundred years have passed since Hobson wrote these words, and today China is an economic superpower that has spent $1 trillion since 2013 on its famous Belt and Road Initiative (BRI). This innocent-sounding Chinese project is like a Marshall Plan of huge resources, but unlike the Marshall Plan, the money is not *given* to poorer nations – it is *loaned* to them for the construction of infrastructure like bridges and roads and tunnels. If the recipients cannot pay the money back, they soon find themselves trapped in debt, and often forced to give the Chinese access to their raw materials and markets. They are therefore stuck in what is called a 'debt trap'. This is not traditional territorial imperialism but the use of soft power, in this case money, to win hearts and minds across Africa, Asia, Latin America and eastern Europe especially.

Today, China is on track to regain its crown as the world's

---

* At the beginning of the 1900s, Hobson had been already predicting a possible rise of China that, in many ways, recalls today's emerging economic dynamics.

biggest economy, and quite soon, in all likelihood before the end of the early 2030s.[3] The former victim of Western imperialism has successfully turned the tables. China has grown its way to the top table of world affairs.

Now that we know more about its history it is perhaps easier to understand why the Chinese today see themselves as currently rightfully reclaiming their place at the top – and just 200 years after China was knocked off its throne as the world's biggest economy by the European imperialists and American free traders.

My friend Kishore Mahbubani from the National University of Singapore has argued eloquently that when viewed against the backdrop of the past 1,800 years, the recent period of the West's relative over-performance against China is 'a major historical aberration'. He noted that all such aberrations eventually come to a natural end.[*] The problem here is that the future of the United States and the entire macro-economic premise upon which Western prosperity is based is now being called into question. For China, this 200-year interval of Western superiority may indeed seem an aberration, but for the United States, and the entire West, it is a far more existential economic and political matter.

In 2001, 100 years after the signing of the Boxer Protocol, China, by now a sleepy giant no more, was admitted to the

---

[*] Kishore Mahbubani, *Has the West Lost it? A Provocation*, Penguin Books, 2019. Mahbubani was among the first analysts to talk about the inescapable rise of China and India in *The New Asian Hemisphere: The Irresistible Shift of Global Power to the East*, PublicAffairs, 2009, where he explains how, given the size of the Chinese and Indian populations, histories and cultures, it is 'much more natural' for these two countries to be the largest powers in the world.

World Trade Organization. Beijing had been undertaking serious economic reforms since 1979, when they had been launched by Deng Xiaoping. The reforms carried out by Deng and his allies gradually led China away from a planned economy and Maoist ideologies, opened it up to foreign investments and technology and introduced its vast labour force to the global market. The process was by no means complete, but Bill Clinton was convinced that the time was ripe for China to be admitted into America's rules-based system. Clinton, the cheerleader for globalisation, pushed hard for China to be admitted despite the fact that it did not meet all the conditions. The United States thought it was directing the show when China joined the World Trade Organization. Instead, China was writing its own script.[*]

China wanted to join the WTO because it would give China access to new trading partners, as well as a seat at the table in a globalising world. The United States wanted China to get on board with a US-led, liberal-democratic order and move away from its communist state-run model. It didn't quite work out the way Washington hoped. China would benefit hugely, and its economy would leap forward after joining the WTO at annual growth rates of 8 per cent at least.[†] But it would also engage in unfair trading

---

[*] On 11 December 2001, China joined the World Trade Organization (WTO). Western countries, the US above all, cautiously assumed that the opening of the Chinese market would soon lead to less authoritarian governments and greater protection of civil rights. So far, Beijing is a concrete example of how an autocratic political system can coexist with a free-market economy.

[†] According to the World Bank, China's GDP had a double-digit growth from 2000 to 2007 and lowered under 10 per cent yearly after 2010. Source https://data.worldbank.org/indicator/

practices, including currency manipulation and the dumping of its products on Western markets, just as Hobson had predicted.

In 2001, the Chinese economy represented 3.8 per cent of the world GDP, with the United States still leading the pack with 30 per cent. Twenty years later, notwithstanding the horrors of the Covid pandemic, the global economy had changed structurally. China now represented 18 per cent of global GDP, with the US at 25 per cent.[*] Consensus forecasts from some of the world's leading economists and banks suggest that China will overtake the United States as the biggest economy in the world in terms of GDP by 2032.[†]

Empire, of course, is about far more than just economics, but the American empire, an accidental empire that became the global superpower by default in 1945, will have been one of the shortest-lived great empires in world history, with a likely duration of less than a century if one takes the starting date as the close of the Second World War in 1945. Even if China is facing terrible economic problems today, at some point toward the 2040s or 2050s the American century will gradually give way to the Chinese century.

The unintended American empire, born in 1945, was

---

[*] As of December 2023, according to the latest IMF–World Bank numbers, China's $18 trillion economy accounted for just under 18 per cent of global GDP, making it the world's second-largest economy after the US.

[†] It is difficult to predict if and when China will surpass its American rival as sudden shifts in geopolitics or breakthroughs in technology would change the picture. However, many research centres, including the Goldman Sachs research bureau, believe that the next decade will be crucial for Beijing to become the world's leading economy. This should happen around 2030, although today's scenario is turning more uncertain as China performed in 2023 well below expectations. See Chris Anstey, 'US Economy Outstrips China, Adds a Korea Worth of GDP', Bloomberg, 26 January 2024.

often grievously mismanaged, both during the Cold War, and especially in the post-Cold War era, and it has now arrived at a key inflection point. That point is located on a trajectory of decline from which it will not be easy to recover. After eighty years of American exceptionalism, the US-designed liberal democratic world order is today under siege, not only from Vladimir Putin's wars and propaganda but also from his new overlord in Beijing, President Xi Jinping. Gradually, but somehow inexorably, the American century seems to be coming to a premature close.

The long arc of history ultimately favours China's rise, and not only in economic but in global political terms. Both Fernand Braudel and Ray Dalio have made the same point about the gravitational power of the arc of history, and a strong case can be made that the twenty-first century will be the Chinese century.[4] That China will overtake the United States to become the biggest economy in the world is a near statistical certainty. That China will equal US political influence seems plausible; it may already be true. The chances of China overtaking the United States in military terms, however, are lower in the near term, at least until the 2050s, according to the experts.[*]

---

[*] In the 2018 annual congressional report, President Xi Jinping called for a possible catch-up with the US military power in 2050. Experts from leading independent think tanks such as GIS Reports, Carnegie Endowment for International Peace and the International Institute for Strategic Studies generally acknowledged that despite Beijing's massive military investments over the last decade, China has caught up with its American rival only under certain military capabilities (i.e., the naval forces, military technologies). However, there is not yet a widespread consensus that today's Chinese advantages (ships, missiles and people) will result within a few decades in China's global military dominance. See Kelly A. Grieco and Jennifer Kavanagh, 'America Can't Surpass China's Power in Asia', *Foreign Affairs*, 16 January 2024.

In Washington, the best and the brightest of the Biden government, Secretary of State Antony Blinken and national security adviser Jake Sullivan, would argue that the inevitable rise of China is not a certainty and that America has the opportunity to maintain its primacy. Or, as Sullivan declared in late 2023, 'Nothing in world politics is inevitable.'[5] But Sullivan, Blinken and the other top US foreign policy officials and presidential advisers in the Biden administration all perceive China as a powerful rival and competitor, as well as an autocracy that regularly violates human rights. They know that the stability of the world requires the smart management of relations between Washington and Beijing. But they are also pressed by domestic electoral politics and the need to grandstand against China in a way that often reduces the perceived threat of China to a campaign slogan.

On his first day in office in 2017, Trump withdrew from the Trans-Pacific Partnership agreement, a move that benefitted China. Trump then imposed 10 per cent tariffs on $300 billion worth of Chinese imports – tariffs that Biden has largely kept in place. Indeed, Biden announced a raft of restrictions on US exports of computers and high-tech equipment in 2022. In May 2024, Biden doubled and quadrupled some of the tariffs on electric cars and solar panels. Biden also turned up the heat on China's human rights abuses in a string of public statements. Predictably, China responded in kind with its own trade restrictions and by harassing US corporations already doing business in China.*

Trump and Biden both focused on retaining American military pre-eminence over China as an overarching goal of US policy. Yet Biden made an effort to placate his Chinese counterpart. At his first meeting with President Xi Jinping during a G20 summit held in Bali in November 2022, Biden promised that there would be 'no new Cold War' with China.[6] The Chinese read-out of the meeting went further and listed five promises that Biden had allegedly made to Xi. According to Beijing, Biden promised that the United States:

- does not seek to change China's system;
- does not seek to start a Cold War with China;
- does not seek to strengthen alliances against China;
- does not support 'Taiwan independence';
- does not intend to break off ties with China, impede China's economic development, or contain China[7]

What Biden did next must have struck the Chinese as pure betrayal. He signed a string of export and investment restrictions on US companies doing business with China. He

---

* The Trump administration, till August 2020, imposed several rounds of tariffs on about $380 billion worth of thousands of Chinese-imported products. China in turn has set tariffs on $185 billion worth of US goods. The United States is currently imposing a 25 per cent tariff on approximately $250 billion of imports from China and a 7.5 per cent tariff on approximately $112 billion worth of imports from China. See Erica York, 'Tracking the Economic Impacts of U.S. Tariffs and Retaliatory Actions', Tax Foundation, 7 July 2023.

worked to build a series of new alliances, like the AUKUS agreement with Australia and the United Kingdom to provide the Australian navy nuclear-powered submarines. The US opened four new military bases in the Philippines, including three in the north of the main island of Luzon, a strategic location near Taiwan. Biden meanwhile established new trilateral intelligence-sharing mechanisms with South Korea and Japan. Biden in particular focused on reinforcing South Korea and Japan as key US alliances, even bringing them together for a special summit at Camp David. The message from each of these alliances was always the same: vigilance against the threat of China, and China should keep its hands off Taiwan.

It was precisely the issue of Taiwan that led to a highly controversial political stunt performed by Nancy Pelosi, the retiring US Speaker of the House of Representatives. Despite Biden personally imploring her not to go to Taiwan, Pelosi went to visit Taiwan anyway in August 2022. Despite the warnings of the White House and the Pentagon that the Pelosi trip would inflame US–China relations, Pelosi didn't care. She persisted in her provocative visit. She had no real mission other than to reassure Taiwan's government that the United States was standing firm against any potential aggression from China. The trip was mainly made to satisfy her own egotistical perception of what she had to do in order to take her rightful place in history while serving her final days as Speaker of the House. It was a farce. The results were disastrous. As expected, tensions between

Beijing and Washington flared. China described the Pelosi visit as 'a gross interference in China's internal affairs' and paraded some gunships off the coast of Taiwan.*

Things got worse in February 2023 when the United States shot a Chinese 'spy balloon' out of the sky at an altitude of 18,000 metres and six miles off the coast of South Carolina. The 61-metre spy balloon, equipped with solar panels and a payload of surveillance devices, had entered US airspace over Alaska on 27 January 2023, and then traversed half of Canada and re-entered the US over Montana a few days later. On 4 February, an F-22 Raptor jet fighter took off from Langley Air Force Base in Virginia and fired one Sidewinder missile at the balloon, which then splashed down in the Atlantic Ocean, in US territorial waters.

As US–China relations went into deep freeze, the anger in Beijing mounted, as did the rhetoric in Washington. The two sides seemed indeed to be on the verge of a new Cold War. In the Spring of 2023, the Chinese Foreign Ministry condemned the AUKUS alliance. The United States, Australia and the United Kingdom were travelling 'down the wrong and dangerous path' for their own geopolitical self-interest, China's Foreign Ministry said. The

---

* On 2 August 2022, following Pelosi's visit to Taiwan the Chinese Foreign Ministry released an official note denouncing what happened 'in disregard of China's grave concerns and firm opposition'. The Speaker's visit to Taiwan 'constitutes a gross interference in China's internal affairs. It gravely undermines China's sovereignty and territorial integrity, seriously tramples on the one-China principle, and severely threatens peace and stability across the Taiwan Strait. In response to Pelosi's egregious provocation China decides to adopt sanctions on Pelosi and her immediate family members in accordance with relevant laws of the People's Republic of China.'

US-engineered alliance was trashed as a 'typical Cold War mentality which will only motivate an arms race, damage the international nuclear non-proliferation regime, and harm regional stability and peace'.[8]

By the end of May 2023, when Biden and other Group of Seven leaders assembled in the historic city of Hiroshima, animosity between China and the West was at a high point. While China was wooing the Global South and increasing its anti-Western alliance with Putin, the United States led a meeting that could only be described as an anti-China workshop. This, by the way, is exactly what Beijing called it.[*]

At the Group of Seven summit in Hiroshima, there was a lot of talk about the threat posed by China's rising power and increasingly aggressive stance. Even the plight of Volodymyr Zelensky's Ukraine took second place to the China-bashing. The G7 leaders criticised China for its use of 'economic coercion', for its 'militarisation of the South China Sea' and for its 'interference activities' aimed at 'undermining the safety of diplomats, the integrity of democratic institutions and economic prosperity'.[9] And the G-7 warned China not to touch Taiwan.

Then Biden rounded up the members of the Quadrilateral Security Group (Australia, Japan, India, USA), a dormant entity that Washington had decided to resuscitate

---

[*] Chinese newspaper *Global Times* called the G7 an 'anti-China workshop'. It happened the day after Beijing summoned Japan's envoy and berated Britain in a fiery response to statements issued by the Group highlighting wide-ranging tensions between Beijing and the rich countries. See Liz Lee and Satoshi Sugiyama, 'Beijing rebukes Japan, Britain over "anti-China" G7 Summit', Reuters, 22 May 2023.

as an anti-China alliance. The 'Quad' met in Hiroshima and promptly issued a thinly veiled attack on China.

The anti-China rhetoric emanating from Hiroshima was immediately perceived, accurately, in Beijing as a significant escalation in rhetorical hostilities. The reaction was prompt and furious, with China's Foreign Ministry saying the G7 used the summit to 'smear and attack China and brazenly interfere in China's internal affairs'.

Beijing also denied accusations of economic coercion, claiming instead that Washington's unilateral sanctions against China and its acts of decoupling and disrupting industrial and supply chains made the US 'the real coercer that politicises and weaponises economic and trade relations'.[10]

Biden was blunt about the threat he perceived from China: China is 'building its military, and that's why I've made it clear that I am not prepared to trade certain items with China', he said. 'We're not looking to "decouple" from China, we're looking to "de-risk" and diversify,' he claimed. 'That means taking steps to diversify our supply chains ... so we're not dependent on any one country for necessary product ... it means protecting a narrow set of advanced technologies critical for our national security.'[11]

What Biden meant is that the United States does not want to abandon China as its trading partner but to reduce America's dependence on China for high-tech strategic products. The de-risking policy is a mix of protectionist trade policy and industrial policies, in essence restricting certain high-tech exports to China while spending a lot of money on large-scale strategic domestic investment projects in America that are aimed at reducing dependence on Chinese goods.

Biden must have known that even many billions of dollars of investment will not reduce US dependence on China for semiconductors and other products by very much. Perhaps in ten years, in the mid-2030s, the capacity of Europe and America to substitute imports from China will increase by 10 per cent.* That is not very much. But it is good electoral politics to speak about such nationalist policies. It wins nationalist votes.

Seen from China, meanwhile, it looks as though the US has cajoled the Japanese and the Europeans into launching a new Cold War-style policy of 'containment' of China, at least in its rhetoric. China is responding by flexing its muscles militarily and with hawkish rhetoric over Taiwan. The risk of escalation is real. This, unfortunately, is what is happening.

By now, it is clear that Xi's China is the world's second most powerful superpower and America's biggest rival on the world stage; China will overtake the United States in terms of size of GDP in the next decade, and within

---

* Through the passing of two Chips Acts – the US CHIPS and Science Act, in 2022, and the European Chips Act, in 2023 – Washington and Brussels have already committed over $90 billion in subsidies to the semiconductor sector over the next decade. However, experts warn that they won't be able to ramp up chip production fast enough to offset any shortage of chips from China in the event of tit-for-tat retaliation. See Hu Weijia, 'EU's semiconductor plan needs China's market amid US dangerous game', *Global Times*, 6 April 2023, and Nik Martin, 'Tech war: China could face US, EU curbs over legacy chips', DW News, 4 May 2024.

twenty-five or thirty years it could match the US in military power. The Chinese have always taken the long view, and Xi is a brutal dictator who can afford to wait for the US presidential elections to pass, and even longer. The good news is that as a follower of Confucian logic he will probably also be patient about trying to take control of Taiwan. He can afford to wait, and the lesson of Ukraine showed Xi that it is in his interest to wait.

The superpower rivalry is real enough. It is a race both in military terms and in the high-tech industries, starting with chips and continuing from critical minerals and other materials, and then right through to the space race and the race for supremacy in artificial intelligence. Trump launched the trade wars with China in 2017, and Biden launched the chip wars in 2022. This American protectionism has led to high-tech competition and rivalry instead of trade and cooperation. Today it is artificial intelligence that is perhaps the most frightening technology, especially if you believe that AI brings enormous opportunity for human progress but also carries huge risks for our species. In the hands of those who wish us ill, a weaponised artificial intelligence system could someday be as dangerous as a nuclear bomb.

The escalating anti-China rhetoric that was part of the 2024 presidential election campaign will only further damage US–China relations, even if Beijing has learned to distinguish between campaign rhetoric and reality. The problem is that in Washington, it is now a bipartisan sport to attack China, a guaranteed vote-getter. Both Republicans and Democrats do it. The rhetoric is likely to escalate even further. Some of it can be laughed off by Xi Jinping; some of it could provoke a reaction.

The problem with all of this, as Henry Kissinger has pointed out, is that the rhetoric feeds into what could ultimately become a self-fulfilling prophecy. Just a few months before his death, Kissinger described his greatest fear as the self-reinforcing nature of perceptions and policies in Beijing and Washington. At the same time that the Group of Seven leaders were meeting in Hiroshima in May 2023, in his office on Park Avenue, Kissinger sat with the editors from *The Economist* for more than eight hours to deliver himself of his final thoughts on the shape of the world. He warned of the risks of military conflict between the United States and China, and he gave special focus to China's role in the twenty-first century.

Kissinger said that the key test for judging future relations would be how China and America behave over Taiwan. He recalled how, during Richard Nixon's first visit to China in 1972, Chairman Mao Tse-tung had been very explicit about Taiwan. He told Kissinger and Nixon, 'We don't need them now. We can wait 100 years. Someday we will ask for them. But it's a long distance away.'[12]

Kissinger believed that the understanding forged between Nixon and Mao was overturned after only fifty of those 100 years because of Donald Trump. The populist President wanted to inflate his tough-guy image by wringing concessions out of China over trade. Biden continued the aggressive stance.

Kissinger said he feared that the leaders of China and the United States have *only five to ten years left* to establish some form of arrangement or détente if they are to avoid military conflict. He cited as a key reason for this the risk of artificial intelligence becoming a weapon of mass destruction, but he also said the problem was one of serious misperceptions among policy-making elites in both capitals.

'We are on the path to great power confrontation,' said Kissinger.

> And what makes it more worrisome to me is that *both sides have convinced themselves that the other represents a strategic danger* [author's itals]. And it is a strategic danger in a world in which the decisions of each can determine the likelihood of conflict. And in such a situation it is natural to attempt to be preeminent, technologically and materially. So a situation can arise in which an issue escalates into a confrontation about the overall relationship. That is the biggest problem, at the moment. And, when you have an issue like Taiwan, in which concessions become very difficult because it involves fundamental principles, that becomes even more dangerous.[13]

These are not encouraging words from the late Henry Kissinger. He may have been controversial, but no American had better insights into the way Beijing perceived the United States than Kissinger.

It is especially troubling that Kissinger felt that 'both sides have convinced themselves that the other represents a strategic danger'. Perceptions are built upon rhetoric and actions, and if the rhetoric is severe enough, it can also trigger an action. This is why engagement is so important and why keeping lines of communication open is the key to world leaders maintaining the peace.

In November 2023, when Joe Biden and Xi Jinping sat down for a long conversation on the fringes of the Asia-Pacific Economic Cooperation summit meetings in San Francisco, the two agreed to reopen certain key lines of communication, especially between their military leaders. But the Chinese President also told Biden to his face that Beijing will eventually reunify Taiwan with mainland China but that the timing has not yet been decided.[14]

Xi even commented on predictions by US military leaders who have said that China plans to take Taiwan in 2025 or 2027, telling Biden that they were wrong, but only because a time frame has not yet been set.

Xi's private warning to Biden had little effect, and the US President has continued to speak out about Taiwan. After the election of a pro-independence candidate in Taiwan's elections in January 2024, Biden carefully noted that Washington was not supporting an independent Taiwan. That placated Beijing. But he then immediately dispatched two unofficial senior emissaries, both of them former top national security officials, to visit Taiwan. Beijing was not pleased at all.

The Chinese century is fully upon us, whether we wish to recognise it or not. This is partly because the managers of the American empire have not had a coherent policy in recent years. Barack Obama promised a 'pivot' to China and was then distracted by the Arab Spring. Trump started a trade war. Biden's policies have veered from harsh public criticism to concerted efforts to keep the lines of communication open. Washington, as a whole, however, has refused to accept the idea of China's ascent, and it appears frightened and uncertain about what to do in the face of China's growing power and influence around the world. The 'big cycle' theory of history shows the American empire on a downward trajectory, while China is clearly rising. This is notwithstanding the current economic woes and shrinking growth that China is facing. The overall trend will continue, even if the 2020s prove to be a relatively weak and erratic decade in China's 21st-century growth story.

In this new and emerging post-Cold War order, China will be one of the two heavyweights; that much is clear. But that does not mean that the new world order is going to be bipolar or that Washington and Beijing will be locked in a new Cold War. The fragmentation of globalised trade and the emergence of the Global South are reshaping great power relations.[15] The reality of war in the heart of Europe can no longer be escaped, as Vladimir Putin plods ahead with his revanchist program. The powder keg of the Middle

East has caused further realignment and shifts in power. The wars in Gaza and in Lebanon have had a traumatic effect on international affairs.

In all of this chaos, China has consistently, albeit disingenuously, presented itself as an honest broker, a great power that is ready and willing to protect global stability. In the spring of 2023, China presided over an historic rapprochement between Saudi Arabia and Iran, which had been longstanding enemies. The ceremony brought together in Beijing the Foreign Ministers of the two great oil-producing rivals of the Middle East. The two nations promised to restore diplomatic ties in the presence of senior Chinese officials. It was an important harbinger of a rapidly changing world order, a new world order that comes in the declining years of the Pax Americana. The China-brokered Saudi-Iran deal was Beijing's first foray into Middle East mediation, a role that for the past few decades had been almost exclusively played by Washington. For both the ayatollahs in Tehran and for Mohammed bin Salman in Riyadh, the Chinese represent a critically important oil market.

For Iran's Supreme Leader, Ayatollah Ali Khamenei and for the Islamic Revolutionary Guard Corps (IRGC), the deal is about far more than normalising ties with the Saudi government in Riyadh. Instead, it is about further facilitating, along with China and Russia, the rise of a new anti-Western global order and excluding the United States from a new regional arrangement. Iran has pursued these goals through its proxies, its puppet terrorist groups like

Hamas, Hezbollah and the Houthis in Yemen. Vladimir Putin has taken the side of the Iranian proxies, and their success is important to Putin. Iran is selling drones and missiles to Russia. The same drones that Iran rained down on Israel in the spring of 2024 were being sent to Moscow for use against Ukraine. Putin has also forged especially strong ties with Saudi Arabia's ruler and linked Russia's oil interests with those of OPEC in the infamous 'OPEC Plus' oil pricing cartel. He is also profiting from his new friendship with North Korean dictator Kim Jong Un.

Thus the world is becoming a more complicated and more dangerous geopolitical environment. Biden has described the state of the world as an existential battle between democracy and autocracy. But the new world order today is even more complex than Biden's depiction.

What is emerging today is a New World Disorder. A world in which the American empire is in decline, not formally ended but declining, a world in which Europe is experiencing an existential crisis because of Vladimir Putin's war, a world in which China and Russia see eye to eye on bringing an end to the Pax Americana. In this new world, there are medium-sized powers emerging as players in the southern hemisphere. In this new world, China and India are competing for leadership of what is now called the 'Global South'. In this new world, nations like South Africa and Brazil often side with Russia and China against Washington. What we are living through is the emergence of a series of new and cross-cutting international political and commercial alliances that tend to exclude the United States and to ignore Europe and that have only one thing in common: a shared rejection of the old world order of Western liberal democracy.

CHAPTER ELEVEN

THE RISE OF THE GLOBAL SOUTH

On a crisp Monday, 20 March 2023, the aircraft of President Xi Jinping, a swanky and well-appointed Boeing 747, touched down at Moscow's Vnukovo Airport. The sky was clear except for a few clouds, but it was just 6°C outside as Xi descended from the jet. During his three-day visit the Chinese leader would be wined and dined by Vladimir Putin and given honour guards of every shape and colour. For the increasingly lonely Putin, still only a year into his invasion of Ukraine, the visit was a welcome boost. Since the start of his war in February 2022, Putin had been living a pariah's life.

Just two days before Xi arrived, Putin had been charged with war crimes. The International Criminal Court (ICC) had issued an arrest warrant for the Russian dictator over the kidnapping and deportation of Ukrainian children to Russia since the start of the war. Xi didn't care. He was a man with a mission. The Chinese dictator, buoyed by his success in brokering a deal between Iran and Saudi

Arabia, had been floating the idea of China mediating a peace accord between Russia and Ukraine. But to Putin's satisfaction, China had never condemned his invasion, and Beijing's platitudes about peace were simply a disguised way of supporting Russia's side. Now he would set about making a deal with China's leader to offload at discounted prices the oil and gas that Europe was no longer buying. Indeed, the way Putin treated the Chinese leader was very much like that of a home heating oil salesman courting his client, or, to switch metaphors, like a vassal curtsying to a visiting emperor.

The Xi visit highlighted what the *Financial Times* called 'Russia's role as junior partner to China'.[1] The result of the Putin–Xi talks was mainly a series of trade deals that were lopsidedly in favour of China, with Russia offering raw exports but seeing little Chinese investment to Russia in return.

As British academic Sam Greene put it, 'Putin tells his people he's fighting for Russia's sovereignty. In truth, he's mortgaged the Kremlin to Beijing.'* Vittorio Emanuele Parsi, an Italian geopolitical analyst, said that from China's point of view, Russia was essentially 'Saudi Arabia with snow'.[2]

But the Xi–Putin meetings of March 2023 had another purpose, one which served the strategic visions of both

---

* As mentioned by Professor John Gray during his conversation with commentator and former Australian Prime Minister John Anderson on 'Russia, China and The Future'. The conversation, which was recorded on 13 May 2022, is part of a web-based interview program, *Conversations with John Anderson*, featuring interviews with high-profile intellectuals.

men: it was a show of unity in their shared challenge to Western liberal democracy and a linking of their geopolitical interests, which were aimed at defying and dismantling both American hegemony and the institutions of the US-designed liberal world order. The rendezvous between Xi and Putin seemed to formalise Russia's role as China's second fiddle, but it also marked a key point amid a series of developments that were redefining the landscape of the existing world order in the early 2020s.

This is why the most important words pronounced by the Chinese leader came at the very end of his visit to Russia, on Wednesday 22 March, as he stood on the steps of the Kremlin. He was beaming with paternalistic friendship for Putin. The two men stood facing one another at a ground floor entrance to Building One of the walled Kremlin complex. They were saying goodbye.

They stand there, Putin on the right side of the huge doorway, listening, and Xi in front of him, now offering a parting piece of his wisdom: 'Right now,' says the Chinese leader, 'there are great changes, the likes of which we have not seen for 100 years. And we are the ones driving these changes, together.' To which a humble Putin replies, 'I agree,' and then wishes the Emperor of China a safe trip back home.*

---

* President Xi Jinping and his Russian counterpart, Vladimir Putin, were filmed while exchanging greetings at the end of their two-day meeting, with China's leader saying they were welcoming a new era of close co-operation following unprecedented global geopolitical changes. The video was published by Al Jazeera on 22 March 2023 (https://www.aljazeera.com/news/2023/3/22/xi-tells-putin-of-changes-not-seen-for-100).

Xi's pithy quote was not at all casual. The expression is one of the Chinese dictator's favourite pet phrases, the line he uses at home to market his strategy for countering America and the West. It is actually a line from a late-nineteenth-century Chinese general, lamenting the changes wrought on the world by Western imperial powers that would eventually bring down the Qing Dynasty. It must be remembered that seen through the eyes of the Chinese, the nineteenth century was one of humiliation. The reference to 'changes unseen in a century' therefore invokes for the Chinese the 'great changes' that shook global geopolitics a century ago: the collapse of the British Empire and the entire European colonial system and the rise of the United States and the Soviet Union after the Second World War.

The expression implies that a similar power transition is now underway, with America playing the role of faltering hegemon and China the rising power. This is official Chinese Communist Party policy, approved by the party's nomenclature as 'Thoughts of Xi' – a kind of 21st-century version of the *Quotations from Chairman Mao Tse-tung*, the little red book that was ubiquitous in China in the 1960s and 1970s.[3]

The significance of President Xi's parting remark should not be underestimated. It was the clearest declaration of war on the Western liberal order since Vladimir Putin himself had forecast oblivion for Western democracy in his notorious *Financial Times* interview of 2019. Xi has used the expression often in his public speeches. He believes that the world order is currently transiting through a turbulent period of world disorder and upheaval, a phase that he refers to as 'Great Changes Unseen in a Century'.* The phrase, with a lengthy explanation, was officially adopted by the Chinese Communist Party in 2018 as a guiding tenet of a collection of speeches entitled 'Xi Jinping Thought on Diplomacy'.†

For many critics in the emerging Global South, and not just Xi, American talk of a 'rules-based system' has long been a fig leaf for Western power. It is only natural, these critics maintain, that now that Western power is declining, this order should be revised and 'reformed' – which means replacing or altering the balance of power at the United Nations, the International Monetary Fund, the World Bank, the World Trade Organization and other institutions that have been, until now, the pillars of the US-designed post-war world order.

Hence Xi's claim that 'changes unseen in a century' are

---

* The phrase 'great changes unseen in a century' was initially used by Chinese academics after the Great Recession (2007–13) and refers to the dangers and opportunities posed by American decline. This phrase was officially elevated into the party lexicon in 2017 and was formally accepted as a central tenet of Chinese foreign policy in a 2018 Central Foreign Affairs Work Conference, where Xi informed the leadership of the diplomatic corps and state security apparatus that China was going through 'the best period for development it has seen since the advent of the modern era' while 'the world was facing great changes unseen in a century' and these two [trends] were 'interwoven, advancing in lockstep; each stimulates the other'.

† The 'General Secretary Xi Jinping's Thought on Diplomacy', as it has been originally presented, is the current Chinese diplomatic and foreign policy doctrine, which is, of course, approved by the Chinese Communist Party led by Xi Jinping. Foreign Minister Wang Yi referred to it as 'the fundamental guideline for China's diplomatic work is an epoch-making milestone in the diplomatic theory of New China'. 'Xi Jinping Thought on Diplomacy' mostly aims at reorienting China's international relations on the bilateral level, while still supporting the existing architecture of the international order. Xi Jinping's doctrine in diplomacy has replaced the 'Deng Xiaoping low-profile' era and has legitimised a more active (and competitive) role for Beijing in the world.

coming to pass. For the Chinese, the shifts in the world order now underway are leading to a curious mix of multipolarity and chaos, with the West's decline accelerated by technology and demographic shifts.

Xi's core insight is that the world is increasingly defined by *disorder* rather than order. China, according to this view, now has the chance to emerge as the predominant superpower of the twenty-first century.

This narrative has great appeal in the Global South, which includes around 100 countries in Asia, the Middle East, Africa and Latin America. Among these are the BRICS countries: Brazil, Russia, India, China, South Africa, Saudi Arabia, Egypt, the United Arab Emirates, Iran and Ethiopia. Some of the newly emerging second-tier powers of the Global South are becoming major regional or even international players. They are not great powers, but they are certainly disrupters of the existing liberal world order.

Beijing has laid its claim to be the leader of the Global South, although it has a noisy rival in India.[4] China has, however, worked assiduously for decades to strengthen its global influence by using developing countries as stepping stones. Today, China occupies the dominant position in the United Nations bloc called the 'Group of 77', or G77. These are the 134 developing countries, once known by the crude and derogatory term of 'Third World countries', all of them part of the 'Global South'. China has cultivated these countries with its extensive Belt and Road Initiative, the previously mentioned financial give-away that comes with many strings attached. Call it soft power, call it Chinese neo-imperialism; whatever you call it, it works, especially in Africa and Latin America.

In political terms, the Global South has tended to side with China and Russia in recent years. Each time the UN votes on a resolution criticising Russia over the Ukraine conflict, many of these developing countries abstain or vote the way China votes. They are voting against the Pax Americana and the Bretton Woods system each time they express themselves. When it comes to voting on a matter related to Israel and the Palestinians, the Global South votes against the United States and Israel. When the Iran-backed Houthi rebels in Yemen began firing missiles at container ships that were sailing past them in the Red Sea, the terrorists made an exception for Chinese and Russian ships; these tankers got safe passage from Iran's puppets. And when the disruption to shipping got too severe and threatened to really damage the global economy in early 2024, it was China that quietly asked the ayatollahs in Tehran to tell the Houthis to stop their attacks.[5]

The expanded BRICS grouping and the entire Global South is today firmly committed to living in a post-American world, a world order that supersedes the post-Cold War period of unipolar American power. In this world order, China is positioning itself as the peacemaker, even as it militarises the South China Sea and threatens Taiwan.

China has meanwhile forged increasingly strong ties with Brazil. It has not been difficult. President Lula da Silva has always tended to embrace America's enemies, using rhetoric that casts the West as a malignant force in world affairs and even pushing for the reduced use of the US dollar in international trade in favour of the Chinese currency, the yuan. Lula has allowed Iranian warships to dock in Rio de Janeiro, he has embraced Iranian President Ebrahim Raisi, and he has trooped loyally to Beijing to kiss the ring of Emperor Xi. He has attacked the United States and Israel over the war in Gaza, and he has expressed sympathy for Russia's Vladimir Putin, even going so far as to purposely snub Ukraine's leader Volodymyr Zelensky twice, by cancelling two consecutive meetings with him that had been scheduled at world summits, while inventing obviously fake excuses.[6] Lula is a Latin American leftist of the old school. This school of thought has always seen American influence in the region as 'imperialistic'.*

South Africa is another accomplice of the Chinese and a good friend to Russia and to terrorist groups like Hamas and Hezbollah. In May 2023, the US Ambassador to South Africa Reuben Brigety publicly accused Pretoria of supplying weapons to Moscow. South Africa has repeatedly refused to criticise Putin for the invasion of Ukraine.

South Africa's ruling party, the African National

---

* President Luiz Inácio Lula da Silva, seventy-seven at the time of writing, a former factory worker and trade unionist, became the symbol of the South American left during his first two terms, between 2003 and 2011. His presidency coincided with the so-called South American 'pink tide', which was marked by the consolidation of social welfare and by radical reforms to fight against poverty. In foreign politics, he played a prominent role on a regional level as one of the leaders of the BRICS countries, supporting an 'active non-alignment' between China and the United States.

Congress (ANC), has historical ties to Moscow, which date back to the Cold War when the Soviet Union supported its anti-apartheid struggle, and to China, which considers South Africa a top priority. Xi Jinping has called South Africa a 'strategic partner' for Beijing.

The ANC leaders remember bitterly that Washington not only designated the ANC a terrorist organisation but also refused to impose sanctions against the apartheid government until 1986 – much later than many other countries. Beyond its historical ties with Russia, South Africa's membership in BRICS also facilitates friendly relations with the Kremlin.

South Africa's leadership also has deep ties to the Palestine Liberation Organization (PLO), stretching back to the 1990s, when its former leader and South Africa's first post-apartheid President, Nelson Mandela, first met with Yasser Arafat. The ANC aligned itself with the PLO and other revolutionary causes while Mandela was in prison.

In December 2023, just two months after the Hamas terrorist attack on Israel, Mandela's grandson Mandla Mandela and senior ANC officials welcomed three Hamas officials to South Africa, including the group's top representative in Iran. They attended a ceremony marking the tenth anniversary of Nelson Mandela's death and fondly remembered his support for the Palestinian cause. Shortly thereafter, South Africa brought a case to the International Court of Justice accusing Israel of genocide in Gaza.[7] But it was not just about shared history; the South African move at the ICJ was also a signal that the Global South was no longer backing Washington in the Middle East; indeed, it was showing that it was more aligned with its rivals.

Today, China and India are the key rivals for the leadership of the Global South. Unlike China, which is a brutal dictatorship, India is still, nominally, a democracy. Sadly, its illiberal leader, the aforementioned extremist Hindu supremacist Narendra Modi, is anything but a democrat. As we have covered, he is a Trump admirer, firmly anti-democratic, similar to Erdoğan in his intimidation of the media and similar to Orbán and Netanyahu in his efforts to pack the Supreme Court with cronies. Modi is similar to Trump in his racist xenophobia and Hindu suprematism, especially in his violent and incendiary rhetoric against India's 220 million Muslim citizens.

Modi faced the wars in Ukraine and Gaza with cynical self-interest. He maintained friendly ties with Putin and bought up as much discounted Russian energy as he could. He cancelled – at the last minute – a meeting that he was supposed to have with Ukraine's Zelensky.* As an arch anti-Muslim, Modi was loathe to criticise Israel. Indeed, he reacted with strong support for Israel after the Hamas attack of October 2023. At a BRICS meeting a month later, the group agreed to condemn Israel's invasion of Gaza,

---

* Narendra Modi closed the door on Volodymyr Zelensky's participation as a guest speaker at the G20 summit in New Delhi hosted by India on 9–10 September 2023. Under his leadership, the country has broken a de facto tradition that saw Zelensky and the Ukrainian dossier on the working tables of major global summits, with the Ukrainian President participating in person. For an in-depth analysis on US–India bilateral relations, read Ashley J. Tellis, 'America's Bad Bet on India', *Foreign Affairs*, 1 May 2023.

with South Africa leading the charge. But India took a milder approach, simply reiterating calls for a two-state solution but refusing to hold Israel accountable for the civilian deaths in Gaza.[8] Modi, after all, was a strongman, and a part of the extended network of Donald Trump and his other miscreant friends. Like Benjamin Netanyahu and Viktor Orbán, he is an illiberal democrat with authoritarian tendencies.

* * *

Taken together, the sum total of all this fragmentation and geopolitical realignment is not merely the decline of American power and influence in a rapidly changing world. The slow death of the Western liberal order is being caused by several factors, all of them coming together in the 2020s as though they were part of a flickering black-and-white newsreel from a century ago, like the 1920s in Italy and the 1930s in Germany. The discontents of globalisation, the victims of income inequalities, the masses, fuelled by fear and anger and willing to submit themselves to strongmen and dictators, the clenched fist, the blackshirts, the cult followers of Nazis and fascists across Europe and America, the appeasement of a dictator at Munich in 1938, the spread of antisemitism and racism and white supremacy on both sides of the Atlantic, the rising amount of political violence and hate crimes, the polarisation of society, the ending of democracies by leaders who were legitimately elected and then became dictators. And then the start of the Second World War and the genocide.

The Second World War began as a result of three separate regional wars: Japan's rampage in China, starting with its invasion in 1937, Hitler's invasion of Poland in 1939, and his quest for hegemony in Europe, and Italy's bid for empire in Africa and the Mediterranean. As American political scientist Hal Brands has put it, 'In some ways, these crises were always linked. Each was the work of an autocratic regime with a penchant for coercion and violence. Each involved a lunge for dominance in a globally significant region.'[9] Professor Brands believes that the situation is analogous today, with brutal wars in the Ukraine and Middle East underway, threats in Asia and Africa and the US distracted by internal problems.

In the Second World War, the bad actors of the day, from Hitler and Mussolini to Hirohito, formed an alliance among themselves. They were axis powers, the bad guys. They committed the atrocities. The United States and its European allies were fighting against a formalised alliance of adversaries. (Stalin first signed a deal with the Nazis in 1939 and then two years later backed the Allies after Hitler invaded Russia.)

In today's world, the bad actors are a more disparate crowd. Some of them are even democratically elected. They also form both formal and unwritten alliances among themselves. The group includes Vladimir Putin, Xi Jinping, Ayatollah Ali Khamenei, Recep Tayyip Erdoğan,

Mohammed bin Salman, to name a few. Add to this club of dictators the authoritarian illiberal democrats Narendra Modi of India and Benjamin Netanyahu of Israel, and an assortment of Gulf potentates. Then add Donald Trump to the mix, and you have a Molotov Cocktail of guaranteed geopolitical danger and uncertainty. Welcome to The New World Disorder.

Inside this disorder, there are regional alliances emerging, especially since the war in Gaza, with an Iran-led grouping and a de facto (anti-Iran) alliance between Saudi Arabia and Israel. The anti-Israel (and anti-American) Axis of Resistance is led by Iran and includes Tehran's puppets in Syria (Assad), in Lebanon (Hezbollah), in the Gaza Strip (Hamas) and in Yemen (the Houthis). One could add to the list the government of Iraq, which is today effectively controlled by Iran. Putin and Erdoğan of course remain important supporters and business partners with Iran's axis. What they have in common is that they all would like to see the end of American hegemony in the Middle East and in the world.

The other sub-group that is emerging is a de facto alliance between Israel, the United States, Saudi Arabia, Jordan, Egypt and the Gulf states. These are the nations that united in April 2024 to shoot down hundreds of Iranian missiles and drones that were launched against Israel. Saudi Arabia even publicly acknowledged its involvement in defending Israel against the Iranian attack.

The bad actors of the 2020s are a tough breed. They don't

abhor violence, political assassination or terrorism; instead they make use of all three as part of their geopolitical game. Putin will do anything necessary to achieve his goals. He is untroubled by ethics. The same is true of the other bad actors, who unfortunately in the 2020s appear to be *in ascesa*.

These leaders tend to favour other totalitarians; they feel more comfortable with each other than with a lame US President who is still pressing them about human rights violations at the margins of another G20 summit. The bad actors have a set of alliances, but in the New World Disorder, the alliances seem less linear and more like a latticework pattern, with transversal and crosscutting economic and political interests.

What they all have in common is that they are proceeding on the assumption that American hegemony is in its final phase, that America is somehow being left behind, trying desperately to tinker with the machinery of the Bretton Woods institutions, trying to add a few billion dollars of funding here and there to placate the Global South. But the attempts to preserve the Western liberal world order are probably futile. As far as the Global South is concerned, that ship has already sailed.

The rise of China in the twenty-first century will meanwhile continue. This will be the Chinese century, notwithstanding the severe economic and social crises of the early 2020s, a period of upheaval and frustration in Xi's China. The long arc of history and demographics still favours the ascending Chinese empire, a 21st-century empire based on the soft (economic) power of suzerainty over its network of friends and allies, rather than sovereignty. By mid-century, or sooner, China could become a formidable military foe of the United States. Intimidation, economic coercion, a false commitment to multilateralism and the blatant use of money will be China's weapons in the war for global influence this century. The greatest rivalry between China and the United States will be about technological innovation and the mastering of artificial intelligence, and this is why Henry Kissinger gravely warned before his death that the leaders of the US and China have 'only five to ten years left' to come to terms or face potential military conflict that could include the use of AI-based weapons.

The two opposing schools of Western thought about the future of US–China relations in the twenty-first century are:

1. Those who believe China's present troubles are a harbinger of a country that is so beset by internal challenges that it will be unable to rival or surpass the United States as the world's leading superpower.
2. Those who believe in the inexorable long arc of history and see present-day problems as a mere blip on a lengthy upward trajectory that will see Chinese power rival and then later on overtake the United States.

In Washington, Jake Sullivan, the national security adviser to President Joe Biden, is among those who fervently believe in the future of American leadership and in the ability of Washington and Beijing to navigate around their difficulties without going to war. 'Nothing in world politics is inevitable,' Sullivan told an audience in Davos in January 2024. 'We are in command of our own choices. So it's up to us to summon the vision, commitment, and sense of shared purpose to make the right choices, to shape the future for the benefit of our fellow citizens and future generations to come.'[10]

On the other side of the spectrum, in Brussels, Mark Leonard, director of the European Council on Foreign Relations, has summed up the state of affairs more bluntly:

> While the West is seeking to preserve the existing rules-based international order by tweaking some of its elements and inviting in a few additional actors, Chinese strategists are increasingly focused on surviving in *a world without order* [author's itals]. And they are offering to help other countries build their own sovereignty and freedom of manoeuvre as Western dominance recedes.[11]

Those who believe in the long arc of history would agree with Leonard's view. The American century is gradually coming to a close, if one considers that it began eighty years ago, in the 1940s, when the term was coined. But even with China as the ascending superpower of the 2040s, or as an equal rival in the new world order, what will take the place of the rusting US-led liberal world order? Can the American empire hang on for a few more decades and perhaps even 'strike back' one more time? Can a deeply divided America, led by an isolationist President, regain a leadership position in world affairs? It seems highly unlikely. For now, it seems that America is severely distracted by its own internal social divisions. This was the case 100 years ago, when dictatorships were spreading around Europe and fascism was growing. Will the 2020s and 2030s be analogous to the 1920s and the 1930s? Back then, an isolationist America first failed to act, and then finally, at the very end, in December 1941, stepped in to defend the values of liberal democracy against the autocratic vision of Hitler and Mussolini. Would Trump step in to defend the values of liberal democracy when he is, in fact, its bitter enemy?

Winston Churchill famously proclaimed, 'You can always count on Americans to do the right thing – after they have tried everything else.'

Today Churchill might take a view closer to that of Kissinger, who warned of the danger of an AI-enhanced military conflict between China and the United States within the next five to ten years. He might not think the Americans can stage an imperial comeback because they are too distracted by deep social and political conflicts at home. He might then assess the centrifugal changes underway in relations among the great powers and conclude that even if it wanted to, America might no longer be in a position to alter the destiny of the world.

The deeply divided America of today reminds many

historians of the societal conflicts that came toward the end of the Roman Empire, or toward the end of the British Empire. In the case of the American empire, the divisions are profound. Trump is a fanatical manifestation of deep discontent, and his style is openly authoritarian. With his return to the White House, the downward trajectory of American leadership can only accelerate, and that in itself will make for a far more dangerous world than one might ever imagine.

CHAPTER TWELVE

THE UNITED STATES OF AMNESIA

The twenty-first century looks like it has the potential to be every bit as violent as the 1900s, and quite possibly worse. We're talking about high-tech violence. In a world of only loosely co-ordinated regulation of AI and increasing competition among the great powers, and with the potential for low-cost access to AI-driven tools rapidly becoming available to bad actors, big and small, the weaponised use of artificial intelligence is more probable than possible. AI, it should be noted, has the potential to create far more death and destruction than the nuclear bomb. Think of it as a dirty bomb with nerve gas, multiplied a million times. Think of what happens when you poison the water supply in a city of 10 or 20 million people. Or turn off the electricity. Think about the potential for chaos, conflict and war in a newly disordered world, in a weakening Western-led order, in a world caught in the middle of epochal change.

Think about what Vladimir Putin or the terrorists of Hamas or Hezbollah or ISIS or al-Qaeda could do with a 'next generation' weapon that is based on artificial intelligence. Think of it: 21st-century, high-tech weapons in the hands of bloodthirsty villains. Sadly, this is probably a part of the near future.

The atrocities committed by Putin's troops in Ukraine, or by the Hamas attack on Israel, are examples of a medieval mentality that persists even in the twenty-first century. The inability of American power to prevent such acts of mass cruelty is becoming clear. We watched Joe Biden's inability to impose a solution. The brutality of Netanyahu against civilians in Gaza has been plain for all the world to see, and it has illustrated the impotence of Washington when faced with an extremist Israeli Prime Minister who has been operating for twenty years thanks to billions of dollars of US aid. Rightly or wrongly, Netanyahu's carpet bombing of Gaza is seen as Biden's failure. By the time Biden finally cut off some arms shipments to Israel, it was too late to make a difference. With Netanyahu's friend Donald Trump at the White House, the terms of peace would be in Israel's favour.

The frustration of the Biden White House and the limits of American influence were apparent as civilians continued to be killed in Gaza. Then, when the Biden administration sought to stop the Iran-backed Houthi attacks on shipping in the Red Sea in early 2024, the United States was forced to turn to China for help. Biden's national security adviser

Jake Sullivan even claimed that China had an 'obligation' to use its leverage with Tehran to rein in the Iranian-backed Houthi rebels.

This is the world we face today. This is the state we find ourselves in. One could argue that American leadership is needed now more than ever. But that leadership is now in doubt with Trump at the helm. America's credibility is in trouble. America's allies are worried. The US may still be the most powerful nation on the planet in military and economic terms, but it is no longer the predominant hyperpower in a unipolar world. That phase is over. Even the former head of the CIA admits it.

'The post-Cold War era came to a definitive end the moment Russia invaded Ukraine in February 2022,' observed William Burns, the director of the Central Intelligence Agency. The CIA chief quoted his boss, President Joe Biden, as saying that the United States is now facing a period of profound change as dramatic as the dawn of the Cold War, or the post-9/11 period. This is true.

'China's rise and Russia's revanchism pose daunting geopolitical challenges in a world of intense strategic competition in which the United States no longer enjoys uncontested primacy and in which existential climate threats are mounting,' admitted Burns.

These challenges will only be exacerbated by the Trump administration. It began with his nominations. By choosing Tulsi Gabbard, a Republican who has been accused of sharing pro-Russian propaganda, as his director of national intelligence, Trump put loyalty to Moscow above his own national security. Gabbard is extreme: she has consistently parroted Kremlin talking points, she has frequently attacked Ukraine and Volodymyr Zelensky, and she has embraced dictators like Syria's Bashar al-Assad. Gabbard may soon oversee the CIA and seventeen other US intelligence agencies. The damage that she can do to US, European and NATO security interests is incalculable. Gideon Rachman, my former colleague at the *Financial Times*, summed up the situation thus: 'So – just to underline – the proposed director of national intelligence for the US, Tulsi Gabbard, is so pro-Putin that she has been described as a Russian agent on Russian TV.' Indeed, in Moscow they were uncorking the champagne after Trump announced Gabbard in November 2024, just a week after his election victory. Bizarre as it may be, Donald Trump is proving to be, in his actions, a loyal ally of the Russian dictator and, in the eyes of many Americans, a traitor to his own country.

In 2026, the United States will celebrate its 250th anniversary as a nation. After two and a half centuries of American democracy, the electorate in 2024 voted overwhelmingly for an autocrat, a man whose own top military advisers described as being a fan of Adolf Hitler and an admirer of Vladimir Putin. General John Kelly, Trump's former Chief of Staff, went so far as to describe Trump as being of a 'fascist' mentality. Then again, Trump has famously called for the 'execution' of the former head of the Joint Chiefs of Staff, General Mark Milley.

Trump has divided the nation, and his presidency will undoubtedly weaken the United States, at home and internationally. Internationally, there are multiple political and military challenges to US authority in Europe, the Middle East, and Asia. At home, social cohesion is breaking down across the country. The glue that is supposed to keep society together is not holding. The social fabric is tearing, and badly. America is becoming an increasingly violent place. The unleashing of extremism as mainstream American politics is threatening the delicate equilibria of democracy.

Trump has glorified the insurrection of 6 January. He has promised pardons for all jailed insurrectionists and, like a tinpot dictator, he has promised to prosecute his political rivals. He has praised white supremacists and he has used the rhetoric of Adolf Hitler to condemn his enemies. He has faced multiple trials for multiple criminal charges. Yet he is the duly elected President of the United States.

Post-election American society is now in the process of shattering. The nation is so divided that many Americans fear a low-density civil war in the near future. There is already so much violence in America that many Americans are unfazed by the prospect of more. The MAGA crowd accepts that insurrection riots and political violence are normal parts of political discourse in America today.

Around a third of the voting public in America is prepared to accept the most outlandish tenets of Trumpism, including conspiracy theories and outright falsehoods.

There are Trump voters who believe that Haitian immigrants in Springfield, Ohio, have been eating cats and dogs. This phenomenon of disinformation is generating more and more extremist sentiment, a phenomenon likely to outlive Trump himself. These people have given up on the American dream. Some are the victims of globalisation; others are openly racist. They are angry. They are frustrated. They are happy to embrace authoritarianism. They don't care about democracy; they care about what they fear, what they have been told to fear by the right-wing media ecosystem of bloggers and Fox News. It must be remembered, however, that many better-educated and upper-middle-class Americans also voted for Trump. The Trump electorate included a large number of Wall Street bankers and suburban households who do not believe in conspiracy theories but who simply see Trump as a way to keep their taxes low and their markets unregulated. They just hold their noses and vote Republican.

The other half of America, like the Democratic Party, is reeling from the trauma of Trump's return to power. The Democrats are leaderless, out of touch with the working class and still governed by a few machine families, like the Clintons and the Obamas. Their liberal elitism is one of the main reasons why Kamala Harris lost the 2024 election, and it made them an easy target for Trump. Like Margaret Thatcher in the 1980s, and the emergence of working-class Tories, Donald Trump has captured the hearts and minds of America's working class. He has done it with lies, demagogy and disinformation, but his voters don't seem to mind.

The other half of the electorate sees Trump as a criminal and fears for the future of American democracy. They fear the apparent drift toward autocracy in an America where, for the time being, traditional checks and balances do not exist.

Trump's America and the other America are separate realities, universes that do not meet, communicate or interact. Each of these two Americas exists in its own political-media ecosystem. Each reads its own websites, follows its own opinion-makers and believes its own news channels. One is based on fact, the other on falsehoods. Each is convinced that their cause is just. They differ on everything, and most of all they differ on the fundamental issue of what America is supposed to be as a nation.

There is a third segment of society that is not at all interested in the debate, or not even aware; this is the non-voting public, which in the election of 2020 and 2024 amounted to a third of eligible US voters, or 80 million people. These people have already given up on democracy.

On top of this, it is worth remembering that more than 70 per cent of Americans get their news, unfiltered, from social media rather than reliable news sites. The abundance of disinformation that is taken as truth and the profusion of conspiracy theories that are given credence across social media means that there is longer a recognition of facts. A fact is now often considered an opinion. Even the *New York*

Times feels compelled to present 'both sides' of the story, even when only one side is based on facts. This is also the state of America today.

The 2024 presidential election was a simulacrum of the existential crisis in American society. Truth doesn't matter. Facts don't matter. The nation feels battered, exhausted, and it is perhaps facing a nervous breakdown. Everything seems broken. The once-mighty Supreme Court now resembles a political clan meeting of far-right hacks; its traditional reputation for impartiality has been destroyed by the three ideological militant judges named by Trump who helped to cancel women's right to abortion. The violence and the pro-Palestinian protest encampments in 2024 across American university campuses were another example of how deeply divided the country is. The ignorance of many of the students who cried 'genocide' and of those who performed acts of antisemitism was patently clear. Here were the results of too much 'woke' and too little common sense.

The idea that the US can maintain its dominant status on the world stage while it is being buffeted at home by such deep social conflict is almost laughable. It is almost impossible to guarantee any continuity or coherence in American foreign policy when America's allies live in fear of a stop-go behaviour pattern by Washington based on four-year electoral cycles. The arrival back on the world stage of Donald Trump is a guarantee of greater uncertainty, impulsive and unpredictable behaviour and serious challenges for America's allies.

* * *

Until very recently, in America, the people who used the term 'American empire' were mainly left-wing intellectuals, like Gore Vidal and Noam Chomsky. Today, the left has lost its monopoly on the phrase; the entire world has seen the United States either fumbling the ball or stepping away from a leadership position in world affairs, and this has emboldened bad actors everywhere, including those inside the United States.

The Trump phenomenon in American politics is particularly frightening because in many ways it mirrors American society all too well. One in three Republicans believe that 'true American patriots' may have to resort to violence to save the country. Among Trump supporters the proportion of those voters approving of violence rises to 41 per cent.[1]

We should remember that Trumpism is not the cause of America's breakdown in social cohesion; it is a manifestation of widespread fear and malcontent. As such, the political movement, and its influence on American culture and society, is likely to transcend Trump himself, continuing to divide America for many years to come. Most populist movements in American history have tended to last at least one to two generations. Periods of European fascism tended to last around twenty years, or more. The result of this prolonged and existential battle between xenophobic isolationists and old-fashioned democratic citizens will accelerate the weakening of America's influence around the world. America's internal divisions will speed up its slippage downward, along the big cycle of history. An inward retreat from the world may be America's short-term destiny, and this will weaken America over time in a further sign that the American century is drawing to a close. The only question left is whether the normally resilient United States of America can stage one last comeback or whether it is truly game over for the American empire. No one should ever underestimate the United States, but the odds of it regaining anything like its past global influence are slim.

Since most Americans do not study history, and since those who fail to learn the lessons of the past are doomed to repeat them, one can be reasonably pessimistic about America's chances of avoiding further decline. In 2004, my friend, the great writer Gore Vidal, declared in a famous essay, 'We are the United States of Amnesia. We learn nothing because we remember nothing.' In that same essay, he gloomily called the United States 'a place where the withered Bill of Rights, like a dead trumpet vine, clings to our pseudo-Roman columns'.

This chapter takes its title from Gore's words, and from a documentary film that was made in 2012 about the life of Gore Vidal. It was, of course, entitled *The United States of Amnesia*. It could have been written about the current state of America.

Gore was a witty man, a great talker as well as a superb writer. I remember him delighting in comparing the Roman Empire to post-Cold-War America and telling me how America had been catapulted from greatness to decadence in just a few generations, which he called the shortest-lived imperial trajectory of a great power in history. He had given up on America long before the end of the Cold War. He had been disillusioned by 'the national security state' and the folly of Vietnam, and he was as critical of American incompetence at managing empire as he was of the underlying hypocrisy he perceived between America's avowed moral superiority and the reality of America's flawed leadership.

If Gore Vidal were alive today, he would undoubtedly spew invective in the direction of Trump, but that does not mean he would have liked Biden or Harris. Vidal would almost certainly agree that Trump represents an existential threat to American democratic norms. He would surely concur with *The Economist*'s declaration that the greatest danger the entire world faces is Trump.

Trump himself appears to be moving ahead with plans to fulfil his threats, promising to round up and deport millions of immigrants and build a series of detention centres, saying that the state should be able to 'monitor' all pregnancies in order to stop abortion and declaring quite plainly that he would use the presidency to orchestrate a full-scale campaign of revenge and retribution against his political enemies. The Trump presidency may turn into America's greatest-ever crisis, a full-on national (and international) nightmare.

There is an old aphorism, which is often attributed to the

American author Sinclair Lewis. His novel about a populist nationalist leader who becomes President, *It Can't Happen Here*, was published long ago, in 1935. The quotation goes like this: 'When fascism comes to America, it will come wrapped in the flag and carrying a cross.'

After a full four-year term of Trump in the White House, two impeachments and a Supreme Court ruling that took away women's reproductive rights, half of the Americans, and most Europeans, agree that Trump was a horrible President. He launched a trade war against Europe, pulled the US out of the international climate accords, threatened to walk out of NATO and seemed to be somehow under the sinister influence of Vladimir Putin. He certainly seemed to love dictators like Putin and Xi Jinping more than his democratic allies in Europe and Asia.

Trump 2: The Vendetta promises to be even more horrific. In the UK and the European Union, it is the view of many that Trump's return to the White House could be the final nail in the coffin of the Western liberal order and a victory for Putin.

What was striking during the 2024 campaign was the way a large segment of the traditional and conservative Republican Party across America opposed Trump, and even actively campaigned for Biden. These so-called 'Never Trumpers' were a mixture of former Reagan, Bush and even Trump White House officials who had already been purged from the party by Trump. They were now sounding the warning about the risks to American democracy that Trump posed.

The leading critic on the right was Republican Liz Cheney, the arch-conservative daughter of the right-wing former Vice President Dick Cheney. As a Member of Congress, she had investigated the 6 January insurrection, and she had no doubt about Trump's role in inciting that violence. She tried to warn America that Trump was a serious threat to democracy, but America was in no mood to listen:

> He has told us what he will do. It's very easy to see the steps that he will take. People who say, 'Well, if he's elected, it's not that dangerous because we have all of these checks and balances,' don't fully understand the extent to which the Republicans in Congress today have been co-opted. One of the things that we see happening today is a sort of a sleepwalking into dictatorship in the United States.

Sleepwalking into dictatorship. Liz Cheney is not a person given to exaggeration.

In broader terms, a key point that may have been lost amid the drama of the 2024 US presidential election campaign is that as far as America's near-term future is concerned, it almost didn't matter who won the election. The 2024 election mattered because it was a choice between an autocratic vision of democracy and a normal liberal democracy. The autocratic vision won the day, with some alarmists saying they heard distant echoes of Berlin in 1933, Hitler's electoral victory. The risk is more Orbán than Hitler. The 'Orbánisation' of the United States may now proceed apace.

America will remain a deeply divided nation for a generation or more. The profound societal schism will continue. The genie is out of the proverbial bottle. Trump may be a far-right extremist with autocratic tendencies, but his movement now represents a significant part of America's body politic, of American society, of the American population. It is a movement based at best on ignorance and at worst on malice and belief in falsehoods. For a large segment of American society, it is now acceptable to cheer for Vladimir Putin, if that is what Trump tells them to do.

In the opinion of Fareed Zakaria, an articulate analyst of geopolitics, the most worrying challenge to the rules-based Western liberal order today does not come from China, Russia, or Iran. It comes from the United States.

'If America, consumed by exaggerated fears of its own decline, retreats from its leading role in world affairs, it will open up power vacuums across the globe and encourage a variety of powers and players to try to step into the disarray,' says Zakaria. 'We have seen what a post-American Middle East looks like. Imagine something similar in Europe and Asia, but this time with great powers, not regional ones, doing the disrupting, and with seismic global consequences.'

Being a keen observer of Washington politics, Zakaria also has this to say about the parallels between today and the 1930s: 'It is disturbing to watch as parts of the Republican Party return to the isolationism that characterised the party in the 1930s, when it resolutely opposed US intervention even as Europe and Asia burned.'

We all know how the 1930s ended, and while there is no reason to think that we are headed for another world war, we should pause to consider that we are already experiencing multiple wars, big and small, in Europe and the Middle East but also in so many other less publicised places. For example, in Africa, where death and destruction have continued for many years. Putin is certainly conducting a hybrid and asymmetric war against the West, via multiple proxies, allies, puppets and with both battlefield and cyberwar tactics. Iran has been operating a multiple terror-state network through its proxies in Syria, Lebanon, Gaza and Yemen. China is in league with most of the world's bad actors. North Korea is deploying thousands of troops on Russia's side in order to do battle with Ukraine. In Europe. On European soil. North Korean soldiers. Alas, it does not seem to matter, in a world where everything moves far too quickly for anything to really matter, or so it appears.

What follows the breakdown of the Western liberal world order? How much damage can Trump do to the multilateral system and NATO in four years? How long does it take for the dust to settle after a geopolitical earthquake? And how long is this earthquake, the one we are currently witnessing in Washington, going to last? We are in a period of epochal flux. There is a hot war on European soil, one caused by a bloodthirsty dictator, and the US President appears to be in some way beholden to this same dictator. Meanwhile, the Global South is rising and aligning itself increasingly with China and Russia. We are facing a hugely difficult period of international realignment and shifting alliances. We are on our way to some other world order, with the slow death of the US-led liberal world order. But what comes in between, while the world order is undergoing asymmetric geopolitical shocks? If the post-Cold War era is over and the American empire is in an inexorable decline, then where are we headed?

Welcome to the New World Disorder.

CHAPTER THIRTEEN

THE NEW WORLD DISORDER

A world without order. What does that even look like? Let us try to imagine it, starting with the present as a baseline.

In the New World Disorder, the machinery of the Western liberal order from the post-war era is rusty. It creaks. There are two great powers competing for global economic and military power: China and the United States. The Global South is playing both sides of the game, knowing that it will always find a friend in Beijing. The United States is increasingly isolated, either by choice or by consequence of its actions. Europe does not speak with one voice and does not really count in world affairs. Putin is meanwhile playing out his Czarist fantasies, at the expense of a horrendous loss of human life, in Europe, in Ukraine and elsewhere. His hybrid war on the West spans twenty countries in Africa, including Libya. His allies include the ayatollahs in Tehran, Hamas, Hezbollah, the Houthis and North Korea. His friends include Brazil,

South Africa and India. His financing of extremist political parties in the European Union continues to pay him dividends.

America is on the defensive. Rather than leading, Washington is mainly reacting to events. China is expanding its soft power while also flexing its military muscle, and it is setting agendas and seeking to displace American influence everywhere it can.

The growing co-operation between China and Russia has made Putin a vassal to Chinese President Xi Jinping, but both share a determination to destabilise the American-led world order. In May 2024, during a visit to Beijing, Putin joined President Xi Jinping in condemning what they called the 'aggressive behaviour' of Washington.

'The United States still thinks in terms of the Cold War and is guided by the logic of bloc confrontation, putting the security of "narrow groups" above regional security and stability, which creates a security threat for all countries in the region,' the two dictators declared in a joint statement.[1]

Likewise, the relationship between Russia and Iran is built on a shared view of Washington as an enemy, alongside the supply of Iranian missiles and drones to Moscow for its war in Ukraine. The friendship between Russia and North Korea is also based on Putin's need for arms supplies to keep his war machine well stocked. North Korea has even dispatched thousands of troops to help Putin attack Ukraine. Yet in broader terms, these relationships are all about the group dynamics of a set of likeminded dictators. China, Russia, North Korea and Iran *all* have a shared contempt for the Western world order. They are all agreed on the need to replace the United States with a different world order, an order in which there is no need to make the world safe for democracy.

In this new world of declining US influence, shifting loyalties and transactional diplomacy, there are six emerging Medium Powers. We could call them 'global swing states.' They are Brazil, India, Indonesia, Saudi Arabia, South Africa, and Turkey. These are all middle-sized powers that together have enough geopolitical weight for their policy preferences to sway the future direction of the international order.'[2]

William Burns, the director of the CIA, has openly admitted the changing nature of world power structures. Writing in *Foreign Affairs*, he has summed up America's waning influence this way:

> In this volatile, divided world, the weight of the 'hedging middle' is growing. Democracies and autocracies, developed economies and developing ones, and countries across the global South are increasingly intent on diversifying their relationships to maximise their options. They see little benefit and plenty of risk in sticking to monogamous geopolitical relationships with either the United States or China.

In the New World Disorder, the United States is no longer the preferred partner, and nor is it the indispensable nation. Nobody is interested in hearing about American exceptionalism. In this parlous period of shifting geopolitical sands, the proclivity toward greater conflict can only increase, and if Western norms don't count anymore, then there will be fewer ways to prevent war. The rule of law will be less relevant than the survival of the fittest. Might will make right. Power politics will prevail. The liberal democracies of the West will be like a large island or an archipelago. At a certain point, at a turning point, there may come to be more illiberal democracies and dictatorships and rogue states than liberal democracies. That is quite possible, even likely, in the near term.

The world we are describing is not in some distant future. We have already arrived at a moment in history in which America's credibility and influence are visibly diminished. The election of a President bent on emasculating America's intelligence and national security establishment can only hasten the process.

It seems plain that we are in the twilight of the American empire, not quite at the end but clearly well into the final decades of an American century that began in 1945. Sadly, America's domestic distractions, its racially tinged social conflict and its political turmoil will all conspire to accelerate its downward trajectory as a great power. The Western world order will give way to no particular order in the short term because of the strange death of liberal democracy in many countries. Liberalism has been under siege for more than 100 years. Liberal England died back in 1911, while American liberalism began petering out in the 1990s and 2000s.

Xi Jinping is not wrong about the fact that the world is facing great changes and upheavals and realignments, the likes of which have not been seen for a century. We are clearly entering a prolonged transition phase, with a variable geometry of geopolitics consisting of a series of transactional political, military and economic alliances. The liberal world order is challenged by a world of outlaws, many of them grouped together in anti-American cluster groups of countries.

At the same time, the world is still moving through a phase of great economic and social injustice, dramatic income disparities, war and terrorism, technological disruptions and job eliminating, AI-based systems. Added to this is the ugly spectacle of the United States of Amnesia, afflicted by rising domestic political violence and the breakdown of social cohesion in what until now has been the most important democracy on the planet.

The rise of extremist movements and populist strongmen in the 2020s across Europe and America, not to mention their rhetoric, their tactics and their slogans, bears a chilling resemblance to the 1930s, perhaps even to the late 1930s. Trump has often quoted Adolf Hitler, and his aides recount that he spoke in the White House about how 'Hitler did a lot of good things'.* Apart from Trump, other extremist and pro-Moscow governments have come to power in European countries like Hungary, the Netherlands, Slovenia, Slovakia, Serbia and Georgia.† The invasion of Ukraine has unleashed the prospect of more regional wars occurring in the near term, as Putin probes around the margins of NATO and escalates his provocations. Georgia is once again the victim of Putin's aggression and meddling. Others will follow.

This is all part of the New World Disorder, a world in which dictators and tribal chieftains engage in the age-old practice of fighting over land and borders and religion, but this time without the global policeman, without a convincing and credible Pax Americana. And this time with high-tech and AI-driven arms. The US may still be the most powerful economy in the world and the predominant military superpower, but it can no longer claim the

---

* See Michael Bender, *Frankly, We Did Win This Election: The Inside Story of How Trump Lost*, Twelve Books, 13 July 2021, p. 432. The *Wall Street Journal* reporter writes here that then-President Donald Trump, during a discussion with his Chief of Staff, John Kelly, in 2018 praised the German dictator for having done some 'good things'. In the same book, the author also reminds us that Trump persisted in claiming that under Hitler's leadership Germany made important economic gains. See also Chandelis Duster and Catherine Valentine, 'Trump allegedly praised Hitler as doing "a lot of good things", new book claims', CNN, 7 July 2021.

† As of May 2024, six EU countries – Italy, Finland, Slovakia, Hungary, Croatia and the Czech Republic – have hard-right parties in their government. On the other hand, Serbia and Georgia, two countries who are candidates to join the EU, are led by pro-Russian parties. Serbian President Aleksandar Vučić is the only European leader who never imposed sanctions on Russia after the Ukraine invasion, while the ruling Georgian Dream Party successfully passed on 14 May 2024 a controversial Russian-inspired draft on 'transparency of foreign influence' further complicating Georgia's already bumpy road to EU membership. See Giovanna Coi, 'Mapped: Europe's rapidly rising right', Politico, 24 May 2024, and Kacper Rekawek, Thomas Renard, and Bàrbara Molas (eds), *Russia and the Far-Right: Insights from Ten European Countries*, The Hague, ICCT Press, 2024.

mantle of global leadership. Nor do most Americans want to get involved in 'forever wars' that cost American lives in faraway places the names of which they cannot even pronounce. The American empire is divided at home, isolationist in spirit, abdicated in terms of leadership and thus less credible abroad. The American empire is coming to a gradual close.

We are heading toward a world that is no longer based on America's 'rules-based system' – except where a piece of the old Bretton Woods IMF or World Bank or WTO or UN machinery still remains of use to the Global South. In the new world trade order, national and regional commercial interests will replace some of the old multilateral rules. Globalisation will not be dismantled, but geopolitics will alter some of our future supply chains. New trading blocs will emerge. Fragmentation will continue. The arms trade will change. The world will remain interdependent, but shipping routes and supply chains will be subject to geopolitical risk and to the outbreak of small- and medium-sized wars. The aim will be to shorten supply chains and become less dependent on key imports from potentially hostile countries. The evidence, however, suggests this cannot be achieved in the short term, if five to ten years is short term.[*]

---

[*] Recent studies suggest that the trend towards preferential trade agreements has dangerous systemic implications. If, in a fraught geopolitical environment, multilateral rules are allowed to fail, world trade will become increasingly regionalised and fragmented. This implies a substantial loss of efficiency and a greater risk of trade conflicts within and between regions. See Uri Dadush and Enzo Dominguez Prost, 'The problem with preferential trade agreements', Bruegel, 9 May 2023.

If the United States is wavering as a great power, this is not merely because of the challenge from Putin or Xi. It is also because of the fifth columnists in Washington who support Donald Trump. The war in Ukraine has seen Trump order his Congressional minions to vote against sending any more military supplies to Ukraine. Incredible as it may seem, a large part of the Republican Party in America has become, in de facto terms, pro-Putin. As President, we can expect Trump to further his warped relationship with Putin, which will in turn weaken American influence around the world, encouraging and legitimising dictators everywhere.

More than a third of America is becoming a society that is essentially bereft of reason, a society that blindly embraces Trump's conspiracy theories and his dystopian vision.[3] Alongside the MAGA nucleus of Trump voters, there are Republican voters who simply vote for low taxes and Wall Street billionaires like Stephen A. Schwarzman, the chairman and chief executive of Blackstone who endorsed Trump.[4] In the same category of cynical enablers is JPMorgan Chase's CEO Jamie Dimon, who has fawned over Trump.[5] The money men don't care about illiberal democracy; they just want to be free to make money without regulation to pay low taxes.

And then there is Elon Musk. The world's richest man spent $120 million on Trump's campaign, made a cool $15 billion thanks to the election and then began to play 'First

Buddy' to Trump in Mar-a-Lago. After 20 January 2025, he will presumably continue to do so at the White House. The South African-born tech billionaire, father of Tesla, SpaceX, xAI and Neuralink, is a 21st-century supervillain, a Lex Luthor, a Penguin, a Marvel miscreant. His neo-fascist and anti-woke brand of politics plays well with the MAGA crowd and with the Boss. Except that the Boss is beholden to Putin while Musk has a symbiotic relationship with Putin, which may be even worse. Musk, who has been charged with slashing the size of the federal government and firing federal employees, is a clear and present danger to American democracy. The toxic mix of Trump and Musk may be the start of a new phase in American politics, where the country becomes less of a representative democracy and more of a Russian-style top-down oligarchy led by an autocrat, with plenty of crony capitalism, repression and inequality. An emblematic story is the tale of how Jeff Bezos of Amazon was so frightened of Trump, even before the election, that he cancelled a *Washington Post* editorial endorsement of Kamala Harris. Oligarchs need not serve at the King's court; they simply need to acknowledge his power and stay in his graces. In the case of Bezos, like Musk, being in Trump's good graces means billions of dollars of government contracts.

As Washington begins to devour itself, and as Britain and the rest of the Western world look on with dismay, the United States will not be able to shore up the increasingly defunct Western-led, rules-based order. Indeed, Trump may do everything in his power to sabotage and dismantle the post-war norms and institutions that have kept the peace since the Second World War.

British geopolitical expert John Gray has argued that a divided America is destined to decline in power and influence. The main challenge for the future will be to avoid catastrophic conflict. 'The idea that a nation now so intractably divided could construct a new international order is far-fetched,' he has noted.[6]

The United States of America today is in no position to design or dictate a new world order; it is finding it hard enough to react to the various wars that are being perpetrated by bad actors. Most of all, America in 2024 is battered, even partially paralysed, by its deep internal divisions.[7]

* * *

Back in the early seventeenth century, there lived one of Europe's forgotten statesmen, a Swedish count who in his own way was a statesman on a par with Otto von Bismarck and Klemens von Metternich. His name was Axel Oxenstierna, and he became a counsellor to kings and queens, a regent and chancellor for the monarchs and a protagonist of the Thirty Years' War between 1618 and 1648. Finally, in 1648, following a calamitous period of European history that saw 8 million people killed, Oxenstierna joined the rulers of Europe to sign the Peace of Westphalia, which he had helped to craft.* In that year, Oxenstierna is said to have written a lengthy letter to his son. It was written in Latin, and the letter included a most memorable line, which was probably influenced by Oxenstierna's vast experience as a man who had advised monarchs, made war and wielded enormous power: 'Do you not know, my son, with how little wisdom the world is governed?'

Oxenstierna's homily could well be applied to the story of the management of the de facto American empire that has ruled the world since 1945.

In the case of the parabola of American power, or the opening and closing of the American century, Oxenstierna's words cover a multitude of sins. The lack of wisdom can be seen in exaggerated over-reactions, in a lack of sophistication, in the use of foreign policy for domestic political purposes, in the incompetent management of unnecessary wars and in the enduring schizophrenia of American exceptionalism, caught in a chokehold of self-proclaimed moral superiority and a tendency toward dirty wars and dirty tricks.

With how little wisdom…

Axel Oxenstierna's admonition serves as a poignant reminder of the pivotal role of leadership decisions in shaping the trajectory of nations. The narrative of the American empire, from its inception in the late eighteenth century to

---

* The Peace of Westphalia, signed in 1648, ended one of the longest and most destructive conflicts in European history, lasting from 1618 to 1648. It is estimated that the Thirty Years' War, fought primarily in Central Europe, caused up to 8 million deaths among soldiers and civilians.

the turbulent 2020s, is replete with instances of a lack of wisdom, and even folly.

The infant American empire emerged from the crucible of revolution in the late eighteenth century, guided by visionary leaders who laid the foundations of a fledgling democracy. But the ensuing century was one of westward imperial expansion, fuelled by slavery and a rolling genocide of much of the indigenous population.

Woodrow Wilson's mismanagement of the Versailles Peace Conference in 1919 and his punitive approach to Germany sowed the seeds of resentment and instability in Europe, laying the groundwork for the rise of totalitarian regimes and the outbreak of the Second World War.

Truman's embrace of containment and the National Security State during the Cold War era set the stage for decades of militarisation and interventionism. It kept the Soviets at bay, and eventually triumphed, but America also dragged itself into a string of failed wars because of ignorance and poor leadership. John F. Kennedy's hawkish Cold War rhetoric and ill-fated entanglement in Vietnam undermined America's moral authority and squandered precious lives and resources in a futile quagmire.

George H. W. Bush's shortsighted approach to the end of the Cold War era, marked by complacency and a lack of strategic vision, allowed for the resurgence of geopolitical tensions and the proliferation of global conflicts. Bill Clinton's blind embrace of globalisation, and his accompanying failure to address its inherent inequities and vulnerabilities, exacerbated economic disparities and contributed to the financial crisis of 2008 and the income inequalities and job dislocations that fuelled 21st-century populism.

Jimmy Carter's humiliation in the Iran hostage crisis of 1980 was not his fault, but it underscored the perils of diplomatic missteps and the consequences of foreign policy blunders. The prolonged captivity of American diplomats in Tehran exposed the vulnerabilities of American leadership and emboldened anti-American sentiment across the globe, dealing a significant blow to Carter's presidency and to America's image as a superpower.

George W. Bush's reckless imperial overreach, epitomised by the disastrous invasion of Iraq under false pretences, as well as his war in Afghanistan, plunged the nation into protracted and costly conflict. His two failed wars showed the limits of American power. His incompetence, together with that of his successor as President in 2009, would cause the rise of ISIS and would ultimately hand control of Iraq to the ayatollahs in Iran. Barack Obama's failure to effectively manage the US reaction to the Arab Spring revolutions further eroded America's credibility and influence on the world stage.

Between 2017 and 2021, Donald Trump's isolationism, his trade wars, his anti-NATO stance and his disdain for multilateralism undermined the liberal world order and left a US leadership void in global governance. Trump's first presidency emboldened all of the autocrats, everywhere.

His disregard for democratic norms at home exacerbated domestic polarisation, and diminished America's standing as a beacon of democracy and human rights. His second presidency is just getting underway.

Joe Biden's disastrous withdrawal from Kabul in August 2021 laid bare the recklessness of Trump's deal with the Taliban, as well as the folly of Biden's refusal to listen to his defence and intelligence advisers. Biden's inability to control Israel's Netanyahu will be remembered as a sign of American weakness. Biden's escalation of Trump's trade war with China in the spring of 2024, based on his desire to appear as tough as Trump in a presidential election year, was another sign that China-bashing is now a bipartisan US policy. Trump's love of trade wars will lead to disastrous economic results for the US, mainly in the form of higher inflation, higher unemployment and slower growth.

* * *

The *ending* of the American empire is thus a reality, and for those who feel this is an exaggerated claim, we can specify that the American empire is not quite over, it has not yet ended, but it does appear to be coming to a close. America is still strong and it will remain the world's predominant power for at least another two or three decades. But it already is possible to perceive the horizon of history.

The American empire won't come to an end with a whimper. Nor should we rule out a comeback moment (or two), because America has proven its extraordinary resilience as a nation many times.

Putin's aggression has proven that NATO allies still very much need Washington's military protection. For Europeans, the aim is to revitalise and strengthen NATO. For Trump, it is to cajole the Europeans into spending more on defence. But the key is not about spending a certain percentage of GDP on defence, as Trump demands; it is about fulfilling the vision of Luigi Einaudi, the Italian statesman who in 1954 first suggested a common European defence policy. Europe could achieve Einaudi's dream without spending more money, but it would require the kind of political will that does not exist in individual European countries. Sadly, in 2024, a divided Europe still seems unable and unwilling to create a common European defence structure. This is a huge problem for Europe. As the head of the CIA himself noted, the post-Cold War world ended in February 2022, with Putin's invasion of Ukraine. Europe cannot defend itself without America, and America is currently living through an existential crisis.

What awaits us is therefore not easily definable; it is not a bipolar or a multipolar world with clearly defined power blocs. We will probably spend the 2020s, and even the 2030s, living through a prolonged period of uncertainty and disorder. We are entering an extended period in world history where the norms and practices of the liberal world order are under constant attack, where the new war of ideologies is no longer between communism and capitalism, nor is it about Samuel Huntington's idea of a 'Clash of Civilization' between the West and the Muslim world;[8] nor is it as simple as Biden's paradigm of 'democracy vs autocracy'.* If the Global South were given what it wants and were to take control of the United Nations and Bretton Woods systems, would that be enough to appease their anger? Or is it the spirit of post-colonialism and resentment against America that helps fuel the Big Bang we are currently experiencing in geopolitical power arrangements?

In the New World Disorder, we are witnessing the breakdown of the rules-based system. We are experiencing in real time what happens when America steps back from its leadership position, practises isolationism or is distracted by internal divisions. The power vacuum is being filled; there is no lack of pretenders for chunks of the American empire. The problem is that those who will come to divvy up the spoils of the Pax Americana over the next decade are likely to be an array of jackals and scoundrels and dictators. In the New World Disorder, the bad guys will sometimes win.

In the New World Disorder, the world will be less global, less synchronised, less globalised. The economic growth cycles of Europe and America and Asia may not move in

---

* Since the very beginning of his administration, Biden has told the world that the primary challenge of international politics is ideological: 'In the battle between democracy and autocracy, democracies are rising to the moment, and the world is clearly choosing the side of peace and security,' Biden has said. See Sam Roggeveen, 'Democracy vs autocracy: Biden's "inflection point"', Lowy Institute, 23 February 2021.

lockstep, and the competition with China to produce strategic technologies will make the new 'Space Race' a race for control of truly dastardly and horrible weaponised systems that are created with artificial intelligence.

It will be a less global world, a world of geopolitical uncertainty, a world of geopolitical tension and of scattered conflicts, big and small. Unfortunately, this new period we are entering could last for a number of years, perhaps for ten or twenty. It will be a more uncomfortable world, a much bumpier ride for the next couple of generations. A period of turmoil and realignment. For the hedge funds of Wall Street, this will represent numerous opportunities to make money. For the middle-class family living in America or Europe, it will be a time of peril and uncertainty. High technology job displacement at home and constant geopolitical tension abroad.

In all of this, as CIA director William Burns put it, the United States is now facing supremely daunting geopolitical challenges, truly frightening choices, and it is doing so in a world of intense strategic competition 'in which the United States no longer enjoys uncontested primacy'.

Europe is today the beacon of liberal democracy, and it probably stands a better chance of protecting the remains of Western multilateralism than the United States itself. Notwithstanding the various Orbáns or Wilders or (Marine) Le Pens who dominate some parts of Europe, much of the continent still believes in Western liberalism.

It is America, sadly, that today represents the world's

greatest source of uncertainty and risk. Distracted, sleep-walking through a period of social conflict, culture wars and mounting political violence. Led by an autocratic narcissist who favours Putin *über alles*. Lacerated by internal divisions. Weakened.

As I wrote in the opening pages of this book, we Americans have never really been very good at managing empire. It is not one of our skill sets. But what is coming next may be a great deal worse than the naive and incompetently managed American empire of the past eighty years. We may come to view the American century, with its rules-based system and multilateralism, with great nostalgia. We are clearly coming to the end of the American empire. We may also be coming to the end of America as we knew it. America's empire is gradually being displaced. What comes next is a murky and unstable period of great uncertainty, fraught with peril, a New World Disorder.

ACKNOWLEDGEMENTS

When I began working on this book, back in 2023, I wanted to tell the story of the decline of American power and leadership in an increasingly dangerous world, one in which Russia had invaded Ukraine and Hamas had attacked Israel. I wanted to try and make sense, in an accessible way for the average reader, of the dramatic and changing geopolitical backdrop we are living through. I wanted to explain the profound mistakes made by many American Presidents and the failures of American foreign policy. Finally, I wanted to provide a glimpse into a murky and uncertain future and imagine what the next couple of decades could look like.

In all of this turmoil, I wanted to examine how so many Americans consistently fail to learn the lessons of history and are therefore doomed to repeat it. I wanted to delve into the social, political and cultural schisms that have shattered American society and to show how Trump and the MAGA phenomenon pose an existential threat to the model of American democracy we have known until now.

It is no coincidence that in various chapters of this book I make more than a fleeting reference to the similarities between the populism, extremism, illiberal democracy and dictatorship of the 1930s. I also discuss the treacherous 2020s, a period of Trump populism and extremism, spreading illiberal democracy, dictatorship and war. I wanted to describe a world in which the most basic values of Western democracy are under siege, both externally and from within.

In order to undertake such an ambitious project, I needed a first-class team of researchers and fact-checkers with a sophisticated understanding of the geopolitics of the past few decades. I was blessed to have at my side Susanna Bonini, an experienced political and economic journalist who worked with me in my early days in Italian television, producing my early economic and political talk shows. Susanna was tireless in assisting the research, the fact-checking, the footnoting and the planning, for which I am deeply grateful.

In Milan, Elisabetta Sgarbi has been a friend, a mentor and, as always, a brilliantly insightful publisher. La nave di Teseo is not only my favourite Italian publishing house; it is a wonderful home for creativity and intellectual exploration. Alongside Elisabetta, my thanks go to Oliviero Toscani, a super-intelligent editor with an excellent bedside manner. Every writer needs an editor, and I have had plenty of them over the years. Oliviero is one of the best! Thank you also to Eugenio Lio and Stefano Losani of La nave di Teseo team.

ACKNOWLEDGEMENTS

Their professionalism – and their enthusiasm – make it a pleasure to be with this independent publishing house.

In London, my thanks go to Olivia Beattie and Ryan Norman of Biteback Publishing. This is my third book for Biteback, following *My Way: Berlusconi In His Own Words* (2015) and *This Is Not America* (2017). Ryan's editing was masterful and his attention to detail superb.

As always, my thanks to my agent and lawyer Avv Niccolò Rositani-Suckert, a Florentine gentleman of the old school, but also a man not to be messed with.

I would also like to thank those special friends who took the time to read the manuscript and offer me their comments, including Richard Mescon and Chris Todd, two of America's most brilliant lawyers; my sister Anita Friedman; former House Judiciary Committee staffer David Lachmann; former head of the Italian secret services Giampiero Massolo; and in Switzerland my friends Giampaolo Naccari and Lanfranco Casartelli.

Dulcis in fundo, my deepest thanks go to my indomitable, patient and always supportive Tuscan wife, Gabriella Carignani, to whom this book is dedicated.

Grazie, Gabriella!
Ruvigliana
27 November 2024

BIBLIOGRAPHY

Alex Alvarez, *Native America and the Question of Genocide*, Rowman & Littlefield, 2015

David Armitage, *The Declaration of Independence: A Global History*, Harvard University Press, 2008

Andrew Bacevich, *The Age of Illusions: How America Squandered Its Cold War Victory*, Picador Paper, 2021

Ray A. Billington, *Westward Expansion: A History of the American Frontier*, Macmillan, 1967

Ian Bremmer, *Us vs. Them: The Failure of Globalism*, Portfolio Penguin, 2018

Clark M. Clifford and Richard Holbrooke, *Counsel to the President: A Memoir*, Anchor Books, 1992

Francis D. Cogliano, *Emperor of Liberty: Thomas Jefferson's Foreign Policy*, Yale University Press, 2014

Michael Cox, *Agonies of Empire: American Power from Clinton to Biden*, Bristol University Press, 2022

Ray Dalio, *Principles for Dealing with the Changing World Order: Why Nations Succeed or Fail*, Simon & Schuster, 2021

George Dangerfield, *The Awakening of American Nationalism: 1815–1828*, Waveland Press, 1994

Colin Dueck, *The Obama Doctrine: American Grand Strategy Today*, Oxford University Press, 2015

Niall Ferguson, *Colossus: The Rise and Fall of the American Empire*, Penguin Press, 2009

Niall Ferguson, *Civilization: The West and the Rest*, Penguin, 2012

Lawrence Freedman, *Kennedy's Wars: Berlin, Cuba, Laos, and Vietnam*, Oxford University Press, 2001

Joshua B. Freeman, *American Empire: The Rise of a Global Power, the Democratic Revolution at Home, 1945–2000*, Viking Press, 2012

Alan G. Friedman, *This Is Not America*, Biteback Publishing, 2017

Alan G. Friedman, *Spider's Web: The Secret History of How the White House Illegally Armed Iraq*, Bantam, 1993

Walter Isaacson and Evan Thomas, *The Wise Men: Six Friends and the World They Made*, Simon & Schuster, 2013

Robert Kagan, *The Ghost at the Feast: America and the Collapse of World Order, 1900–1941* (vols 1–2), Knopf, 2023

Stanley Karnow, *Vietnam: A History*, Penguin, 1997

George F. Kennan, *The Long Telegram: A 1946 Call for Containment of the Soviet Union*, Cosimo Classics, 1946

Stephen Kinzer, *Overthrow: America's Century of Regime Change from Hawaii to Iraq*, Times Books, 2007

Henry A. Kissinger, Eric Schmidt and Daniel Huttenlocher, *The Age of A.I. and Our Human Future*, Back Bay Books, 2023

Charles A. Kupchan, *The End of the American Era: U.S. Foreign Policy and Geopolitics of the Twenty-First Century*, Knopf, 2002

Kai-Fu Lee, *A.I. Super-Powers: China, Silicon Valley and the New World Order*, Mariner Books, 2021

James W. Lowen, *Lies Across America: What Our Historic Sites Get Wrong*, New Press, 2019

Edward Luce, *The Retreat of Western Liberalism*, Little, Brown, 2018

Angus Maddison, *The World Economy: A Millennial Perspective*, Organization for Economic Co-operation and Development (OECD), 2010

Henry Magdoff, *The Age of Imperialism: The Economics of U.S. Foreign Policy*, Monthly Review Press, 2011

Kishore Mahbubani, *Has the West Lost it? A Provocation*, Penguin, 2019

Michael Mandelbaum, *The Four Ages of American Policy: Weak Power, Great Power, Superpower, Hyperpower*, Oxford University Press, 2022

Jon Meacham, *Destiny and Power: The American Odyssey of George Herbert Walker Bush*, Random House, 2016

Reinhold Niebuhr, *The Irony of American History*, University of Chicago Press, 2008

Peter S. Onuf, *Jefferson's Empire: The Language of American Nationhood*, University of Virginia Press, 2000

Patricia O'Toole, *The Moralist: Woodrow Wilson and the World He Made*, Simon & Schuster, 2019

Stuart Rollo, *Terminus: Westward Expansion, China, and the End of American Empire*, Johns Hopkins University Press, 2023

Jim Sciutto, *The Return of Great Powers: Russia, China and the Next World War*, Dutton, 2024

William Shawcross, *The Shah's Last Ride: The Story of the Exile, Misadventures and Death of the Emperor*, Chatto & Windus Ltd, 1989

William Shawcross, *Sideshow: Kissinger, Nixon, and the Destruction of Cambodia*, Cooper Square Press, 2002

Oswald Spengler, *The Decline of the West (Volume One): Form and Actuality*, Arktos Media Ltd, 2021

David E. Stannard, *American Holocaust: The Conquest of the New World*, Oxford University Press, 1993

Anders Stephenson, *Manifest Destiny: American Expansionism and the Empire of Right*, Hill & Wang, 1999

Evan Thomas, *The Very Best Men: The Daring Early Years of the CIA*, Simon & Schuster, 2006

Evan Thomas, *War Lovers: Roosevelt, Lodge, Hearst, and the Rush to Empire, 1898*, Back Bay Books, 2011

Alexis de Tocqueville, *Democracy in America*, David Campbell, 1994

Daniel Yergin, *Shattered Peace: The Origins of the Cold War and the National Security State*, Penguin, 1977

Gore Vidal, *The Decline and Fall of the American Empire*, Odonian Press, 1992

Tara Zahra, *Against the World: Anti-Globalism and Mass Politics Between the World Wars*, W. W. Norton & Company Ltd, 2023

Fareed Zakaria, *The Post-American World: Release 2.0*, W. W. Norton & Company Ltd, 2012

Kenneth N. Waltz, *Theory of International Politics*, Waveland Press, 1979

William E. Odom and Robert Dujarric, *America's Inadvertent Empire*, Yale University Press, 2012

William A. Williams, *The Tragedy of American Diplomacy*, W. W. Norton & Company Ltd, 2011

NOTES

CHAPTER ONE

1. Declaration of Independence, signed by representatives of the thirteen United States of America in the General Congress on 4 July 1776.
2. Niall Ferguson, *Colossus: The Rise and Fall of the American Empire*, Penguin, 2012, pp. 35–7. Also see Angus Maddison, *The World Economy: A Millennial Perspective*, Development Centre Studies OECD, 2010
3. See F. D. Cogliano, *Emperor of Liberty: Thomas Jefferson's Foreign Policy*, Yale University Press, 2014
4. R. Kagan, *The Ghost at the Feast: America and the Collapse of World Order, 1900–1941*, Knopf, 2023, p. 76
5. Ibid., p. 78

CHAPTER TWO

1. See Robert Kagan, *The Ghost at the Feast: America and the Collapse of World Order, 1900–1941*, Knopf, 2023, p. 341
2. Ibid.
3. See P. M. H. Bell, *The Origins of the Second World War*, 2nd edition, London, 1997, pp. 44–54
4. Franklin D. Roosevelt, campaign address delivered in Boston, Massachusetts, 30 October 1940, https://www.presidency.ucsb.edu/documents/campaign-address-boston-massachusetts
5. See Arthur D. Morse, *While Six Million Died: A Chronicle of American Apathy*, Harry N. Abrams, 1983
6. Walter Isaacson and Evan Thomas, *The Wise Men: Six Friends and the World They Made*, Simon & Schuster, 2013
7. Quoted by Niall Ferguson, Ibid., p. 68; Arnold J. Toynbee, *America and the World Revolution*, Oxford University Press, 1962
8. Ibid.
9. Letter from President Harry Truman to his daughter, Margaret Truman Daniel, 3 March 1945. National archives, Harry S. Truman Library and Museum, www.trumanlibrary.gov
10. Harry Truman's Diary Entry, 12 April 1945, *Memoirs by Harry S. Truman, 1945: Year of Decisions*, Smithmark, 1995, pp. 10–11
11. Walter Isaacson and Evan Thomas, Ibid., p. 266
12. Ibid., p. 267
13. Andrew Glass, 'Truman confronts Molotov at White House, April 23, 1945', Politico, 24 April 2018

CHAPTER THREE

1. See Daniel Yergin, *Shattered Peace: The Origins of the Cold War and the National Security State*, Penguin Books, 1977, p. 346

2   Ibid., p. 158. Also see *Memoirs by Harry S. Truman, 1945: Year of Decisions*, Smithmark, 1995, pp. 547–50, quoted in George Lenczowski, *American Presidents and the Middle East*, p. 10
3   See Daniel Yergin, Ibid., pp 150–60
4   Jongsoo J. Lee, *The Partition of Korea after World War II: A Global History*, Palgrave Macmillan, 2006, pp. 70–129
5   See George F. Kennan, *Memoirs 1925–1950*, Little Brown, 1967, p. 583
6   Letter from President Harry S. Truman to Secretary of State James Byrnes, 5 January 1946. Harry S. Truman Library, National Archives, Collection: Harry S. Truman Papers: President's Secretary's Files, also available on www.trumanlibrary.gov
7   Ibid.
8   Ibid.
9   Quote in Walter Isaacson and Evan Thomas, *The Wise Men: Six Friends and the World They Made*, Simon & Schuster, 2013, p. 348
10 Ibid.
11 Ibid., pp. 354–6
12 Ibid., p. 448
13 Ibid.
14 Ibid.
15 Ibid., p. 476
16 Joshua B. Freeman, *American Empire: The Rise of a Global Power, the Democratic Revolution at Home, 1945–2000*, Viking Press, 2012, p. 68
17 Ibid., p. 441
18 Daniel Yergin, Ibid., pp. 206–8, and Alexander Wooley, 'The Fall of James Forrestal', *Washington Post*, 23 May 1999

CHAPTER FOUR

1   Cft. Lawrence Freedman, *Kennedy's Wars: Berlin, Cuba, Laos, and Vietnam*, Oxford University Press, 2002 and John Garofano, 'Tragedy or Choice in Vietnam? Learning to Think outside the Archival Box: A Review Essay', *International Security*, vol. 26, issue 4, Spring 2002, pp. 143–68, the MIT Press
2   Howard Jones, *Death of a Generation: How the Assassinations of Diem and JFK Prolonged the Vietnam War*, Oxford University Press, 2003, p. 319. Also quoted, among the others, in Walter Isaacson and Evan Thomas, Ibid.
3   David Oshinsky, 'The Strength of His Weakness', *New York Times*, 29 October 1995
4   See William Shawcross, *The Shah's Last Ride: The Story of the Exile, Misadventures and Death of the Emperor*, Chatto & Windus, 1989

CHAPTER FIVE

1   James R. Blaker, United States Overseas Basing, Praeger, 1999 (Table 1.2) Also see www.davidvine.net/unitedstatesofwar and www.basenation.us/maps.
2   Joe Meacham, *Destiny and Power: The American Odyssey of George Herbert Walker Bush*, Random House, 2015, p. 379
3   'President Bush Comments on the Relaxation of East German Border Controls', Ibid.
4   Edmund L. Andrews, 'Greenspan Concedes Errors on Regulation', *New York Times*, 23 October 2008. See also Sebastian Mallaby, *The Man Who Knew: The Life and Times of Alan Greenspan*, Bloomsbury, 2016
5   Michael Mandelbaum, *The Four Ages of American Foreign Policy: Weak Power, Great Power, Superpower, Hyperpower*, Oxford University Press, 2022, pp. 390–400
6   Remarks delivered by President Clinton in his State of the Union address at the Congress on 4 February 1997
7   Francis Fukuyama, 'The End of History?', *National Interest*, issue 16, Summer 1989, pp. 3–18
8   James Atlas, 'What is Fukuyama Saying? And to Whom Is He Saying It?', *New York Times*, 22 October 1989
9   Ibid.

NOTES

CHAPTER SIX

1. Jytte Klausen, *Western Jihadism: A Thirty Year History*, Oxford University Press, 2021
2. 'Human and Budgetary Costs to Date of the U.S. War in Afghanistan, 2001–2022', figures in 'Costs of War', Watson Institute International & Public Affairs, Brown University
3. Ron Suskind, 'Faith, Certainty and the Presidency of George W. Bush', *New York Times*, 17 October 2004
4. President George W. Bush delivered the Graduation Speech at the U.S. Military Academy of West Point, New York, 1 June 2002. The text of the speech is available on George W. Bush White House Archive (https://georgewbush-whitehouse.archives.gov/)
5. Edward Luce, 'Was Blair Bush's Poodle?', *Financial Times*, 10 May 2007

CHAPTER SEVEN

1. Remarks by President Barack Obama at the press conference after the GCC Summit, Camp David, 14 May 2015
2. See Tony Duheaume, 'ANALYSIS: The Nazi Roots of Muslim Brotherhood', Al Arabiya, 27 June 2018
3. Helene Cooper and Robert F. Worth, 'In Arab Spring, Obama Finds a Sharp Test', *New York Times*, 24 September 2012. See also Colin Dueck, *The Obama Doctrine: American Grand Strategy Today*, Oxford University Press, 2015, p. 77
4. President Obama Statement on the Situation in Egypt, 3 July 2013, published by the Office of the Federal Register National Archives and Records Administration, 'Public Papers of the Presidents of the United States: Barack Obama 2013'. See also Patricia Zengerle and Warren Strobel, 'When is a coup not a coup? Obama faces tricky call in Egypt', Reuters, 4 July 2013
5. See Alan Friedman, *Berlusconi: The Epic Story of the Billionaire Who Took Over Italy*, Hachette Books, 2015, pp. 188–9
6. See Michael Mandelbaum, Ibid., pp. 444–5
7. See Ian Traynor, 'Obama highlights Putin threat to EU during keynote speech in Brussels', *The Guardian*, 26 March 2014

CHAPTER EIGHT

1. President Donald Trump Inauguration Speech, 20 January 2017, Washington D.C.
2. Francesco Guarascio and Emma Farge, 'U.S. funding to WHO fell by 25% during pandemic', Reuters, January 26, 2022
3. See David A. Fahrenthold and Jonathan O'Connell, 'Saudi-funded lobbyist paid for 500 rooms at Trump's hotel after 2016 election', *Washington Post*, 5 December 2018, and Carolyn Kenney and John Norris, 'Trump's Conflicts of Interest in Saudi Arabia', Center for American Progress, 14 June 2017
4. See Ihsan Yilmaz, 'Erdoğan's Political Journey: From Victimised Muslim Democrat to Authoritarian, Islamist Populist', ECPS Leader Profiles. European Center for Populism Studies (ECPS), 14 February 2021, and Soner Cagaptay, 'Erdoğan's Russian Victory: Turkey Is Shifting from Illiberal Democracy to Putin-Style Autocracy', *Foreign Affairs*, 29 May 2023
5. Jill Colvin and Peter Prengaman, 'Trump buddies up with Bolsonaro, the "Trump of the Tropics"', Associated Press, 20 March 2019
6. Vanessa Barbara, 'The "Trump of the Tropics" Goes Bust', *New York Times*, 9 January 2023
7. Figures taken from updated Human Rights Watch research on the Philippines' war on drugs taking place from 30 June 2016
8. See Damien Gayle, 'Barack Obama cancels meeting after Philippines president calls him "son of a whore"', *The Guardian*, 6 September 2016
9. Julie Hirschfeld Davis, 'Trump Lauds "Great Relationship" With Duterte in Manila', *New York Times*, November 13, 2017
10. 'The 2002 Gujarat Genocidal Massacres: A Report by Genocide Watch', Genocide Watch 2 August 2023
11. Xander Landen, 'Trump Repeats Praise of "Smart" Putin, Touts Xi's "Iron Fist" Rule of China', Newsweek, 4 September 2022.

12. 'The Trump–Ukraine Impeachment Inquiry Report: Report of the House Permanent Select Committee on Intelligence, Pursuant to H. Res. 660 in Consultation with the House Committee on Oversight and Reform and the House Committee on Foreign Affairs', December 2019
13. Jacob Knutson, 'Trump Officials Back Away from 2020 Taliban Peace Deal after withdrawal chaos', Axios, 20 August 2021
14. Mark Mazzetti, Julian E. Barnes and Adam Goldman, 'Intelligence Warned of Afghan Military Collapse, Despite Biden's Assurances', *New York Times*, 17 August 2021. Also see 'U.S. Withdrawal from Afghanistan', White House document available on www.whitehouse.gov.
15. Larisa Brown, *The Gardener of Lashkar Gah: The Afghans who Risked Everything to Fight the Taliban*, Bloomsbury Continuum, 31 August 2023, p. 288

CHAPTER NINE

1. See Alan Friedman, 'Silvio Berlusconi and Vladimir Putin: the odd couple', *Financial Times*, 2 October 2015. Friedman's interview of Putin was an excerpt of the writer's biography of Silvio Berlusconi, published in 2015 by Hachette Books (U.S.), Biteback Publishing (U.K.) and Rizzoli (Italy)
2. Lionel Barber, Henry Foy and Alex Barker, 'Vladimir Putin says liberalism has "become obsolete"', *Financial Times*, 28 June 2019
3. Courtney Kube and Carol E. Lee, 'Russia is providing "unprecedented" military support to Iran in exchange for drones, officials say', NBC News, 9 December 2022
4. Stephen Braun and Bernard Condon, 'Behind Cohen plea: Trump's longtime dream of a Moscow tower', Associated Press, November 30, 2018
5. Jared Gans, 'Half of Americans expect a civil war "in the next few years"', The Hill, 21 July 2022
6. Peter Fibiger Bang, 'Empire – A World History: Anatomy and Concept, Theory and Synthesis', in Peter Fibiger Bang, C. A. Bayly and Walter Scheidel (eds), *The Oxford World History of Empire: Volume One: The Imperial Experience*, Oxford University Press, 3 March 2021

CHAPTER TEN

1. John A. Hobson, *Imperialism: A Study*, Routledge, 2018, pp. 313–4
2. Ibid.
3. See 'China 2030: Building a Modern, Harmonious, and Creative High-Income Society', The World Bank, Development Research Center of the State Council, the People's Republic of China, 2013
4. See Fernand Braudel, *A History of Civilizations*, Penguin Books, 1995, and Ray Dalio, *Principles for Dealing with the Changing World Order*, Simon & Schuster, 2021
5. Jake Sullivan, 'The Sources of American Power. A Foreign Policy for a Changed World', *Foreign Affairs*, 24 October 2023
6. Tessa Wong, 'Xi Biden meeting: US leader promises "no new Cold War" with China', BBC, 14 November 2022
7. See the statement released by the Chinese Ministry of Foreign Affairs on the sidelines of the meeting in Bali, on 14 November 2022. https://www.mfa.gov.cn/eng/zxxx_662805/202211/t20221114_10974686.html
8. See 'China says AUKUS on "dangerous path" with nuclear subs deal', Associated Press, 14 March 2023
9. G7 Hiroshima Leaders' Communiqué, pp. 35–6
10. See Gabriel Dominguez, 'China and Russia lash out at G7 "double containment" attempt', *Japan Times*, 21 May 2023
11. Remarks by President Joe Biden at a Press Conference, Hiroshima, Hilton Hotel, 21 May 2023
12. Zanny Minton Beddoes and Edward Carr, 'A conversation with Henry Kissinger', *The Economist*, 17 May 2023

NOTES

13 Ibid. See also Henry Kissinger, Eric Schmidt and Daniel Huttenlocher, *The Age of AI: And Our Human Future*, Back Bay Books, 2022
14 Kristen Welker, Courtney Kube, Carol E. Lee and Andrea Mitchell, 'Xi warned Biden during summit that Beijing will reunify Taiwan with China', NBC News, 20 December 2023
15 See Hiroyuki Akita, 'China and India Battle for Leadership of Global South', www.asia.nikkei.com, 1 April 2023

CHAPTER ELEVEN

1 Max Seddon and Joe Leahy, 'Xi Jinping–Vladimir Putin talks highlight Russia's role as "junior partner" to China', *Financial Times*, 21 March 2023
2 Alan Friedman and Vittorio Emanuele Parsi, 'The New World Disorder in Crisis. A conversation on 2024 forecasts', *La Stampa*, 17 January 2024. See also Vittorio Emanuele Parsi, *Madre patria. Un'idea per una nazione di orfani*, Saggi Bompiani, 2023
3 Mingfu Liu and Zhongyuan Wang, *The Thoughts of Xi Jinping*, American Academic Press, 2017
4 Hiroyuki Akita, 'China and India battle for leadership of Global South', Nikkei Asia, 1 April 2023
5 Jon B. Alterman, 'What the Red Sea Crisis Reveals About China's Middle East Strategy', Foreign Policy, 14 February 2024, and 'China Calls on Houthis to Stop Red Sea Attacks', Bloomberg News, 26 January 2024.
6 Christopher S. Chivvis and Beatrix Geaghan-Breiner, 'Brazil in the Emerging World Order', Carnegie Endowment for International Peace, 18 December 2023
7 Gerald Imray, 'South Africa Asks UN Court to Urgently Examine Israel's Targeting of Rafah in Ongoing Genocide Case', Associated Press, 13 February 2024
8 Jonathan Fenton-Harvey, 'Why India has embraced Israel amid the Gaza war', The New Arab, 5 December 2023
9 Hal Brands, 'The Next Global War: How Today's Regional Conflicts Resemble the Ones That Produced World War II', Foreign Policy, 26 January 2024
10 The White House, 'Remarks and Q&A by National Security Advisor Jake Sullivan at the 2024 World Economic Forum, Davos, Switzerland', 16 January 2024
11 Mark Leonard, 'China's Game in Gaza: How Beijing Is Exploiting Israel's War to Win Over the Global South', *Foreign Affairs*, 8 January 2024

CHAPTER TWELVE

1 PPRI, 'Threats to American Democracy Ahead of an Unprecedented Presidential Election', 25 November 2023

CHAPTER THIRTEEN

1 Bernard Orr, Guy Faulconbridge and Andrew Osborn, 'Putin and Xi pledge a new era and condemn the United States', Reuters, 16 May 2024
2 Andrea Kendall-Taylor and Richard Fontaine, 'The Axis of Upheaval: How America's Adversaries Are Uniting to Overturn the Global Order', *Foreign Affairs*, May/June 2024
3 See Brandy Zadrozny, 'Disinformation poses an unprecedented threat in 2024 – and the U.S. is less ready than ever', NBC News, 18 January 2024, and Donie O'Sullivan, 'MisinfoNation: The Trump Faithful' documentary for *The Whole Story with Anderson Cooper*, CNN, 22 April 2024
4 Steff Chávez and Alex Rogers, 'Blackstone chief Stephen Schwarzman backs Donald Trump', *Financial Times*, 25 May 2024
5 Robert Reich, 'Jamie Dimon thinks Trump was "kind of right" about a lot of things. What?', *The Guardian*, 21 January 2024
6 John Gray, 'The New Age of Tragedy: Great-power rivalry, resource scarcity and the crumbling of the liberal rules-based order', *New Statesman*, 26 April 2023
7 See Steven Levitsky and Lucan Way, 'America's Coming Age of Instability: Why Constitutional Crises and Political Violence Could Soon Be the Norm', *Foreign Affairs*, 20 January 2022
8 Samuel P. Huntington, *The Clash of Civilizations and the Remaking of World Order*, Simon & Schuster, June 2002

INDEX

9/11 attacks 99, 101–5, 115, 132, 138, 219

Afghanistan 91, 106, 142
    Kabul (fall of) 153, 154
    war 103–5, 112, 115, 245
    withdrawal from 152–4, 165
AI (artificial intelligence) 191, 193, 213, 215, 217, 218, 237, 238, 249
Al-Assad, Bashar 128, 129, 159, 163, 211, 220, 233
Ali, Ben 117
Al-Qaeda 102, 103, 127, 153, 218
Al-Sisi, General Abdel Fattah 121, 164
'America First' movement 24, 134, 143, 144, 215
American
    century xii, 30, 182, 183, 214, 226, 236, 243, 250
    civil war 173, 221
    decline 113, 129, 132, 136, 162, 173, 209
    democracy 7, 13, 135, 220, 223, 227, 229, 241
    dream 222
    electorate 82, 221–3
    exceptionalism 101, 183, 236, 243
    expansionism 9, 10, 14
    foreign policy 6, 16, 36, 48, 56, 69, 224
    hegemony 74, 102, 201, 211, 212
    history 8, 16, 225
    imperialism xii, xviii
    influence 69, 86, 126, 129, 132, 162, 206, 218, 234, 240
    leadership 78, 85, 86, 101, 127, 154, 214, 216, 219, 245
    liberalism 237
    military power 21, 108
    moral superiority 18, 52, 87, 227, 243
    power 78, 99, 101, 103, 136, 159, 205, 209, 218, 243, 245
    protectionism 191
    republic 8
    society 73, 83, 135, 170, 172, 221, 224, 225, 230
    soft power 113
    sovereignty 139
    values xii
American empire 5, 73, 78, 84, 101, 127, 171, 215, 216, 236, 239, 244, 248
    decline of 81, 113, 116–17, 129, 136, 162, 173, 197, 209, 232
    end of 246, 250
    management of 68, 69, 86, 92, 94, 95, 98, 104, 195, 243
ANC (African National Congress) 206, 207
Angleton, James Jesus 53, 54
anti-China 188, 189, 191
anti-communist 49, 54, 61, 142
anti-imperialism 51, 52, 86
Arab Spring 115–32, 195, 245
AUKUS agreement 186, 187, 188
austerity 21, 22, 23, 97, 98
Australia 186–8
authoritarian 77, 117, 134, 143, 146, 149–51, 169, 171, 211, 216
authoritarianism 23, 26, 222

Ba'ath Party 111
Bahrain 117, 118, 119, 124
Baker, James 90, 91, 96
'banana wars' 19, 84
Barber, Lionel 160
Barr, William 84
benign neglect 90
Berlin Wall xiv, 59, 87–91, 93, 96, 99, 101
Berlusconi, Silvio 122, 125, 126, 158, 159
Bezos, Jeff 241
Biden, Joe 136, 151, 154, 195, 197, 219, 228, 248
    Afghanistan 152, 153, 159, 165, 246

265

Biden, Joe *cont.*
    China 184, 185, 186, 188–91, 193, 194, 246
    Hamas attacks 172, 218, 246
    Ukraine 164, 165, 166, 169
'big cycle' theory xiv, 32, 101, 195, 226
bin Salman, Mohammed 143, 144, 145, 170, 196, 211
Blair, Tony 110
Blinken, Anthony 164, 184
Bolsonaro, Jair 145, 147
Bonaparte, Napoleon 6
Bouazizi, Mohamed 117
Brands, Hal 210
Braudel, Fernand 183
Bremer, Lewis Paul III 111, 112
Bretton Woods 30, 31, 205, 212, 239, 248
BRICS xiv, 204–8
Brigety, Reuben 206
Bryan, William Jennings 11, 14
Brzezinski, Zbigniew 76
Buchanan, James 176
Bulgaria 25, 29, 41, 42, 43, 44
Burns, William 219, 235, 249
Bush Doctrine 106, 107
Bush, George H. W. 84, 85, 88, 89, 90, 91, 92, 244
Bush, George W. 99, 101–13, 115, 127, 132, 153, 245
Byrnes, Jimmy 39–43, 45

Cable 243 64
Cambodia 71–2
Cameron, David 123–5
Canada 1, 2, 28, 74, 83, 187
Carter, Jimmy 75–7, 82, 245
Chamberlain, Neville 27
Cheney, Dick 105, 107, 229
Cheney, Liz 229
Cherokee tribe 4, 9
China 32, 175–98, 208, 218–19
    Belt and Road Initiative (BRI) 179, 204
    Biden promises 185, 186
    Boxer Rebellion 177
    Brazil 205, 206
    Chinese century 175, 182, 183, 195, 212
    economic superpower 179, 180, 190
    GDP 190
    Group of 77 (G77) 204
    Opium Wars 176, 177
    reform 88, 96
    rising power 188, 195, 202, 212, 214
    Russia 174, 197, 199–202
    Saudi–Iran deal 196
    soft power 179, 205, 234
    South Africa 206
    spy balloon 187
    Taiwan 186, 187, 188, 192, 193, 194
    tariffs 184
    Trump 136, 142, 150, 191, 246
    US dependence on 189, 190
    US–China relations 186, 187, 189, 191, 213
    world leader 175
    World Trade Organization 180
Chinese Communist Party (CCP) 202, 203
chip wars 191
Chomsky, Noam xii, 225
Christianity 7, 12
Churchill, Winston 28, 29, 34, 48, 49, 50, 60, 215
CIA (Central Intelligence Agency) 53–4, 56, 59, 61–3, 65, 84, 120, 140, 152, 219–20
Civil Disobedience 8
Clinton, Bill xi, 92–9, 181, 244
Clinton, Hillary 124–6, 133, 140
Cold War 36–7, 52, 58–60, 79, 87–96, 159, 188, 207, 234, 244
colonisers 5
communism 37, 46, 47, 51, 53, 68, 69, 248
communist 36, 50, 57, 58, 59, 60, 90, 181
    anti-communist 49, 54, 61, 142
Communist Party 51, 55, 202, 203
Comprehensive and Progressive Agreement for Trans-Pacific Partnership 136, 184
conspiracy theories 161, 221, 222, 223, 240
containment 37, 45–52, 60, 69, 95, 151, 190, 244
Coolidge, Calvin 25
covert operations 53, 59, 61, 68, 85
Covid-19 142, 147, 182
Crimea 130–32, 51, 159, 160, 162
Cuba 11, 12, 14, 15, 17, 28, 70, 92
Cuban Missile Crisis 59, 70

Dalio, Ray xiv, 32, 183
de facto empire xviii, 86
Declaration of Independence 2, 3
Deng, Xiaoping 181
Depression of 1893 10
deregulation 83, 93, 98
Dewey, Admiral Thomas 12, 57
dictatorships 25, 215, 236
Diem, Ngo Dinh 61–4, 66, 67
Dimon, Jamie 240
domino theory 60
Donilon, Thomas E 124
Dulles, Allen 53
Duterte, Rodrigo 145, 147, 148

Economic Consequences of Peace, The 22
economic growth 7, 10, 83, 98, 248
economic imperialism 83
Economist, The 192, 227
Egypt 115, 117, 119–21, 164, 204, 211
Eight-Nation Alliance 177
Einaudi, Luigi 247
Eisenhower, Dwight 58, 97
'Empire of Liberty' 1, 2, 6

INDEX

Erdoğan, Recep Tayyip 145, 146, 147, 149, 164, 171, 208, 210, 211
European Union (EU) 130, 166, 170, 228, 234
expansionism 9, 14, 53
extremism 22, 23, 25, 221, 252

failed nation/state 110, 125, 126, 163
Federal Employee Loyalty Program 51
financial crisis of 2008 93, 245
Financial Times 160, 200, 202, 220
First World War 19, 21, 24, 25, 27, 166
Ford, Gerald 70
Foreign Affairs 48, 95, 235
Forrestal, James 47, 48, 54, 56–8
Forrestal, Michael 63–6
Franco, General Francisco 25
free market 83, 179, 181
free trade 10, 83, 94, 98, 142, 180
Friedman, Tom 96, 97
Fukuyama, Francis 95, 96, 97, 98, 102, 106

G7 meeting 188, 192
Gabbard, Tulsi 219, 220
Gaddafi, Muammar 85, 122, 123, 125, 126, 163
GATT (General Agreement on Tariffs and Trade) 31
Gaza 120, 150, 172, 174, 196, 206–9, 211, 218, 231
genocide 7, 207, 210, 224, 244
Georgia 162, 238
German reunification 87, 91
Gilded Age, the 10, 97
glasnost 86–7
global governance 29, 30, 31, 245
Global Compact for Migration 139
Global South 69, 171, 188, 195, 197, 199–216, 232–3, 235, 239, 248
'global swing states' 235
globalisation 10, 22, 79, 83, 94–9, 146, 181, 209, 239, 244
Gorbachev, Mikhail 86, 87, 89, 90
Great Britain 4, 103
Great Depression, the 16, 24, 26
Greene, Sam 200
Greenspan, Alan 93
Grenada 85
Group of 77 (G77) 204

Haftar, General Khalifa 163
Haines, Avril 165
Haley, Nikki 139
Hamas 102, 120, 147, 150, 171–2, 197, 206–8, 211, 218, 233, 251
Harding, Warren 25
Harriman, William Averell 34, 35, 45, 60, 61, 63–5
Harris, Kamala 164, 172, 222, 227, 241
Hay, John 12, 178

Hearst, William Randolph 10, 11, 12
Helsinki Commission 140, 141
Hemings, Sally 3
Hezbollah 102, 147, 171, 197, 206, 211, 218, 233
Hilsman, Roger 60, 61, 63, 64, 65
Hitler, Adolf 24–7, 29, 56, 120, 210, 215, 220, 221, 230, 237, 238
Hobson, John 178, 179, 182
Hoover, Herbert 25, 26
Hoover, J. Edgar 57
Houthis 197, 205, 211, 218, 219, 233
Huntington, Samuel 248
Hussein, Saddam 84, 91, 92, 105, 107, 108, 109, 111, 126
hyperpower 88, 94, 96, 98, 172, 219

ICC (International Criminal Court) 142, 199
illiberal democracy 145, 240, 252
immigration 10, 134, 139
imperial overreach xiii, 68, 101, 104, 112, 153, 245
imperialism 5, 14, 51, 52, 83, 107, 176, 178–80, 205
India 149, 171, 176, 188, 197, 204, 208–9, 234–5
Indian Removal Act (1830) 8
INF (Intermediate-Range Nuclear Forces) treaty 137
International Monetary Fund (IMF) 46, 182, 239
internationalism 45
interventionism 18, 19, 244
Iran–Contra scandal 83, 85
Iranian hostage crisis 78
Iranian Revolution 75, 76
Iraq 211
  invasion of 105–11, 115, 245
  withdrawal from 127
Iraqgate 84, 85
ISIS 102, 103, 111, 112, 127, 129, 218, 245
isolationist/isolationism 24, 26, 134, 143, 215, 225, 231, 239, 245, 248
Israel 74, 150, 197, 205–9, 211, 218
It Can't Happen Here 228

Jackson, Andrew 8, 9
Jefferson, Thomas 1–6
Johnson, Chalmers xii
Johnson, Lyndon 64–7
Johnson, Mike 167, 168, 169

Kelly, General John 220
Kennan, George 35, 42, 45–8, 50, 53, 54, 56, 60, 95
Kennedy, Joe 70
Kennedy, John F. 58, 59–70, 87, 244
Keynes, John Maynard 22
Khamenei, Ayatollah Ali 196, 210
Khashoggi, Jamal 143, 144
Khmer Rouge 71, 72

Khomeini, Ayatollah Ruhollah 75, 78
Kim, Jong Un 197
Kipling, Rudyard 12, 13
Kissinger, Henry 67, 71–3, 76, 77, 111, 152, 192–4, 213
Kohl, Helmut 87
Korean War 51, 58
Kristol, Irving 96
Kushner, Jared 143, 144
Kuwait 90, 91, 92

laissez-faire capitalism 98
Laos 60, 61, 71
League of Nations 17, 21, 26, 28
Leahy, Admiral William 40
Lehman Brothers 93
Leonard, Mark 214
Lewis, Sinclair 228
liberal democracy xiv, 31, 96, 98, 145, 161, 165, 198, 201, 215, 229, 237, 249
liberal world order 97, 102, 106, 136, 140, 204, 212, 214, 231–2, 245, 247
liberalism 160, 237, 249
Libya 117, 119, 121–7, 129, 159, 163–4, 174, 233
Life magazine xii, 30
Lincoln, Abraham 8, 131
Lodge, Henry Cabot 11, 13, 63
'Long Telegram', the 46, 47, 48
Louisiana Territory 2, 6
Lovett, Robert 54, 57
Luce, Henry xii, 30
Lula da Silva, Luiz 147, 171, 205, 206

McCain, John 141
McCarthy era 51, 58
McCarthy, Eugene 66
McCarthy, Joe 51, 58
McCone, John 62, 65
McGovern, George xi
McKinley, William 11–15, 177
McMaster, H. R. 152
McNamara, Robert S 62, 65, 67
Madison, James 6
MAGA (Make America Great Again) 141, 221, 240, 241
Mahbubani, Kishore 180
management of empire 68, 69, 86, 92, 94, 95, 104, 243
Mandela, Nelson 207
'manifest destiny' xvi, 6, 7, 8, 82
Mao, Tse-tung 192
Marshall Plan, the 55, 56, 179
Marshall, George 54
Merkel, Angela 125, 140
Mexican revolution 19
Mexican–American War 7, 8
Mexico 7, 8, 17, 18, 77, 83, 137

Milley, General Mark 164, 220
Modi, Narendra 145, 149, 150, 171, 208, 209, 211
Molotov, Vyacheslav Mikhailovich 35, 36
Monroe Doctrine 6, 13, 16, 17
Monroe, James 6
moral superiority 18, 52, 87, 119, 227, 243
Morsi, Mohamed 120, 121
MS *St Louis* 28
Mubarak, Hosni 119, 120
multilateralism xviii, 213, 245, 249, 250
Musk, Elon 240, 241
Muslim Brotherhood 119, 120, 121
Mussolini, Benito 24, 25, 26, 56, 210, 215

NAFTA (North American Free Trade Agreement) 83, 94
National Interest 95, 96, 97
National Security Council 53, 56
national security state 45, 56, 227, 244
National Security Strategy of the United States 106
nationalism 134, 145, 147
nationalist(s) 15, 22, 23, 32, 146, 149, 150, 167, 190, 228
Native Americans 3, 4, 7, 8, 9
NATO (North Atlantic Treaty Organization) 55, 90, 122, 131, 147, 153, 165–6
  Article 5 138
  creation 31, 53
  Trump and 138, 146, 165, 220, 228, 231, 245, 247
neoliberal policy 79, 82, 97
Netanyahu, Benjamin 145, 150, 172, 208, 209, 211, 218, 246
'Never Trumpers' 228
New Deal, the 26, 43
'New World Disorder' xv, xvii, xviii, 197, 211, 212, 232, 233–50
New York Times 96, 108
Nixon, Richard 66, 67, 70, 71, 73, 74, 192
Noriega, Manuel 92
North Korea 197, 231, 233, 234, 235

Obama, Barack 115–32, 133, 148, 151, 195, 245
Obama, Michelle 133
'Office of Special Projects' 53
OPEC (Organization of Petroleum Exporting Countries) 74, 13, 171, 197
open borders 10, 160
Operation Desert Storm 91
Operation Eagle Claw 77
Operation Iraqi Freedom 109
Operation Linebacker 71
Operation Menu 71
Operation Switchback 59
Orbán, Viktor 140, 145, 161, 167–70, 208, 209, 230, 249

INDEX

Osama bin Laden 102, 153
Oxenstierna, Axel 242, 243

Panama 16, 77, 92
Paris Agreement 137
Paris Peace Accords 72
Parsi, Vittorio Emanuele 200
Pax Americana xv, xvii, 30, 67, 75, 81, 101, 136, 196–7, 205, 238, 248
'peace with honour' 73, 112
Pelosi, Nancy 186, 187
Persian Gulf 90, 102
Peskov, Dmitry 158, 169
Philippine–American War 15
PLO (Palestinian Liberation Organization) 207
Poland 25, 29, 33, 36, 41, 43, 95, 210
political violence 173, 209, 221, 237, 250
Polk, James K. 7, 8
Pompeo, Mike 152
post-American world 205
post-Cold War 91, 98, 101, 102, 151, 195, 205, 226
  era 93, 183, 219, 232
  world 88, 171, 247
Pot, Pol 71, 72
Potsdam Conference 30, 33, 34, 43
Powell, Colin 105, 109
'pre-emptive war' 106, 107
protectionist/protectionism 134, 142, 189, 191
Psaki, Jen 121
Putin, Vladimir 157–74
  China 199, 200, 201, 202, 234
  Crimea 130–32, 51, 159, 160, 162
  Financial Times interview 160, 161
  Libya 163, 164
  Middle East allies 170, 171, 197
  Musk, Elon 241
  other allies 171, 172
  Syria 128, 129, 151, 162, 163
  Trump, Donald 137, 138, 140, 141, 145, 151, 154, 168, 169, 170, 220, 228, 230, 240
  Ukraine invasion 2021 159, 162, 163, 164–70

Quadrilateral Security Group 188, 189

Rachman, Gideon 220
Raisi, Ebrahim 206
Reagan, Ronald 78, 79, 82–8, 92, 93, 94, 97, 101, 228
Reaganomics 83
regime change 17, 18, 43, 62, 68, 75, 81, 84, 108, 165
Regime Fascista 23
regional alliances 211
Republican Party 15, 141, 142, 167, 170, 228, 231, 240
Rockefeller, David 77

Romania 25, 29, 41, 42, 43
Roosevelt Corollary 16, 17
Roosevelt, Franklin Delano (FDR) 2, 16, 26–8, 29, 34, 35, 43, 45, 60
Roosevelt, Theodore 'Teddy' 11–14, 15, 16, 17, 105
Rubin, Bob 93
rule of law 106, 142, 146, 169, 170, 236
rules-based system 30, 31, 142, 181, 203, 239, 248, 250
Rumsfeld, Donald 105, 107
Rusk, Dean 65
Russian empire 166
Ryan, Paul 141

Sarkozy, Nicolas 122, 123, 125, 126
Saudi Arabia 74, 102, 117–19, 143, 170, 171, 196–7, 204, 211, 235
Schwarzman, Stephen A 240
Scowcroft, Brent 88
SDI (Strategic Defense Initiative) 86
Second World War 16, 29, 30, 56, 60, 67, 78, 136, 182, 210, 244
Shah of Iran 75–8
slavery xvi, 2, 3, 7, 8, 10, 244
Slidell, John 8
Smoot–Hawley Tariff Act (1930) 24
social conflict 32, 173, 224, 236, 250
soft power 113, 179, 205, 213, 234
South Africa 197, 204, 206, 207, 209, 234, 235
Soviet Union 28–9, 29, 42, 46, 48–50, 60, 67, 86–8, 98, 102, 159, 202
  dissolution of 90, 91, 93
  expansionism 53
  glasnost 86–7
Spain 6, 11–13, 15, 25, 105, 125
Spanish Civil War 25
Spanish–American War (1898) 12
spheres of influence 28, 29, 30
stagflation 74
Stahl, Lesley 88
Stalin, Joseph 26, 28–9, 33–6, 39, 41–2, 47, 50, 52, 55, 60, 210
Sullivan, Jake 165, 184, 213, 214, 219
Sullivan, William 75
Summers, Larry 93
superpower 29, 31, 81, 82, 88, 92, 173, 190, 191, 213, 245
  ascending 32, 214
  economic 179
  military 238
  predominant 32, 204, 238
Syria 117, 127–30, 132, 151, 159, 162–3, 174, 211, 220, 231, 233

Taft, William 84
Tahrir Square 119, 120, 124
Taiwan 185–8, 190–95, 205

Talbott, Strobe 96
Taliban, the 102, 103, 151–4, 246
Tehran conference (1943) 28
Thatcher, Margaret 222
Third Reich, the 23
Thoreau, Henry David 8
Time magazine 96
Toynbee, Arnold 31
Trade Expansion Act (1962) 138, 139
trade war 138, 191, 195, 228, 245, 246
Tragedy of American Diplomacy, The 131
'Trail of Tears' 9
Treaty of Paris 4
Treaty of Versailles 21, 22
Treaty on the Prohibition of Nuclear Weapons 137
trickle-down economics 82
Truman Doctrine 50, 51
Truman, Harry 29, 31, 33–7, 39–48, 50–53, 55–7, 70, 244
Trump, Donald 133–55, 216, 222–231, 237, 238, 240–42
   affinity for dictators 140, 143, 145–50
   anti-immigrant measures 137, 139
   China 136, 142, 150, 191, 246
   ICC 142
   impeachment 136, 151, 228
   inauguration speech 133–5
   January 6 insurrection 135, 136, 220
   NATO 138, 146, 165, 220, 228, 231, 245, 247
   Putin 137–8, 140–41, 144–5, 151, 154, 159, 167, 168–70, 220, 228, 230, 240
   Taliban deal 151, 152, 246
   tariffs 138, 139, 184
   Trumpism 173, 221, 225
   WHO 142
   withdrawal from agreements 136, 137, 138, 139, 142, 184
Tunisia 117, 118
Tyler, John 176

Ukraine 130–31, 151, 155, 159, 162–74, 199–200, 205–6, 210, 218–20, 231, 233
UN (United Nations) 28, 35, 137, 139, 203, 204, 248
UN Arms Trade Treaty 137
UN General Assembly 108, 118
UN Human Rights Council 137
UN Security Council 31, 50, 109, 110
UNESCO (United Nations Educational, Scientific and Cultural Organization) 137
US Embassy, Tehran 76, 77
US presidential election (2024) 168, 170, 191, 220, 222–4, 228, 229
US–China relations 186, 187, 189, 191, 213
USS *Maine* 11

Vance, J. D. 168
Vidal, Gore xi, xii, xiii, xv, 225, 226, 227
Vietnam War xi, 51, 59–64, 66–9, 71–4, 78, 152, 227, 244

Wagner Group 159, 163, 164
Wall Street 93, 222, 240, 249
War of 1812 2
War on Terror 103, 104
Warsaw Pact 91
Washington consensus 135
Washington Post 143, 241
Washington, George 1, 5
Watergate 71, 74
weapons of mass destruction 107, 109
Western liberal democracy xiv, 31, 96, 98, 161, 165, 198, 201
Western liberal order 97, 102, 161, 174, 202, 209, 212, 214, 228, 230, 231, 233
westward expansion 1, 2, 6, 7, 10
'white man's burden' 13
white supremacy 18, 141, 209, 221
WHO (World Health Organization) 142
Williams, William Appleman 131
Wilson, Woodrow 17–22, 24, 26, 27, 120, 244
Wolfowitz, Paul D. 96, 105, 107
World Bank 31, 46, 203, 239
World Is Flat, The 96, 97
World Trade Organization 94, 142, 181, 203

xenophobia xv, 134, 139, 145, 208, 225
Xi, Jinping 150, 174, 183, 185, 190–94, 199–207, 210, 212, 228, 234, 237, 240

Yalta Conference 28, 29, 30, 33, 35, 36, 41
Yanukovych, Viktor 130
yellow journalism 10
Yeltsin, Boris 90
Yemen 117, 118, 197, 205, 211, 231
Yom Kippur War 74

Zakaria, Fareed 230, 231
Zapatero, Rodriguez 125
Zelensky, Volodymyr 151, 166, 171, 188, 206, 208, 220